THE TURKISH LANGUAGE REFORM

The Turkish Language Reform

A Catastrophic Success

GEOFFREY LEWIS

OXFORD
UNIVERSITY PRESS

OXFORD

UNIVERSITY PRESS

Great Clarendon Street, Oxford OX2 6DP

Oxford University Press is a department of the University of Oxford.
It furthers the University's objective of excellence in research, scholarship,
and education by publishing worldwide in

Oxford New York

Athens Auckland Bangkok Bogotá Buenos Aires Calcutta
Cape Town Chennai Dar es Salaam Delhi Florence Hong Kong Istanbul
Karachi Kuala Lumpur Madrid Melbourne Mexico City Mumbai
Nairobi Paris São Paulo Singapore Taipei Tokyo Toronto Warsaw

and associated companies in Berlin Ibadan

Oxford is a registered trade mark of Oxford University Press
in the UK and certain other countries

Published in the United States
by Oxford University Press Inc., New York

First published 1999

British Library Cataloguing in Publication Data

Data available

Library of Congress Cataloging in Publication Data
Lewis, Geoffrey L.
The Turkish language reform: a catastrophic success / Geoffrey
Lewis.
p. cm.
Includes bibliographical references (p.   ).
1. Turkish language—Reform.   2. Turkish language—History.
I. Title.
PL115.L47 1999
494'.35—dc21   99-24289
ISBN 0-19-823856-8

1 3 5 7 9 10 8 6 4 2

Typeset by Best-set Typesetter Ltd., Hong Kong
Printed in Great Britain
on acid-free paper by
Bookcraft (Bath) Ltd., Midsomer Norton

Acknowledgements

To all the many friends who supplied me with material, my deep gratitude. Most of them said that if I criticized the language reform too harshly they would not mind a bit. My especial thanks to Fuat M. Andic, Emre Aracı, Çiğdem Balım, Ruth Davis, Sıtkı Egeli, Şükrü Elçin, Selim İlkin, Iverach McDonald, Andrew Mango, Bengisu Rona, and Ali Suat Ürgüplü.

Contents

Abbreviations

[A]	Arabic
ATD	*Atatürk ve Türk Dili* (Ankara: TDK, 1963)
AKDTYK	Atatürk Kültür, Dil ve Tarih Yüksek Kurumu
AÜDTC	Ankara Üniversitesi Dil Tarih-Coğrafya Fakültesi
DLT	*Dīwān Luġāt al-Turk*
[F]	French
[G]	Greek
JRAS	*Journal of the Royal Asiatic Society of London*
[M]	Mongolian
OT	Old Turkic
[P]	Persian
TBMM	Türkiye Büyük Millet Meclisi
TDK	Türk Dil Kurumu
TDTC	Türk Dili Tetkik Cemiyeti
TL	Türk Lirası (Turkish lira)
TTK	Türk Tarih Kurumu

Note on the Text

Turkish words under discussion are in italic unless there is no possibility of confusion with a similar English word. Words from other languages, as well as book titles, are also shown in italic, likewise words of Arabic or Persian origin in some of the quotations, words of native origin being in roman.

An [A], [P], [F], [G], or [M] after a word shows its origin as Arabic, Persian, French, Greek, or Mongolian respectively; [PA] after a two-word phrase means that the first word is of Persian origin, the second Arabic. Square brackets are also used (*a*) to enclose the author's comments within translations of quotations, (*b*) to cite the original wording where the full text is not included (which happens rarely, only when there is nothing particularly noteworthy about the Turkish), and (*c*) round surnames later assumed by people who come into the story before the Surnames Law of 1934. Logic would demand that the founder of the Republic should be called Mustafa Kemal (or just Kemal, which he preferred) until the story comes down to the time of that law; nevertheless he is sometimes referred to anachronistically as Atatürk, the name by which he is best remembered.

In transliterations of Arabic and Persian words, *č* stands for the sound of English *ch*; *ḍ* for English *th* in *this*; *ǧ* for English *j*; *ġ* for Arabic *ghayn*, the gargling sound of the Parisian and Northumbrian *r*; *ḥ* for *kh* as in *Bukhara*; *j* for French *j*; *š* for English *sh*; *ṭ* for English *th* in *think*. (In the Chaghatay passage quoted in Chapter 2 I have followed Levend's transliteration; he uses *ç* and *ş*, not *č* and *š*.)

While most references to *Türk Dili*, the Türk Dil Kurumu's monthly journal, are by volume number and page, some give the number or date of the individual monthly part, because volume numbers were not always shown and because the pagination was not always cumulative, so that a volume may contain, say, a dozen pages numbered 27. The aim has been to make the references clear, though not necessarily consistent.

A pair of forward strokes encloses a representation of pronunciation, for which ordinary characters, not the symbols of the International Phonetic Alphabet, are used: /gʸāvur/.

An asterisk preceding a word shows it to be a hypothetical form.

OT stands for Old Turkic, Turkic (the current Turkish for which is Türkî [A]) being the unattractive but generally accepted term for the family of which Turkish, the language of Turkey, is a member. The term Old Turkic is properly applied to languages of the family from the eighth to the tenth century, while the period from the eleventh to the fifteenth century is Middle Turkic. I beg the reader's indulgence if on occasion I have misapplied 'OT' to a Middle Turkic word.

1

Introduction

This book has two purposes. The first is to acquaint the general reader with the often bizarre, sometimes tragicomic, but never dull story of the Turkish language reform. The second is to provide students of Turkish at every level with some useful and stimulating reading matter. With both purposes in mind, no word, phrase, or sentence of Turkish has been left untranslated, apart from names of books and articles, as it is assumed that the reader who wishes to chase up bibliographical references will understand the meaning of the titles. The second purpose accounts for the references to the author's *Turkish Grammar* and for the abundance of footnotes and digressions.

The language reform is not so well known abroad as other aspects of the Kemalist revolution because, having lasted for more than half a century, it is not the stuff of which headlines are made, but its effects are evident if we compare the Turkish of today with that of even thirty years ago.

Not a few nations have gone in for linguistic engineering. By this I mean tinkering with language with the express purpose of changing people's speech habits and the way they write. I am not referring to the introduction of new words for technical innovations such as vaccination, radar, or the modem, or to the creation of new non-technical words by individuals intending to amuse or to express ideas for which they find no words in the existing language. The names that come to mind in these last two categories are, on the one hand, Lewis Carroll, on the other hand, James Joyce, and, in the middle, the American Gelett Burgess, whom we have to thank for the word *blurb*. In his *Burgess Unabridged: A New Dictionary of Words You Have Always Needed* (1914), he defines it as '1. A flamboyant advertisement; an inspired testimonial. 2. Fulsome praise; a sound like a publisher.' An earlier (1906) success of his had been to popularize *bromide*, previously meaning a sedative, in the sense of a boringly trite remark. He gives as an example: 'It isn't the money, it's the principle of the thing', and points out that what makes it a bromide is not just its triteness but its inevitability. He was by no means the first such benefactor of humanity; there was, for example, the unknown seventeenth-century genius who combined *dumbstruck* and *confounded* to make *dumbfounded*. Nor was he the last; the earliest recorded appearance in print of *guesstimate*, later *guestimate*, was in 1936, in the *New York Times*, and such inventions keep coming. During the Gulf War of 1991 we were reminded by an American general of the existence of *bodacious*, apparently a combination of *bold* and *audacious*, first recorded in British English in 1845.

These, however, are not what I intend by linguistic engineering. I mean the sort of deliberate campaign that has been carried out at various times by Germans, Swedes, Hungarians, Finns, and Albanians, among others, for nationalistic reasons, to purge their languages of foreign words and substitute native words for them. In lands of German speech the encroachment of French began at the end of the sixteenth century. The first stirrings of protest came a century later, although clearly with no effect on King Friedrich Wilhelm I of Prussia (1713–40), to judge by his celebrated declaration to his nobles: 'Ich stabiliere die Souveraineté wie einen Rocher de Bronze.' The modern German vocabulary shows the results of another such campaign, with *Fernsprecher* and *Kraftwagen* replacing the international *Telefon* and *Auto*, though the latter two have staged a comeback. A movement to eliminate German and Latin words from Hungarian began in the second half of the eighteenth century and had considerable success. The French Academy has long been fighting a losing battle against the inroads of Franglais.

Attempts have been made to purge English too. *Inwit* was used for *conscience* in the *Ancrene Riwle*, written about 1230. In 1340 Dan Michel wrote his *Ayenbite of Inwit*, *ayenbite* being a Middle English translation of the late Latin *remorsus* 'remorse'; James Joyce partially modernized it into *agenbite* in his *Ulysses* (1922). In the nineteenth century came the Saxonisms, native substitutes for words of Greek and Latin origin. *Birdlore* was invented in 1830 to replace *ornithology*, and *folklore* in 1846 to encapsulate 'traditional beliefs, legends and customs of the common people'. *Foreword* for *preface* is first recorded in 1842. But nowhere has such a campaign been so long sustained and effective as in Turkey.

The aim of the Turkish language reform was to eliminate the Arabic and Persian grammatical features and the many thousands of Arabic and Persian borrowings that had long been part of the language. It comprised two different phases of activity: isolated attempts from the mid-nineteenth century on, undertaken mostly by private individuals and groups, and the government-inspired campaign that began around 1930. The latter could more accurately be termed a revolution than a reform, since 'reform' implies improvement. *Dil devrimi* (the language revolution) is what Turks call it, but Western writers have always called it the language reform, and the practice is followed in this book. Although it is less accurate to call the proponents of *dil devrimi* 'language reformers' rather than 'linguistic revolutionaries', it is also less cumbersome.

Why the subtitle 'A Catastrophic Success'? The author recognizes that not every reader who knows the story will share his view, but some of them may do so by the time they have read to the end. There is no denying the success. An incontrovertible proof is that *Nutuk*, Mustafa Kemal's thirty-six hour Speech on the end of the Ottoman Empire and the rise of the Turkish Republic, which he delivered over six days in 1927, became less and less comprehensible to the young until in the early 1960s it had to be 'translated into the present-day language'. A single paragraph is enough to show the extent of the changes that thirty odd years had wrought. First, Kemal's own words:

Muhterem Efendiler, İnönü muharebe meydanını, ikinci defa olarak mağlûben terk ve Bursa istikametinde eski mevzilerine ricat eden düşmanın takibinde, piyade ve süvari fırkalarımızın gösterdikleri şayanı tezkâr kahramanlıkları izah etmiyeceğim. Yalnız, umumî vaziyeti askeriyeyi itmam için müsaade buyurursanız Cenup Cephemize ait mıntakada cereyan etmiş olan harekâtı hulâsa edeyim. (Kemal 1934: ii. 106)[1]

Honoured gentlemen, I shall not give an account of the notable acts of heroism shown by our infantry and cavalry divisions in pursuit of the enemy, who, vanquished for the second time, was abandoning the İnönü battlefield and retreating in the direction of Bursa, to its old positions. With your permission, however, to complete the general military picture let me summarize the movements which had proceeded in the region of our southern front.

Here is the corresponding text in the 1963 version (Tuğrul *et al.*: ii. 427), with a translation using words of Anglo-Saxon rather than of Latin origin wherever possible, to try to convey the flavour of the neologisms:

Sayın baylar, İnönü Savaş alanını ikinci kez yenilerek bırakan ve Bursa doğrultusunda eski dayangalarına çekilen düşmanın kovalanmasında piyade ve süvari tümenlerimizin göster-dikleri anılmaya değer yiğitlikleri anlatmayacağım. Yalnız, askerlik bakımından genel durumun açıklanmasını tamamlamak için, izin verirseniz, Güney Cephemiz bölgesinde yapılan savaşları özetleyeyim.

Distinguished sirs, I shall not tell of the noteworthy deeds of bravery done by our infantry and cavalry divisions in chasing the enemy, who, beaten for the second time, was leaving the İnönü battlefield and withdrawing towards Bursa, to its old standings. With your leave, however, to fill out the sketch of the general situation from the military viewpoint, let me outline the struggles carried out in the section of our southern front.

The neologism *dayanga* (here rendered 'standing'), manufactured from *dayanmak* 'to be based, to hold out', was intended to replace *mevzi* in the sense of a position held by troops. It did not gain acceptance, has not replaced *mevzi*, and does not appear in recent dictionaries. Nor has a substitute been found for *harekât*, an Arabic plural still current for 'troop movements'; the *savaşlar* of the text, 'struggles' or 'battles', does not convey Kemal's meaning. For 'permission' in the final sentence, his *müsaade* has been replaced by *izin*, which is equally Arabic but less obviously so.

The language did not remain static after the 1960s. Not twenty years later, the need was felt for an even more up-to-date version. *Nutuk-Söylev* (Arar *et al.* 1986) gives the 1934 and 1963 texts in parallel, with some amendments to the latter, although, in the paragraph quoted above (at ii., 777 in *Nutuk-Söylev*), there happens to be only one change from the 1963 version: *Sayın*, now no more of an honorific than Mr, Mrs, Miss, or Ms, has been replaced by *Saygıdeğer* 'respectworthy'.

---

[1] The first publication was in the old alphabet (Ankara: Türk Tayyare Cemiyeti, 1927).

And consider this, from the introduction to the 1982 edition of a book first published in 1968 (Yücel 1982), explaining why the author thought a revised version was necessary: 'Bir kez, şimdi olduğu gibi o günlerde de yazılarımı oldukça arı bir Türkçe yazmama karşın, on üç yıl önceki dilim bayağı eskimiş göründü bana' (For one thing, although I wrote then as I do now, in quite a pure Turkish, my language of thirteen years ago seemed to me downright antiquated).

What gives the success its catastrophic aspect is not just the loss of Ottoman Turkish—its time had long passed and only a fast-disappearing company of elderly Turks and the few foreigners who love the language for its own sake are shedding any tears over it—but also the loss of its natural development, the Turkish of the 1920s and 1930s, the language of Halide Edip Adıvar, Sabahattin Ali, Yakup Kadri Karaosmanoğlu, and Reşat Nuri Güntekin.[2] The loss affects every Turk who now, in speaking or writing, gropes for the precise word to express the required meaning and does not find it, because it is as dead as Etruscan and has not been replaced. Moreover, many of the neologisms were constructed arbitrarily, with little or no regard for the rules and conventions of Turkish, with the result that any Turk with a feeling for language finds at least some of them excruciating and cannot bear to use or to hear them. Several of my friends cannot stand *iletişim* for 'communications', while many more cannot abide the use of *neden* 'from what?' as a noun meaning 'cause'.

In 1984 I attended a lecture in Ankara by a social anthropologist. It was entitled 'Differing Mentalities and Culture' and it was a good lecture, but I confess to having been more interested in the medium than the message. The speaker began by drawing a distinction between local cultures and universal culture. For 'universal' he first used the Ottoman 'küllî', and then, when a stirring in the audience showed that it was not intelligible or not acceptable to everyone, he tried 'tümel', the neologism for 'universal' as a philosophical term. A similar reaction from the audience, and he said 'üniversel'. Later on he used 'genel' 'general'. He did not try 'evrensel', the prescribed neologism for 'universal, cosmic', which was subsequently used by a questioner from the floor. After a while he took to rattling off three words for each concept: for example, when he wanted to express 'causality' he used the Ottoman borrowing from Arabic, the neologism which may be literally rendered 'fromwhatishness', and the French: 'illiyet–nedenlilik–causalité'.

How the language got into that state is the subject of this book.

---

[2] Turkish cynics say that the young do not read works written more than ten years ago anyway, but this is belied by the number of 'translations into modern Turkish' and 'simplified versions' of standard authors to be seen in the bookshops. See, however, the quotation from Fuat M. Andic on page 143.

2

Ottoman Turkish

By the beginning of the eleventh century, most of the ancestors of the present Turks of Turkey had become Muslim. It is evident that their introduction to Islam was due to peoples of Iranian speech, because the basic religious terms in Turkish come not from Arabic but from Persian or other Iranian languages: *namaz* 'prayer', *oruç* 'fasting', *peygamber* 'prophet'. The apparent exceptions, the Arabic *hac* or *ziyaret* for 'pilgrimage', are no exception, because those are the words used in Persian too. Once settled within the civilization of Islam, the Turks took into their language as much of the Persian and Arabic vocabularies as they needed, and more. As the perception that they were Turks was supplanted by an awareness that they were members of the Ümmet-i Muhammed, the Community of Believers, so the tide of Arabic and Persian flowed. It was not just a matter of borrowing foreign words for foreign concepts. They had a perfectly good word for 'city', *balık*, as in Marco Polo's name for Pekin, Cambaluc—i.e. *Ḥānbalık* 'Emperor's City'. By the fourteenth century they had abandoned it for *şehir* (Persian *šahr*), and *kend* (Sogdian *kn̠d*), which forms the last element of the names Tashkent, Yarkand, and Samarkand. They had two words for 'army', *çerig* and *sü*, both of which were ousted from general use by *asker*, Arabic *ʿaskar* (originally the Latin *exercitus*), though *çerig* was preserved in *Yeniçeri* 'New Troops', whence *Janissary*. Even the word for 'fire', *ōd*, gradually fell out of use; it survived in poetry until the early twentieth century but had hardly been used in prose for four hundred years, its place having been taken by *ateş*, Persian *āteš*. This process had begun in the empire of the Seljuk Turks (1040–1157). Mehmet Fuat Köprülüzade (1928: 10–11) wrote:[1]

Anadolu'da . . . klâsik Acem şi'rini model ittihaz eden 'Saray şairleri'ni daha Selçukîler sarayında görmeğe başlıyoruz . . . İran tesiratının mütemadi kuvvetle nemasına ve Acem modellerinin taklidinde daimî bir terakki gösterilmesine rağmen, Türkçe yazan şairler ve müellifler, eserlerinde hemen umumiyetle: 'Türkçe'nin Arapça ve Acemce'ye nispetle daha dar, daha kaba, ifadeye daha kabiliyetsiz olduğunu, ve binaenaleyh kendi kusurların bakılmamak lâzım geldiğini' söylüyorlar, hatta bazan zımnî bir mazeret şeklinde 'Arabî ve Farsî bilmeyen halkın anlaması için Türkçe yazmağa mecbur olduklarını' ilâve ediyorlardı.

Already at the Seljuk court in Anatolia we begin to see the 'Palace poets', who took classical Persian poetry as their model . . . But almost all those poets and prose-writers who

---

[1] This great historian of Turkish literature (1890–1966) changed his name to Mehmet Fuat Köprülü in compliance with the Surnames Law of 1934, which required every family to choose a Turkish surname; the *zāde* ('-son') in his time-honoured patronymic was Persian.

wrote in Turkish despite the continuing vigorous growth of Persian influences and a steady advance in the imitation of Persian models, used to say in their works that Turkish, in comparison with Arabic and Persian, was limited, crude, and inexpressive, and that their own shortcomings must therefore be overlooked. They would sometimes even add as an implicit excuse that they were obliged to write in Turkish in order to be understood by the common people, who were ignorant of Arabic and Persian.

Huge though the influx of Persian words was, a bigger invasion came from Arabic, and not only because as the language of the Koran it naturally became the language of religion and theology and because the Persian vocabulary was itself replete with Arabic borrowings, but also because when an Arabic word was borrowed it brought its whole family with it. This calls for a brief explanation, which Arabists may skip.

Arabic words generally are based on triliteral roots—that is, roots consisting of three consonants, for example, *K–T–B* and *J–B–R* expressing the concepts of writing and compulsion respectively. These consonants are fitted into patterns of short and long vowels, sometimes with a doubling of the second or third consonant, sometimes with prefixes or infixes. Each pattern has a specific grammatical function: *KaTaBa* 'he wrote', *KāTiB* 'writer', *maKTūB* 'written'; *JaBaRa* 'he compelled', *JāBiR* 'compelling', *maJBūR* 'compelled'. Once one knows the patterns, learning a new root can increase one's vocabulary by as many as a dozen new words.

It was natural that the Turks should borrow so fundamental a word as ʿ*ilm*: 'knowledge', more particularly 'religious knowledge'. So along came ʿ*ālim* 'scholar' with its plural ʿ*ulamā*', *maʿlūm* 'known', *muʿallim* 'teacher', *taʿlīm* 'instruction', *istiʿlām* 'request for information', and lots more. And every new importation of a foreign word meant that the corresponding Turkish word was forgotten or became restricted to the speech of the common people. A good example is *sin* 'grave, tomb', found in popular poetry from the thirteenth to the twentieth century and still widely used in Anatolia, but hardly ever found in elevated writing, having long ago been supplanted by *mezar* [A].

But there was more to the rise of Ottoman than the suppression of native words. With the Arabic and Persian words came Arabic and Persian grammatical conventions. Turkish was born free of that disease of language known as grammatical gender; Arabic was not. Further, whereas Turkish adjectives precede their nouns, Arabic and Persian adjectives follow them.[2] Nor is that the whole story. When Persian took nouns over from Arabic, it usually took their plurals as well: with ʿ*ilm* 'knowledge, science', came its plural ʿ*ulūm*, which is grammatically

---

[2] While students of Turkish may be cheered to find the occasional similarity with English, they should remember that Turkish adjectives *invariably* precede their nouns. In English, however, besides the locutions exemplified in 'He is well versed in matters archaeological' and 'The boiler is in an outbuilding, not in the house proper', we have such anomalies as 'court martial', 'time immemorial', 'Princess Royal', 'Heir Apparent', and 'President Elect', while 'law merchant' and 'rhyme royal' still figure in the vocabularies of experts in jurisprudence and literature respectively.

feminine. Moreover, in Persian an *i* (termed 'Persian izafet', from *iḍāfaʾ* [A] 'attachment') is interposed between a noun and its qualifier. *Āb* is 'water', *sard* 'cold', *ḥayāt* 'life'; 'cold water' is *āb-i-sard* and 'the water of life' is *āb-i-ḥayāt*. The Arabic for 'natural' is *ṭabīʿī*, the feminine of which is *ṭabīʿīya*. So in Persian 'the natural sciences' was ʿ*ulūm-i-ṭabīʿīya*, and this became the Ottoman Turkish too (in modern spelling, *ulûm-i tabiiye*). The New Literature movement at the end of the nineteenth century was known as Edebiyat-ı Cedide; *edebiyat* 'literature' was feminine in Arabic, so *cedid* 'new', the Arabic *jadīd*, was given the Arabic feminine termination, and noun and adjective were linked by the Persian izafet. One of the names of what we call the Ottoman Empire was 'The Guarded Dominions'. 'Dominion' in Arabic is *mamlaka*, plural *mamālik*, which again is feminine. So *maḥrūs̤*, the Arabic for 'guarded', was put into the feminine form, *maḥrūṣa*. In Arabic, 'guarded dominions' was therefore *mamālik maḥrūṣa*, but in Ottoman Turkish it became *memalik-i mahrusa*, for that was how it was done in Persian.

Persianization continued unabated under the Ottomans. Although they did not go as far as their Seljuk predecessors in despising their mother tongue enough to make Persian their official language, the fifteenth century saw a huge increase in the Persian influence on Turkish writers of prose and poetry. They took Persian writers as their models and filled their works with Persian borrowings. Latifî (1491–1582) of Kastamonu relates that the poet and historian Leâlî was sufficiently proficient in the Persian language to pass as a Persian. He moved from his native Tokat to the capital, where he became a literary lion and won the favour of Sultan Mehmed the Conqueror, but immediately lost it when it transpired that he was not a Persian but a Turk (Latifî 1314/1898: 289–90). True, Latifî was writing in 1546, almost a century after Leâlî's time, and there is no guarantee that his account was factual, but it shows how depreciated at least one Turkish literary man, Latifî, felt *vis-à-vis* the Persians.[3]

The situation is thus summed up by Gibb (1900–9: i. 8):

It is not too much to say that during the whole of the five and a half centuries [fourteenth to mid-nineteenth] covered by the Old School [of poetry], more especially the Third Period [the seventeenth century], every Persian and every Arabic word was a possible Ottoman word. In thus borrowing material from the two classical languages a writer was quite unrestricted save by his own taste and the limit of his knowledge; all that was required was that in case of need he should give the foreign words a Turkish grammatical form.

By this he meant that Turkish suffixes could be added to foreign words. As indeed they were, but not always in profusion; in classical Ottoman poetry one may see whole lines where the only indication that they are in Turkish and not Persian is

---

[3] Of interest in this context is an observation on language in fourteenth-century England in the introduction (signed 'H.M.') to Maundeville (1886: 3): 'In the days of Maundeville Latin, French and English were the three languages written in this country. Latin was then and long afterwards the common language of the educated, and it united them into a European Republic of Letters; French was the courtly language; English was the language of the people.'

a final -*dir* 'is' or -*di* 'was'. Sometimes even that much is wanting. The three following couplets, containing not one syllable of Turkish, form part of an ode in honour of Sultan Süleyman by Bakî (1526/7–1600), the most highly esteemed poet of the classical age:

> Bālānişīn-i mesned-i şāhān-i tācdār
> Vālānişān-i maʿreke-i ʿarşa-i keyān
> Cemşīd-i ʿayş ü ʿişret ü Dārā-yı dār ü gīr
> Kisrā-yı ʿadl ü re'fet ü İskender-i zamān
> Sulṭān-ı şarḳ u ġarb şehinşāh-i baḥr u berr
> Dārā-yı dehr Şāh Süleymān-ı kāmrān.

> Seated above the thrones of crownèd monarchs,
> High o'er the fray of battlefields of kings,
> Jamshid of feasting and carousing, Darius of war,
> Chosroes of justice and clemency, Alexander of the age,
> Sultan of east and west, King of Kings of sea and land,
> Darius of the time, King Süleyman, of fortune blessed.[4]

The mixture of Turkish, Arabic, and Persian, which Turks call Osmanlıca and we call Ottoman, was an administrative and literary language, and ordinary people must have been at a loss when they came into contact with officials. But while they must often have been baffled by Ottoman phraseology, they were capable of seeing the funny side of it. In the shadow theatre, the running joke is that Karagöz speaks Turkish while his sparring partner Hacivat speaks Ottoman. In the play *Salıncak*, Karagöz keeps hitting Hacivat. Hacivat asks him why, but receives only nonsensical answers sounding vaguely like his—to Karagöz—unintelligible questions. Eventually he asks, 'Vurmanızdan aksâ-yı murâd?' (What is your ultimate object in hitting me?). To which Karagöz replies, 'Aksaray'da murtad babandır' (The turncoat at Aksaray is your father) (Kudret 1968–70: iii. 54.) A rough English parallel would be, 'Explain your bellicose attitude.'—'How do *I* know why he chewed my billy-goat's hat?'

Following in the footsteps of Karagöz are today's taxi-drivers who refer to their battery-chargers not as *şarjör*, the French *chargeur*, but as *carcur* 'chatter'.[5] They are displaying not ignorance but a sense of fun, like those who in the days of the Democrat Party pronounced 'Demokrat' as 'Demirkırat' 'Iron-Grey Horse'.[6] The British sailors who served on the ship taking Napoleon to St Helena knew very well that her name was not *Billy Ruffian*; in calling her that, they were just cutting the fancy foreign *Bellerophon* down to size, like those people in England who used to Anglicize *asparagus* as *sparrow-grass* and *hysterics* as *high strikes*. In fact the

---

[4] A translation of the whole ode will be found in Gibb (1900–9: iii. 147–51).

[5] According to Erkilet (1952), soldiers were already saying *carcur* instead of *şarjör* in the 1920s, though this was another kind of *şarjör*, an ammunition-belt for machine-guns. (See p. 101 of the 1967 reprint.)

[6] When the party was outlawed (see Chapter 12), its reincarnation, the Justice Party, chose as its logo the figure of a horse.

Turkish vocabulary still includes not a few originally foreign words that the tongue of the people has converted into more Turkish shapes: from Persian, for example, *çamaşır* 'linen' (*jāmešūy*), *çerçeve* 'frame' (*čarčūba*), *gözde*[7] 'favourite' (*guzīde*), *köşe* 'corner' (*gūša*), *çarşamba* 'Wednesday' (*čāršanbih*), and *merdiven* 'staircase' (*nardubān*); and, from Arabic, *rahat lokum* 'Turkish Delight' (*rāḥat al-ḥulḳūm* 'ease of the gullet'), now abbreviated to *lokum*, *muşamba* 'oilskin' (*mušammaʿ*), and *maydanoz* 'parsley' (*maḳdūnis*). *Maydanoz* was transformed by some into *midenüvaz* [AP] 'stomach-caressing', a Persian compound that cannot be called a popular etymology; one is reminded of the English people who turned 'Welsh rabbit' into the more genteel-seeming 'Welsh rarebit'. The essayist and novelist Peyami Safa (1899–1961) must have taken *midenüvaz* to be the correct form, for he wrote:

Geçenlerde de bir muharrir arkadaşımız, gazetesinde, türkçeleşmiş bir fransızca kelimeyi türkçe imlâ ile yazdığım için bana tariz etmişti. 'Çıkolata' kelimesine 'şokola' ve 'şimendifer' kelimesine 'şömendöfer' diyenler arasında bulunmaktan çekinirim. Bu yolun sonunda maydanoza 'midenüvaz' demek vardır. O çıkmaza girmek istemem ben. (Safa 1970: 47)

A writer friend recently took me to task in his newspaper for spelling a Turkicized French word in the Turkish way. I am reluctant to join the ranks of those who pronounce 'çıkolata' as 'şokola' and 'şimendifer' as 'şömendöfer' [*chemin de fer*]. What lies at the end of that road is pronouncing *maydanoz* as *midenüvaz*, a dead end which I have no wish to enter.

On the theme of the bewilderment of ordinary people when confronted by speakers of Ottoman, there is the tale of the *sarıklı hoca* (the turbanned cleric), who, wishing to buy some mutton, addresses a butcher's boy with the words 'Ey šāgird-i ḳaṣṣāb, laḥm-i ġanemden bir ḳıyye bilvezin bana ʿiṭā eyler misin?' (O apprentice of the butcher, wilt thou bestow on me one oke avoirdupois of ovine flesh?). The perplexed boy can only reply 'Amīn!' (Amen!). On the other hand, there is the story of one occasion when the uneducated were not baffled by someone who spoke differently from them. It is said to have happened in 1876, at a time of rioting by the *softas* (students at the *medreses* (religious schools)), when the police were chasing a crowd of them. Despairing of outdistancing the pursuit, one *softa* had the bright idea of sitting down on the pavement. When the police asked him, 'Which way did they go?', he replied, giving full weight to the Arabic pronunciation of his words, as was second nature for a *softa*: 'Baʿḍısı şu ṭarafa, baʿḍısı o ṭarafa' (Some went this way, some that)—and was quite surprised to find himself in custody.

Tahsin Banguoğlu, having mentioned (1987: 325) that the poet and sociologist Ziya Gökalp (1876–1924) had wanted the new Turkish to be Istanbul Turkish as spoken by the intellectuals, adds a comment containing an interesting piece of information that the author has not seen recorded elsewhere:

---

[7] Turkish for 'in the eye', an obvious popular etymology.

Evet ama, o zaman aydınların konuştuğu Türkçe eski yazı dilinin çok etkisinde kalmış bir Türkçe idi. Onu da halk pek anlamıyordu. Halk buna *istillâhi konuşma* derdi. Meselâ 'müdür bey, kâtibe bir şey söyledi, ama anlayamadım. İstillâhi konuşuyorlar.'

Yes, but the Turkish spoken by intellectuals at that time was a Turkish still very much under the influence of the old written language. And this the people did not understand very well. They called it 'talking istillâhi'. For example: 'The manager said something to the clerk, but I couldn't understand it. They're talking istillâhi.'

İstillâhi is another example of the phenomenon discussed above: giving a more familiar shape to high-flown words with which one does not feel at home, the word in this case being *ıstılahî*, the adjective of *ıstılah*. *Istılah paralamak* (to tear technical terms to pieces), once meant talking over the heads of one's hearers. The meaningless but Arabic-looking *istillâhi* is made up of familiar elements: the first two syllables are in imitation of words such as *istiklâl* 'independence' and *istikamet* 'direction', while *llah* is from the Arabic name of God. As we might say, or might have said a generation or two ago, 'They're parleyvooing.'

Even before the rise of the Ottomans there had been expressions of dissatisfaction with the dominance of Arabic and Persian.[8] In 1277 Şemsüddin Mehmed Karamanoğlu, the chief minister of the ruler of Konya, decreed that thenceforth no language other than Turkish would be spoken at court or in government offices or public places. Unfortunately he was killed in battle a few months later.

Few Turks who write about the history of their language can forbear to quote the two following couplets from the *Garipnâme* ('Book of the Stranger') of the Sufi poet Âşık Paşa (1272–1333).[9] The purpose of the work is to illustrate Sufi doctrine through discourses on passages from the Koran, tradition, and the sayings of Sufi masters.

> Türk diline kimesne bakmaz idi
> Türklere hergiz gönül akmaz idi
> Türk dahi bilmez idi bu dilleri
> İnce yolı, ol ulu menzilleri.

> None had regard for the Turkish tongue;
> Turks won no hearts.
> Nor did the Turk know these languages,
> The narrow road, those great staging posts.

It is doubtful, however, whether every reader of these lines has a clear idea of their meaning. Of which languages was the Turk ignorant; what are the narrow road and those great staging posts? One scholar (Sılay 1993) translates the fourth line as 'these styles of elegant and elevated discourse', which does no more than raise another question: what styles? The context makes it plain that Âşık Pasha is not talking about literary style. He has been discussing Koran 14. 4: 'We have sent no messenger save with the language of his people.' The Koran was revealed to the

---

[8] A valuable source on this topic is Yavuz (1983).
[9] The relevant portion of the text is most readily accessible in İz (1967: i. 584–5).

Arabs, in Arabic; neither Persians not Turks have had a prophet bearing them the revelation in their own tongues.

> Bu *Garipnâme* anın geldi dile
> Ki bu dil ehli dahi mânâ bile.
>
> Therefore has this *Garipnâme* been uttered
> That those who speak this tongue may also know the hidden wisdom.

The identity of the languages in question is shown in a previous couplet:

> Çün bilesin cümle yol menzillerin[10]
> Yirmegil sen Türk ü Tacik dillerin.
>
> To know all the staging posts of the road,
> Do not despise the Turkish and Persian languages.

The languages of which the Turk was ignorant are Turkish and Persian, the implication being that so far the language of religion has been Arabic, but Arabic is not the only language through which spiritual knowledge can be attained. Persian is the language of the *Mesnevî* of the great Sufi poet Jalāl al-Dīn Rūmī; the Turk should learn to read that language and his own, so that he can make use of the *Mesnevî* and of the *Garipnâme*. The road is the progress towards enlightenment, the staging posts are the stages in that progress.

To Mīr ʿAlī Šīr Nevāī (1441–1501) of Herat in Afghanistan belongs the distinction of having raised the Chaghatay dialect of Turkish to the status of literary language of Central Asia. In his *Muḥākamat al-Luġateyn* ('The Judgment between the Two Languages') he sets out to demonstrate that Turkish is in no way inferior to Persian as a literary medium. At one point he says:

Ve hünersiz Türkniñ sitem-ẓarīf yigitleri āsānlıḳḳa bola Fārsī elfāẓ bile naẓm ayturġa meşġūl bolupturlar. Ve fi'l-ḥaḳīḳa kişi yaḫşı mülâḥaẓa ve te'emmül ḳılsa, čūn bu lafẓda munça vüsʿat ve meydānıda munça füsḥat tapılur, kirek kim munda her süḫan-güzārlıġ ve faṣīḥ-güftārlıġ ve naẓm-sāzlıġ ve fesāne-perdāzlıġ āsānraḳ bolġay, ve vāḳiʿ āsānraḳdur. (Levend 1965–8: iv. 203)

Among untalented Turks, would-be artistic young men have occupied themselves with verse composition using Persian vocabulary, as being the easy course. Truly, if one considers and reflects well, since such scope and range are found in our own language, it follows that all eloquence and expression, all versification and story-telling, are bound to be easier in it and are in fact easier.

Like seventeen others of the thirty-six Ottoman sultans, Selim I (1512–20) wrote poetry. Most of his was in Persian. On the other hand, his arch-enemy Shah Ismail of Persia (1501–24) wrote poems in Turkish, some of which, set to music, may still be heard today on Turkish radio. It has been suggested that his purpose was to endear himself to the Turcomans in his territories, but the simpler explanation is that he was a Turk by birth and that writing in his mother tongue came naturally to him.

---

[10] In modern Turkish, the *-in* at the end of this line and the next would be *-ini*. See Lewis (1988: 41) and, for the *-gil* of *yirmegil*, ibid. (137).

In the fifteenth and sixteenth centuries came the school of *Türkî-i basit* ('plain
Turkish' poetry), associated with the names of Aydınlı Visâlî, Tatavlalı Mahremî,
and Edirneli Nazmî, whom it did not outlive. Readers of poetry expected it to
be in Ottoman, not *kaba Türkçe* (crude Turkish), whereas those whose everyday
language was indeed *kaba Türkçe*, while they might enjoy listening to poetry
that they could understand, were not generally readers. Yet even such a dyed-in-
the-wool Persianizing poet as Nabî (*c.*1630–1712), whom Gibb (1900–9: iii. 325)
speaks of as 'writing verses which can by courtesy alone be described as Turkish',
was moved to write:

> Ey şi'r miyanında satan lafz-ı garibi
> Divan-ı gazel nüsha-ı kamus değüldür.

> (Levend 1972: 78; Korkmaz 1985: 388)

> O you who sell outlandish words wrapped in poetry!
> A book of odes is not a copy of the dictionary!

It will be seen that only three—*ey, satan, değüldür*—of the eleven words in which
Nabî expresses this laudable sentiment are Turkish. Indeed, long after Ottoman
chroniclers had taken to writing in Ottoman instead of Persian, they persisted in
using pure Persian for their chapter headings.

The political changes introduced by the Tanzimat-ı Hayriye, the 'Propitious
Regulations' of 1839, and even more by the reform charter of 1856, gave hope that
the manifold grievances of various sections of the Sultan's subjects might be
rectified. Some were, but by no means all. For our purposes it is enough to say
that the spirit of the Tanzimat (the term applied to the period as well as to the
reforms) gave rise to the first serious stirrings of Turkish nationalism and to a
flowering of journalism, and from then on the tide of language reform flowed
strongly. A newspaper proprietor or editor does not have to be as devoted to the
ideal of a well-informed public as the pioneers of Turkish journalism were (most
if not all of them were driven into exile at some time in their careers), or indeed
devoted to any ideal at all, to see the necessity of making the language of his paper
understandable by as many people as possible; if he fails to see it, he will soon be
enlightened by his circulation manager.

The father of Turkish journalism was the writer and poet İbrahim Şinasi
(?1824–71), co-founder in 1860 with Agâh Efendi (1832–85), a civil servant and
diplomat, of *Terceman-ı Ahvâl*, founded in 1861, the second non-official newspaper
to be published in the country (the first was the weekly *Ceride-i Havâdis*, started
in 1840 by an Englishman, William Churchill).[11] Şinasi declared the paper's policy
in his first editorial (Levend 1972: 83):

[11] For a concise history of the Turkish press, see *The Encyclopaedia of Islam* (1960), ii. 465–6,
473–6. As for Churchill, see Koloğlu (1986), an entertaining account of how, despite being
miyop (short-sighted), he went out pigeon-shooting one Sunday afternoon in May 1836 and
wounded a shepherd boy and a sheep. There were diplomatic repercussions. An earlier account was
Alric (1892).

Ta'rife hacet olmadığı üzre, kelâm, ifade-i meram etmeğe mahsus bir mevhibe-i kudret olduğu misillü, en güzel icad-ı akl-ı insanî olan kitabet dahi, kalemle tasvir-i kelâm eylemek fenninden ibaretdir. Bu i'tibar-ı hakikate mebni giderek, umum halkın kolaylıkla anlayabileceği mertebede işbu gazeteyi kaleme almak mültezem olduğu dahi, makam münasebetiyle şimdiden ihtar olunur.

There is no need to explain that, while speech is a divine gift for the expression of thought, writing is the finest invention of the human intelligence, consisting as it does in the science of depicting speech by means of the pen. Proceeding from a regard for this truth, editorial notice is hereby given that it is a bounden duty to write this newspaper in a way that will be easily understood by the public at large.

Among the other pioneers were Namık Kemal (1840–88), a selfless patriot and distinguished writer in many fields, and his friend the great statesman Ziya Pasha (1825–80). This is from Namık Kemal's article 'Observations on Literature in the Ottoman Language':

İstanbul'da okuyup yazma bilenlerden dahi belki onda biri, sebk-i ma'ruf üzre yazılmış bir kâğıddan ve hattâ kâfil-i hukuku olan kanun-ı devletten bile istifade-i merama kaadir değildir. Çünki edebiyatımıza şark u garbın bir kaç ecnebî lisanından müstear olan şiveler galebe ederek ıttırâd-ı ifadeye halel vermiş ve edevât ü ta'birât ü ifâdat-ı takrirden bütün bütün ayrılmıs olan üslûb-ı tahrir ise bayağı bir başka lisan hükmüne girmiştir . . .
Elfazda garabet o kadar mu'teberdir ki, meselâ Nergisî gibi milletimizin en meşhur bir te'lif-i edîbânesinden istihrâc-i meal etmek, bize göre ecnebî bir lisanda yazılmış olan Gülistan'ı anlamaktan müşkildir. Türkçenin eczâ-yı terkibi olan üç lisan ki, telâffuzda oldukça ittihad bulmuşken tahrirde hâlâ hey'et-i asliyyelerini muhafaza ediyor. Akaanîm-i selâse gibi sözde gûya müttehid ve hakikatte zıdd-ı kâmildir.[12]

Even of literates in Istanbul, perhaps one in ten is incapable of getting as much as he would like from a normally phrased note or even from a State law, the guarantor of his rights. The reason is that our literature is swamped with locutions borrowed from several foreign tongues of east and west, which have damaged the flow of expression, while the style of composition has become totally detached from the particles and terms and forms of discourse and has fallen, to put it plainly, under the domination of another language.
So prevalent is foreignness in our vocabulary that it is harder, in my view, to extract the meaning from one of our nation's best-known literary compositions, for example that of Nergisî, than to understand the *Gulistān*, which is written in a foreign language. While the three languages of which Turkish is compounded have attained a certain unity in speech, they still preserve their original forms in writing. Like the three persons of the Trinity, they are said to be united but are in fact the reverse of integrated.

The poems of Nergisî (d. 1635) are more intelligible than his prose works. Gibb (1900–9: iii. 208–9) refers to him when speaking of Veysî's *Life of the Prophet*: '[It] is written in the most recherché Persian style, and shares with the prose Khamsa of Nergisé [*sic*] the distinction of having been gibbeted by Ebu-z-Ziyá Tevfíq Bey, one of the most stalwart champions of the Modern School, as a composition the continued study of which will land the nation in disaster.' The *Gulistān* of Saʿdī

---

[12] *Tasvir-i Efkâr*, 416, 16 Rebiyülâhır 1283/29 Aug. 1866; Levend (1972: 113–14).

(?1213–92), in a mixture of verse and rhymed prose, is regarded as one of the masterpieces of Persian literature. One might think that Namık Kemal was exaggerating, but in his day Arabic and Persian were a regular part of secondary education (and remained so until 1 October 1929). Anyone who has learned Persian, which is not a challenging language, can understand the *Gulistān*, but Nergisî's convoluted Ottoman prose presents much greater difficulty.

Ziya Pasha wrote the following in an article in *Hürriyet*, the newspaper he and Namık Kemal founded while exiles in London:

Elyevm resmen ilân olunan fermanlar ve emirnâmeler âhâd-ı nas huzurunda okutuldukta bir şey istifade ediliyor mu? Ya bu muharrerat yalnız kitabette melekesi olanlara mı mahsustur? Yoksa avâm-ı nas devletin emrini anlamak içün müdür? Anadolu'da ve Rumeli'de âhâd-ı nastan her şahsa, devletin bir ticaret nizamı vardır ve a'şarın suret-i müzayede ve ihalesine ve tevzi-i vergiye ve şuna buna dair fermanları ve emirnâmeleri vardır deyü sorulsun, görülür ki biçarelerin birinden haberi yoktur. Bu sebebdendir ki hâlâ bizim memâlikte Tanzimat nedir ve nizâmât-ı cedide ne turlü islâhat hâsıl etmiştir, ahali bilmediklerinden ekser mahallerde mütehayyizân-ı memleket ve zaleme-i vülât ve me'-murin ellerinde ve âdeta kable't-Tanzimat cereyan eden usûl-i zulm ü i'tisaf altında ezilir ve kimseye derdini anlatamazlar. Amma Fransa ve İngiltere memâlikinden birinde me'murun birisi nizâmât-ı mevcude hilâfında cüz'î bir hareket edecek olsa avâm-ı nas derhal da'vâcı olur.[13]

Today, when decrees and orders are read out in the hearing of the common people, can anything be made of them? Are such compositions meant exclusively for those with a mastery of the written word, or is it intended that ordinary people should understand what the State commands? Try talking to any commoner in Anatolia and Rumelia about a commercial regulation, or the decrees and orders relating to the auctioning and awarding of the right to collect tithes, or establishing the amount of tax due from each household, or any matter at all; you will find that none of the poor creatures knows anything about any one of them. This is why dwellers in our territories still do not know what the Tanzimat is and what kind of reforms the new regulations have given rise to, and in most places therefore suffer oppression at the hands of local dignitaries, tyrannical governors and officials, under the same bullying system and with all the injustices that prevailed in pre-Tanzimat times. Nor is the population able to tell anyone its troubles, whereas if an official in any of the French or English realms were to infringe the current regulations in the slightest degree, the commoners would immediately have the law on him.

Two lines from Chesterton's 'The Secret People' come irresistibly to mind:

We hear men speaking for us of new laws strong and sweet,
Yet is there no man speaketh as we speak in the street.

Ali Suavi (1837–78) was one of the first to take a nationalist stand in the matter of language: he urged the avoidance of non-Turkish words for which there were good Turkish equivalents and, like Süleyman Pasha and Şemsettin Sami after him,

---

[13] *Hürriyet* (London), 20 Cemâdî'l-ûlâ 1285/7 Sept. 1868; Levend (1972: 119).

spoke out against calling the language Ottoman. He went further than Şinasi, who did not explicitly advocate the use of Turkish in preference to non-Turkish words. This is how he ended the introductory editorial he wrote for his newspaper *Muhbir* (1 (1867); Levend 1972: 115): 'Tasrihi câiz olan herşey'i, Âsitâne'de kullanılan âdî lisan ile ya'ni herkesin anlıyabileceği ifade ile yazacaktır' (Everything which can legitimately be expressed, [this journal] will write up in the ordinary language used in the capital; that is to say, in terms that everybody will be able to understand).

Although the new newspapers and magazines frequently carried articles urging the use of simple Turkish, they tended to urge it in very complicated language. The domestic news sections of the newspapers went on for many years under the heading *Havâdis-i Dâhilîye*, because *havâdis* 'news' is an Arabic feminine, so *dâhilî* 'internal' had to be in the feminine too, not forgetting the Persian *-i*. As late as 1896, a contributor to the newspaper *İzmir* wrote an article appealing for the use of straightforward Turkish, one paragraph of which should suffice to prove this point (Levend 1972: 275). The Persian izafet compounds (which is what the writer meant by 'unfamiliar and ponderous foreign locutions') are identifiable in the modern transcription by the *-i* or *-ı*. Words in italic are of non-Turkish origin. '*Safvet-i ifade*mizi *ihlâl* eden *elfaz-i gayr-ı me'nuse ve sakile-i ecnebiyyeye mukabil servet-i mevcude-i lisaniyye*mizden *istifade* etmiş olsak, *daire-i safvet-i ifade*yi, *binaenalyh daire-i terakki*yi *tevsî*' etmiş oluruz' (*Had we made use of* our *existing linguistic wealth instead of* the *unfamiliar and ponderous foreign locutions* that *corrupt* our *purity of expression*, we would have *broadened the compass of purity of expression and consequently the compass of progress*).

Ahmet Midhat (1844–1912), most prolific of Turkish journalists,[14] wrote this in 1871, with not a single Persian izafet:

En evvel kalem sahiblerine şunu sormak isterim ki, bizim kendimize mahsus bir lisanımız yok mudur? Türkistan'da söylenmekte bulunan Türkçeyi gösterecekler, öyle değil mi? Hayır, o lisan bizim lisanımız değildir. Bundan altı yedi asır mukaddem bizim lisanımız idi, fakat şimdi değil. O Türkçe bizim lisanımız olmadığı gibi Arabî ve Farisî dahi lisanımız değildir.

Amma denilecek ki, bizim lisanımız her halde bunlardan haric olamıyor. Haric olamadığı gibi dahilinde de sayılamıyor. Türkistan'dan bir Türk ve Necid'den bir Arab ve Şiraz'dan bir Acem getirsek, edebiyyatımızdan en güzel bir parçayı bunlara karşı okusak hangisi anlar? Şübhe yok ki hiç birisi anlıyamaz.

Tamam, işte bunlardan hiç birisinin anlıyamadığı lisan bizim lisanımızdır diyelim. Hayır, anı da diyemeyiz. Çünki o parçayı bize okudukları zaman biz de anlıyamıyoruz . . .

Pek a'lâ, ne yapalım? Lisansız mı kalalım? Hayır, halkımızın kullandığı bir lisan yok mu? İşte anı millet lisanı yapalım . . .

---

[14] Ahmet Midhat's work was more remarkable for its extent than for its originality. His output, of close on 200 books and countless articles, won him the appellation 'kırk beygir kuvvetinde bir makina' (a forty-horsepower engine). Nevertheless he was an effective and widely read popularizer of new ideas. Over half of *Türk Dili*, 521 (May 1995) was devoted to him.

Arabça ve Farsçanın ne kadar izafetleri ve ne kadar sıfatları varsa kaldırıversek, yazdığımız şeyleri bugün yediyüz kişi anlıyabilmekte ise yarın mutlaka yedi bin kişi anlar. (*Basiret*, 4 Apr. 1871; Levend 1972: 123)

The first thing I should like to ask our writers is, don't we have a language of our own? They will point to the Turkish spoken in Turkestan, won't they? No, that is not our language. It was, six or seven centuries ago, but not now. That Turkish is not our language, nor are Arabic and Persian our language. But some will say, surely our language cannot lie outside these? It cannot lie outside them and it cannot be considered as inside them. If we were to bring a Turk from Turkestan, an Arab from Nejd, and a Persian from Shiraz, and read in their presence some exquisite passage from our literature, which of them would understand it? There is no doubt that none of them would. All right, let us say that this language which none of them can understand is our language. No, we cannot say that either, because when they read that passage to us *we* cannot understand it . . .

Very well, what are we to do? Are we to be left without a language? No! There is a language that our people speak, isn't there? Let us make that the national language . . . If we were to sweep away all the izafets and all the adjectives there are in Arabic and Persian, if seven hundred people today understand what we write, tomorrow it will surely be seven thousand.

Ahmet Midhat lived to see his wish well on the road to fulfilment. People who had been used to calling the natural sciences *ulûm-i tabiiye* came to see that there was no harm in using the Turkish plural instead of the Arabic, dropping the Persian *i* and the Arabic feminine ending of the adjective, and putting the adjective first: *tabiî ilimler*. Even so, M. A. Hagopian found it necessary to devote over 40 per cent of his *Ottoman-Turkish Conversation-Grammar* (1907) to the grammar of Arabic and Persian.

Süleyman Pasha (1838–92) deserves the palm for being the first Turk to publish a grammar of Turkish and to name it accordingly: *İlm-i Sarf-i Türkî* (1874). Credit is also due to Abdullah Ramiz Pasha, whose *Lisân-ı Osmânî'nin Kavâ'idini Hâvi Emsile-i Türkî* ('Paradigms of Turkish, Containing the Rules of the Ottoman Language') had appeared in 1868. In 1851, Ahmed Cevdet Pasha (1825–95) and Fuad Efendi, later Pasha (1815–68), had published *Kavâ'id-i Osmâniye* ('Ottoman Rules'), a grammar that went through a number of editions. The 1875 edition was named *Kavâ'id-i Türkiye* ('Turkish Rules').

Article 18 of the Constitution of 1876 named the official language as Turkish, not Ottoman: 'Tebâ'a-i Osmâniyenin hidemât-ı devlette istihdam olunmak için devletin lisân-ı resmîsi olan Türkçeyi bilmeleri şarttır' (A prerequisite for Ottoman subjects' employment in State service is that they know Turkish, which is the official language of the State).

Şemsettin Sami (1850–1904), famous for his excellent dictionary *Kamus-i Türkî* (1316/1901) (though it is not as comprehensive as Redhouse (1890)), was of Süleyman Pasha's way of thinking. The following extracts are from his article 'Lisân-ı Türkî (Osmânî)', published in an Istanbul weekly in 1881.

Osmanlı lisanı ta'birini pek de doğru görmüyoruz . . . Asıl bu lisanla mütekellim olan kavmın ismi 'Türk' ve söyledikleri lisanın ismi dahi 'lisân-ı Türkî' dir. Cühelâ-yı avam indinde mezmum addolunan ve yalnız Anadolu köylülerine ıtlak edilmek istenilen bu isim, intisabiyle iftihar olunacak bir büyük ümmetin ismidir. 'Osmanlı' ile 'Türk' isimleri beynindeki nisbet, tıpkı 'Avusturyalı' ile 'Alman' isimleri beynindeki nisbet gibidir. 'Avusturyalı' unvani Avusturya devletinin taht-ı tâbiiyyetinde bulunan kâffe-i akvâma ve onların biri ve ümmet-i hâkimesi olan Avusturya Almanlarına ıtlak olunduğu halde, 'Alman' ismi bu ümmet-i azîmenin gerek Avusturya'da, gerek Prusya ve Almanya'da ve gerek İsviçre ve Rusya ve sair taraflarda bulunan kâffe-i akvam efradına ıtlak olunur. Devlet-i Osmaniyyenin zîr-i tâbiiyyetinde bu lunan kâffe-i akvam efradına dahi 'Osmanlı' denilüp, 'Türk' ismi ise Adriatik denizi sevahilinden Çin hududuna ve Sibirya'nın iç taraflarına kadar münteşir olan bir ümmet-i azîmenin unvanıdır. Bunun içün, bu unvan, . . . müstevcib-i fahr ü mesâr olmak ıktıza eder. Memâlik-i Osmaniyye'de söylenilen lisanların cümlesine 'elsine-i Osmaniyye' denilmek caiz olabilirse de, bunların birine ve hususiyle ekseriyyet-i etrafı bu memâlikin haricinde olup bu devletin teessüsünden çok daha eski bulunan bir lisana 'lisan-ı Osmanî' denilmek tarihe ve ensâb-ı elsineye asla tevafuk etmez . . .

Bana kalırsa, o aktâr-ı ba'îdeki Türklerin lisaniyle bizim lisanımız bir olduğundan, ikisine de 'lisan-ı Türkî' ism-i müştereki ve beyinlerdeki farka da riayet olunmak istenildiği halde, onlarınkine 'Türkî-i şarkî' ve bizimkine 'Türkî-i garbî' unvanı pek münasibdir . . .[15]

I do not think the term 'the Ottoman language' is quite correct . . . The name of the people who speak this language is really 'Turks' and their language is Turkish. This name, which is regarded as a reproach by the ignorant masses and which some would like to see applied only to the peasants of Anatolia, is the name of a great community which ought to take pride in being so termed. The relationship between 'Ottoman' and 'Turk' is just like that between 'Austrian' and 'German'. 'Austrian' is applied to the totality of peoples who are subjects of the Austrian State, among them the Germans of Austria, the dominant community. 'German' is applied to all members of this great community, both in Austria and in Prussia and Germany, as well as in Switzerland, Russia and elsewhere. So, too, members of all the peoples subject to the Ottoman dynasty are called Ottomans, while 'Turk' is the title of a great community extending from the shores of the Adriatic to the borders of China and the interior of Siberia. This title, therefore . . . should be a reason for pride and joy. Though it may be permissible to give the name 'the Ottoman languages' to the totality of languages spoken in the Ottoman dominions, it is quite inconsistent with history and the relationships of languages to apply the name 'the Ottoman language' to one of them, particularly one whose boundaries for the most part lie beyond those dominions and which antedates by far the foundation of this State . . .

As I see it, since the language of the Turks in those distant regions is one with ours, it is perfectly proper to give them the common name of Turkish and, in cases where it is desirable for the difference between them to be observed, to call theirs Eastern Turkish and ours Western Turkish . . .

Part of the reaction to the repressive regime of Sultan Abdülhamid (1876–1909) was manifested in the imitation of Western, particularly French, literary works, their content as much as their form, notably by the *Servet-i Fünun* school. Despite its modernist pretensions, this famous journal ('The Riches of Science')

---

[15] *Hafta*, 12, 10 Zilhicce 1298/4 Nov. 1881. Full text in Levend (1972: 130–4).

represents a blind alley, even a U-turn, on the road to making the written language more accessible to the general public. It began its career in 1891 as the weekly magazine of the Istanbul evening newspaper *Servet*. Between 1895 and 1901, when the government closed it down, it was the hub of a circle of young French-oriented writers who became known as the Edebiyat-ı Cedideciler, the exponents of the new literature. The precious style adopted by many of them repelled the common reader. Persuaded as they were that Turkish was incapable of being a literary medium without the aid of Arabic and Persian, they were wedded to the Persian izafet compounds and, not content with those current in the literary language, created new ones. Among their favourites were: *şebnem-i zevk u tesliyet* 'the dew of pleasure and consolation', *hadika-i sükûn* 'garden of tranquillity', and *melâl-i mesâ* 'evening melancholy' (Levend 1972: 349). At the same time they liked to show how Westernized they were by using calques, literal translations of French expressions, such as *ilâç almak* 'to take medicine' instead of the normal *ilâç yemek*. One of their number, the novelist Halit Ziya Uşaklıgil (1866–1945), wrote this in his memoirs forty years on:

Bu maraz hâdisesi, refiklerimin affedeceklerine, hattâ benimle beraber i'tiraf eyliyeceklerine kanaatle söyliyeceğim, zînet ve san'at ibtilâsıydı . . . öyle ki o tarihten uzaklaştıkça hele bugün ben bizzat bunları tekrar okurken sinirlenmekten hâlî kalmıyorum.   (Uşaklıgil 1936: iv. 141; Levend 1972: 238)

This disease—and I shall say this in the conviction that my old colleagues will forgive me and may even join in my confession—was an addiction to ornateness and artifice . . . so much so that the further I am removed from that time, and especially at the present day, the more irritated I become on re-reading what I wrote then.

During the 1897 war with Greece, the poet Mehmet Emin [Yurdakul] (1869–1944) published his *Türkçe Şiirleri*. The title is significant: these were Turkish poems, not Ottoman poems. The first, 'Anadoludan bir ses yahut Cenge giderken' ('A Voice from Anatolia, or Going to War'), began:

> Ben bir Türküm: dinim, cinsim uludur:
> Sinem, özüm ateş ile doludur:
> İnsan olan vatanının kuludur:
> Türk evlâdı evde durmaz; giderim!

> I am a Turk, my faith and my race are great;
> My breast and soul are full of fire.
> He who serves his native land—he is a man;
> The sons of Turks will not stay at home; I go!

It won him the appellation Türk Şairi, meaning not just 'the Turkish poet' but 'the "Turk" poet'. The language of the poem, for the most part simple Turkish, the words 'Ben bir Türküm', and above all his use of the syllabic metres of popular verse rather than the Arabo-Persian quantitative metres of classical poetry, were a slap in the face for the intellectuals who saw themselves as Ottomans, in particular for the élitist Edebiyat-ı Cedideciler. They retorted that he was no poet but a mere versifier and that not all the words he used would be intelligible to the common people. There was some justice in these criticisms: *ceng* [P], for example, was a distinctly high-flown way of saying 'war'. But the common people admired him as a literary man who was not too proud to declare himself a Turk like them.

Türk Derneği, the Turkish Association, was the first nationalist cultural organization to be formed, in January 1908, one of its founders being Ahmet Midhat (Tunaya 1984: i. 414–15; Levend 1972: 301). Its sixty-three members were far from having a shared view about the future of the language. Some of them were Simplifiers (*Sadeleştirmeciler*), who favoured eliminating non-Turkish elements and replacing them with native words current in speech. Some were Turkicizers (*Türkçeciler*), who believed that new words should be created by means of the regular Turkish suffixes and that Arabic and Persian words current in popular speech should be counted as Turkish. Then there were the Purifiers (*Tasfiyeciler*), who did not object to the Turkicizers' view on the latter point but advocated borrowing words and suffixes from other dialects. Their leader Fuat Köseraif was not averse to inventing where necessary; according to Ziya Gökalp, he favoured taking suffixes over from Kirghiz, Uzbek, or Tatar, or even creating them from whole cloth ('büsbütün yeniden yaratılacak'): the adjective suffix -*î* could be replaced by -*kı/ki/gı/gi*, so that *hayatî* 'vital' would become *hayatkı*, and *edebî* 'literary' would become *edebgi*. Unfortunately for anyone trying to sort out the various groups, their contemporaries outside the Dernek tended to call them all Purifiers, which Gökalp (1339/1923: 114–15) found confusing.[16]

Others could not stomach the idea of abandoning even the Persian izafet, and came out strongly against those who would turn Ottomans into *Buharalı* (people of Bukhara). Two prominent members, Mehmet Emin and Halit Ziya, held diametrically opposite views on the course the language ought to take. While the Association was being established, the latter contributed an article to *Servet-i Fünun* in which he poured scorn on those wishing to expel from the language words of non-Turkish ancestry for which Turkish synonyms existed. The first word or phrase in the first two pairs in the following quotation is Arabic, the second Persian; in the others the order is reversed:

Yok, maksud, zaten bizde Türkçe olarak müradifleri mevcud olan kelimeleri atmaksa, meselâ lisanda güneş var diye ufk-ı edebîmizden 'şems ü hurşid' i silmek, yıldız var diye 'nücum u ahter' i söndürmek, göz var diye 'çeşm ü dîde' yi, 'ayn u basar' ı kapamak, yol var diye 'râh u tarik' i seddetmek, su var diye 'âb u mâ' yı kurutmak kabilinden ameliyatı tahribe karar vermekse, buna bir israf-ı bîhude nazarı ile bakmak tabiîdir.

Bu mütalâaya serdedilen yegâne i'tiraz: lisanı sadeleştirmek, onu seviye-i irfan-ı halka indirmek içün bu fedakârlığa lüzum var sözünden ibarettir. Fakat lisan seviye-i irfan-ı halka inmez, seviye-i irfan-ı halk lisana yükseltimeğe çalışılır.   (Levend 1972: 305)

[16] He always spelled his second name as two words: Gök Alp (Sky Hero).

No, if the purpose is to discard the words we have with Turkish synonyms, and to decide on such destructive surgery as effacing *şems* and *hurşid* from our literary horizon because we have *güneş* 'sun', extinguishing *nücum* and *ahter* because we have *yıldız* 'star', closing *çeşm u dîde* and *ayn ü basar* because we have *göz* 'eye', blocking *râh* and *tarik* because we have *yol* 'road', drying up *âb* and *mâ* because we have *su* 'water', one cannot but regard it as wanton waste.

The sole objection raised to this observation consists in the assertion that this sacrifice is necessary in order to simplify the language, to lower it to the cultural level of the people. But the language does not descend to the cultural level of the people; one endeavours to elevate the cultural level of the people to the language.

The majority of the membership must have been of Halit Ziya's way of thinking, for this was how the Association's official attitude was set forth in its journal, which shared its name:

Osmanlı lisanının Arabî ve Farsî lisanlarından ettiği istifade gayr-ı münker bulunduğundan ve Osmanlı Türkçesini bu muhterem lisanlardan tecrid etmek hiçbir Osmanlının hayalinden bile geçmiyeceğinden, Türk Derneği, Arabî ve Farsî kelimelerini bütün Osmanlılar tarafından kemal-i sühuletle anlaşılacak vechile şâyi' olmuşlarından intihab edecek ve binaenaleyh mezkûr Derneğin yazacağı eserlerde kullanacağı lisan en sade Osmanlı Türkçesi olacaktır.   (Levend 1972: 301)

Since the benefit that the Ottoman language has derived from the Arabic and Persian languages is undeniable, and since no Ottoman would even dream of dissociating Ottoman Turkish from these revered languages, the Turkish Association will select Arabic and Persian words from among those that have gained currency enough to be understood with total ease by all Ottomans. Consequently, the language that the Association will use in works it produces will be the simplest Ottoman Turkish.

All very fine for the Ottomans, but not much use to those inhabitants of Turkey who, not presuming to lay claim to that designation, humbly thought of themselves as Turks. Mehmet Emin for one could scarcely have approved. Clearly the disparity of opinions did not augur well for the prospects of the Association, which by 1913 had indeed ceased to exist.

The exponents of simple Turkish still had far to go, not having yet grasped the principle expressed in St Luke's 'Physician, heal thyself.' At this range it is impossible to say whether or not the drafter of the following 'Decision on the Purification of the Language', quoted in the press in November 1909 (Levend 1972: 313), had his tongue in his cheek. Again, the words in italic are of non-Turkish origin:

*Levazimat-ı umumiyye dairesi ta'yînat kısmı ma'rifet*iyle terkim ve tevzi' edilmekte olan *matbu' pusula*lara *envâ'-ı muayyenatı mübeyyin* olmak üzere *der*colunmakta olan '*nân-ı aziz*', '*gûşt*', '*erz*', '*şa'r*' ve '*hatab*' *kelime*lerinin yerlerine, *ba'demâ* 'ekmek', 'et', '*pirinç*', 'arpa' ve 'odun' yazılması *karargir* olmuştur.

It has been *decided* that the *words* '*nân-ı aziz*' [PA] 'precious bread',[17] *gûşt* [P] 'meat', '*erz*' [A] 'rice', '*şa'r*' [A] 'barley', *and hatab*' [A] 'firewood', which are *included* on the *printed slips*

---

[17] The adjective 'precious' does not denote a particular type of loaf; it was a stock epithet of bread.

drawn up and distributed by the rationing section of the *Department of the Commissariat-General* to *indicate the various kinds of rations,* shall *henceforth* be replaced by 'ekmek', 'et', *'pirinç* [P], 'arpa', *and* 'odun'.

But one doubts that members of the Ottoman Parliament had their tongues in their cheeks one month later, when stating their objection to the proposed wording of their response to the Speech from the Throne: '*Arîza-i teşekküriyye*nin *üslûb-ı tahriri* pek *edibane ve Meclis-i Millî*'ye yakışmıyacak *derece*de teşbihat ve elfaz-ı rengin ile *mahmul*' (*The style of composition* of the Grateful Submission is very *literary and laden* with *similes and ornate locutions* to an *extent* unbecoming *the National Assembly*) (Levend 1972: 313).

On the other hand, the poet Mehmet Âkif was not happy with the results of purification as exhibited in the newspaper *İkdam* in 1910:

bir takım makaleler görülüyor ki Türkçe kelimelerin yanıbaşlarında Arapçaları olmasa zavallı ümmet-i merhume hiçbir şey anlamıyacak! Meclis yerine 'kurıltay',[18] meb'us yerine 'yalvaç', a'yan yerine 'aksakal', hal yerine 'idemük', can yerine bilmem ne! . . . Gazetelerde zabıta vukuatı öyle ağır bir lisanla yazılıyor ki avam onu bir dua gibi dinliyor: 'Mehmet Bey'in hanesine leylen fürce-yâb-ı duhul olan sârık sekiz adet kalîçe-i giran-baha sirkat etmiştir' deyüp de 'Mehmed Bey'in bu gece evine hırsız girmiş sekiz halı çalmış' dememek âdetâ maskaralıktır. Avâmın anlıyabileceği meânî avâmın kullandığı lisan ile edâ edilmeli . . . (*Sırât-ı Müstakim,* 4/92, 9 Apr. 1910; Levend 1972: 311–12)

One sees many articles of which the unfortunate public—God have mercy on them—would understand nothing were it not for the Arabic equivalents given alongside the Turkish words! *Kurıltay* for *meclis* 'Parliament', *yalvaç* for *meb'us* 'Deputy', *aksakal* 'greybeards' for *a'yan* 'notables', *idemük*[19] for *hal* 'situation', and I don't know what for *can* 'soul'! . . . The police reports in the newspapers are couched in language so abstruse that ordinary people listen to them as if they were religious formulas. To say 'Depredators who nocturnally effected an opportunist entry into Mehmed Bey's domicile purloined costly tapis eight in number', and not to say 'Last night burglars broke into Mehmed Bey's house and stole eight rugs' is not far short of buffoonery. Concepts for ordinary people to be able to understand should be expressed in the language used by ordinary people . . .

By the end of the nineteenth century some, and by the First World War most, Turkish writers were making a conscious effort to avoid Persian constructions except in stock phrases. They were also ceasing to think of their language as Ottoman, and after 1918 few went on thinking of themselves as Ottomans. Article 7 of the 1908 political programme of the Society for Union and Progress ('the Young Turks') ran: 'Devletin lisan-ı resmîsi Türkçe kalacaktır. Her nevi muhaberat ve müzakeratı Türkçe icra olunacaktır' (The official language of the State will remain Turkish. Its correspondence and deliberations of every kind will be conducted in Turkish) (Tunaya 1952: 209). In 1920, while the War of Independence was still raging and the Sultan's government still ruled in

---

[18] In Levend, *kurıltay* is misspelt *kurultay*.

[19] The author has so far failed to track down this word, even in that wonderful ragbag *Tarama Dergisi* (1934).

Istanbul, schoolteachers had been instructed by the Ankara government's Ministry of Education to collect pure Turkish words in colloquial use that had so far eluded the lexicographers.

But the non-writing classes took a good deal longer to adjust to the new situation. The author was told by Fahir İz that, during his military service in the neighbourhood of Erzurum just before the Second World War, he had got into conversation with a shepherd, whom he shocked by using the words 'Biz Türkler' (We Turks). 'Estağfurullah!' was the reply, 'Ben Türküm, zat-ı âliniz Osmanlısınız' (Lord have mercy! I'm a Turk; Your Excellency is an Ottoman).

Somewhat more effective than Türk Derneği was the literary group that called itself and its journal *Genç Kalemler* (The Young Pens), formed in Salonica (Selânik) in April 1911 (Levend 1972: 313–30). Its members were also known as *Yeni Lisancılar*, the exponents of the new language. Most influential among them were Ziya Gökalp and the short-story writer Ömer Seyfettin (1884–1920).

The latter was the author of an article entitled 'Yeni Lisan' and signed only with a question mark, attacking the *Edebiyat-ı Cedide*, the 'new literature' of the Servet-i Fünun group, and the even shorter-lived group known as *Fecr-i Âtî* (the Coming Dawn), which formed round *Servet-i Fünun* on its reappearance after the Young Turk revolution of 1908. 'Bugünkülerin dünküleri taklid etmekten vazgeçtikleri dakika hakikî fecir olacak, onların sayesinde yeni bir lisanla terennüm olunan millî bir edebiyat doğacaktır . . . Millî bir edebiyat vücuda getirmek için evvelâ millî lisan ister' (The true dawn will break at the moment when today's people stop imitating yesterday's. Thanks to them a national literature will be born, hymned in a new language . . . To bring a national literature into being requires first a national language). He went on to give his recipe for that future national language. In something of a purple passage, he stated his objections to replacing current words of Arabic and Persian origin with native words or with borrowings from further east:

Derneğin arkasına takılup akîm bir irticaa doğru, 'Buhara-yı şerif'deki henüz mebnâî bir hayat süren, müdhiş bir vukufsuzluğun, korkunç bir taassubun karanlıkları içinde uyuyan bundan bir düzüne asır evvelki günleri yaşıyan kavimdaşlarımızın yanına mı gidelim? Bu bir intihardır. Bu serî' ateşli toplarımızı, makineli tüfenklerimizi bırakıp yerine; düşmanlarımız gelince—kavimdaşlarımız gibi—üzerlerine atacağımız suları kaynatmağa mahsus çay semaverleri koymağa benzer. Hayır. Beş asırdan beri konuştuğumuz kelimeleri, me'nus denilen Arabî ve Farsî kelimeleri mümkin değil terkedemeyiz. Hele aruzu atıp Mehmed Emin Bey'in vezinlerini hiçbir şair kabul etmez. Konuştuğumuz lisan, İstanbul Türkçesi en tabiî bir lisandır. Klişe olmuş terkiblerden başka lüzumsuz zinetler aslâ mükalememize giremez. Yazı lisanı ile konuşmak lisanını birleştirirsek, edebiyatımızı ihya veya icad etmiş olacağız . . .

Lisanımızda yalnız Türkce kaideler hükmedecek; yalnız Türkce, yalnız Türkce kaideleri. (*Genç Kalemler* (Apr. 1911); Levend 1972: 314–15)

Are we to tag along behind the Türk Derneği and head for a sterile reaction, joining our fellow members of the Turkish community who still lead a basic existence in 'Bukhara the

Noble', slumbering in the darkness of a dreadful ignorance and horrendous fanaticism, living the life of a dozen centuries ago? That would be an act of suicide. It would be like abandoning our quick-firing artillery and machine-guns and instead, when our enemies arrive, doing as the fellow-members of our people do and putting on the samovars expressly intended to boil the water we're going to throw over them. No, it is impossible; we cannot forsake the Arabic and Persian words, the words we call familiar, that we have spoken for five centuries. Certainly no poet will renounce the classical prosody and accept Mehmet Emin Bey's metres. Istanbul Turkish, the language we speak, is a most natural language. Stereotyped izafet compounds aside, the unnecessary trimmings can never enter our speech. If we unify the language of writing and the language of speaking, we shall have revived our literature or produced a new literature . . .

In our language, only Turkish rules will hold sway; only the Turkish language and only the rules of Turkish.

The spectre of Türk Derneği's failure must have been before his eyes as he wrote that equivocal statement, which in no way justified the term 'new language'. Şemsettin Sami had been far more radical thirty years before.

Most of the literary establishment were less receptive than Ömer Seyfettin to suggestions that the language needed to be reformed; this may have been due to their love of Ottoman for its own sake or as a badge of rank distinguishing them form the commoners. Süleyman Nazif (1870–1927), editor of *Yeni Tasvir-i Efkâr*, published an open letter by way of a rejection slip to a writer who had sent him an article on language. Having said that, if he were the proprietor of the newspaper, he would never open its pages to an article that advocated simplifying the language, he went on:

Lisanını seven bir Osmanlı Türk'ü, hiçbir vakit 'hatavât-ı terakki' makamına 'ilerleme adımları'nı ıs'ad edemez, böyle yaparsak lisanın kabiliyyet ve letafetini elimizle mahvetmiş oluruz . . . Lisanı sadeleştirmek, bizi yedi asır geriye ve dört beş bin kilometre uzağa atmaktır . . . Tekrar ederim ki biz bugün Buhârâlı değiliz ve olamayız. O maziyi iadeye çalışmak mühlik bir irtica'dır. (*Yeni Tasvir-i Efkâr*, 12 July 1909; Levend 1972: 305–6)

An Ottoman Turk who loves his language can never elevate *ilerleme adımları* [going-ahead steps] to the status of *hatavât-ı terakki* [progressive paces]. If we do that, we thereby destroy the capacity and subtlety of the language with our own hands . . . To simplify the language is to throw us seven centuries back and four or five thousand kilometres distant . . . I repeat: today we are not and cannot be Bukharans. Trying to bring back that past is a destructive piece of reaction.

Interestingly, the cudgels were taken up on behalf of simplification by an easterner; not a Bukharan but a man from Kazan, Kazanlı Ayaz.

Bizim mesleğimiz avam tarafdarı bulunmak olduğundan, biz bütün efkâr-ı siyasiye ve icti-maiye avâma anlatmak tarafındayız. Bizce bu meslek bir lisan için değil, bütün mesâil-i hayatiye içündür . . . Memleketin ıslâhı, milletin teceddüdü bütün efrad-ı millet efkârının teceddüdü ile hasıl olacağından bizim nokta-ı nazarımızdan milletini seven her Türk yazdığı her makaleyi Anadolu Türklerinin anlayacağı bir lisanla yazması lâzım gelir. (*Servet-i Fünun*, 9 July 1325/22 July 1909; Levend 1972: 307)

Given that our vocation is to take the side of the common people, we are for acquainting them with all political and social thinking. In my view this vocation does not relate to a language but to all vital problems . . . As the reformation of the country and the renewal of the nation will come about with the renewal of the thinking of every member of the nation, from our point of view every article written by any Turk who loves his nation must be in a language that will be understood by the Turks of Anatolia.

One of the few who joined him was Celâl Sahir [Erozan] (1883–1935), a poet of the Fecr-i Âtî school, who followed Mehmet Emin in making the transition from Arabo-Persian prosody to Turkish syllabic metre, in which he produced some attractive love-poetry:

Şimdi lisanda teceddüd husulü için çalışmak isteyenlerin ilk adımı bu kavaid-i ecnebiyyeyi tard ve imhâ olmalıdır. Bizim kelimeye ihtiyacımız var. Peki, fakat yalnız kelimeye, müfred kelimelerle müfredlerinden ayrı, müstakil bir ma'nâ ifade eden cemi' kelimelere, her kelimenin cem'ine, tesniyesine değil, hele terakibe hiç değil . . . Hele lisanı sadeleştirmenin bizi yedi asır geriye atmak olduğunu hiç kabul edemem.   (*Servet-i Fünun*, 27 May 1326/9 June 1910; Levend 1972: 309)

The first step taken by those wishing to work for renewal in the language should be to cast out and eliminate these foreign rules. We need words. Very well; but *only* words: the singular forms of words and those plurals which express independent meanings, distinct from their singulars,[20] but not the plural or the feminine of every word and above all not izafet compounds . . . In particular I cannot accept that simplifying the language means throwing us seven centuries back into the past.

To leave for a moment the views of established literary figures of the old days, here is a reminiscence of the economist Fuat Andic about his generation's view in the 1940s of what the language of the future ought to be. It centres on a verse by Kemalpaşazade Sait, alias Lâstik ('Galoshes') Sait, who held several senior posts in government service but was best known as a writer of articles on literature for the newspapers *Tarik* and *Vakit*, and as a minor poet. The reason for his nickname was that he was reputed never to take off his galoshes even in summer.[21] He engaged in often vitriolic polemics on literature and language with Namık Kemal, Ahmet Midhat, and the poet Abdülhak Hâmid (1851–1937). The language of his writings was pure Ottoman; does the verse express his real opinion or was it meant sarcastically? Probably the former; he habitually wrote in Ottoman, because in those days it was the only way to write formally, but this time he was rebelling. At any rate, the boys of Fuat Andic's generation took it seriously. And here it is:

[20] The reference is to words like the Arabic *ajzā'*, plural of *juz'* 'part'; its Turkish form *ecza* means not 'parts' but 'chemicals, drugs', whence *eczacı* 'pharmacist'. See Lewis (1988: 27).

[21] I am indebted to Professor Andic, both for drawing my attention to Lâstik Sait and for explaining the origin of his nickname.

Arapça isteyen urbana gitsin
Acemce isteyen İrana gitsin
Frengiler Frengistana gitsin
Ki biz Türküz bize Türkî gerek.

Let the one who wants Arabic go to the Beduin;
Let the one who wants Persian go to Iran;
Let the Franks go to their own land.
For we are Turks; we must have Turkish.

The class used to add a fifth line: 'Bunu bilmeyen ahmak/eşşek demek' (Anyone who doesn't know this, it means he's a silly fool/donkey).[22]

To revert to the grown-ups: Ziya Gökalp believed that, if the Turks were to equip themselves with the vocabulary necessary for coping with the advances of science and technology, the natural way was to follow the example of the Western nations. Just as they had recourse to Greek and Latin, the classical languages of their culture, so the Turks should go back to Arabic and Persian. In practice, he based his creations on Arabic, less frequently Persian, while using the Persian izafet to make compounds. From *rūḥ* 'soul, spirit' he made *ruhiyat*[23] for 'psychology'; from *badī* 'floweriness of style', *bediî* for 'aesthetic' (though in Arabic *badī'ī* means 'rhetorical') and *bediiyat* for 'aesthetics'. From the Arabic *ša'n*, 'matter, affair', he made *şe'nî* 'pragmatic' and *şe'niyet* 'reality'. These two never won much currency, partly because 'pragmatic' does not figure in everyone's vocabulary, and mostly because Turks in general did not distinguish between Arabic *'ayn*, the pharyngal gulp, and *hamza*, the glottal stop, or attempt to pronounce either of them, so that except to a few pedants Ziya Gökalp's *şe'nî* 'pragmatic' sounded exactly like *şenî*, the Turkish pronunciation of the Arabic *šanī'* 'abominable'.

His most successful coinage was a word for 'ideal'. Until his time, the dictionary equivalent had been *gaye-i emel* 'goal of hope' or *gaye-i hayal* 'goal of imagination', though probably most people who talked about ideals used the French *idéal*. He invented *mefkûre* (together with *mefkûreviyat* for 'ideology'), based on the Arabic *fakara* 'to think', which was enthusiastically adopted, surviving long after *Tarama Dergisi* (1934) came up with *ülkü*; indeed, recent dictionaries still use it to define *ülkü*. It survives in another aspect too: in Turkish cities you will see apartment blocks named Mefkûre, as well as Ülkü and İdeal.

After all that, Gökalp (1339/1923: 28) might be accused of inconsistency for writing: 'Lisanın bir kelimesini değiştiremeyiz. Onun yerine başka bir kelime icad edip koyamayız' (We cannot change a word of the language. We cannot invent and substitute another word for it). His creations, however, were intended to express concepts for which no words yet existed.

---

[22] Andic writes, 'The fifth line may or may not belong to him. When I was in high school it was a pastime among us to add one or two lines to well-known poems. I do not know for sure whether the fifth line belongs to me or to Lâstik Sait' (Letter to the author, 13 Apr. 1997). The student should bear in mind that *eşek* is more offensive than 'donkey', and that *eşşek* is more offensive than *eşek*.

[23] For the *-iyat*, sometimes transcribed as *-îyat* or *-iyyat*, see Lewis (1988: 27).

He tells how deeply impressed he was in 1897 at hearing how private soldiers coped with the Ottoman terms for first and second lieutenant. 'Lieutenant' in Arabic was *mulāzim*, 'first' was *awwal*, and 'second' was *ṭānī*. Put together in accordance with the rules of Persian and pronounced in accordance with the rules of Turkish, that made 'mülâzim-i evvel', 'mülâzim-i sani'. The soldiers, however, put the adjectives first, saying 'evvel mülâzim', 'sani mülâzim'. This led him to the following conclusion: 'Türkçeyi ıslâh içün bu lisandan bütün Arabî ve Farsî kelimeleri değil, umum Arabî ve Farsî kaideleri atmak, Arabî ve Farsî kelimeler-den de Türkçesi olanları terkederek, Türkçesi bulunmayanları lisanda ibka etmek' (The way to reform Turkish is not to throw all the Arabic and Persian words out of this language but to throw out all Arabic and Persian rules and abandon all the Arabic and Persian words which have Turkish equivalents, letting those with no Turkish equivalents survive in the language) (Gökalp 1339/1923: 12).

A line from his poem 'Lisan',[24] 'Türkçeleşmiş Türkçedir' (What has become Turkish is Turkish), has often been quoted by those unwilling to see the loss of any Ottoman word. Later on in the same book he states his first principle of *Lisanî Türkçülük* (Linguistic Turkism): 'Millî lisanımızı vücude getirmek için, Osmanlı lisanını hiç yokmuş gibi bir tarafa atarak, halk edebiyatına temel vazifesini gören Türk dilini ayniyle kabul edip İstanbul halkının ve bilhassa İstanbul hanımlarının konuştukları gibi yazmak' (For the purpose of creating our national language, to accept as it stands the Turkish tongue, which serves as the basis for popular liter-ature, and to write as Istanbul people speak, especially Istanbul ladies, discarding the Ottoman language as if it had never been) (Gökalp 1339/1923: 121).

The word *halk* is ambiguous nowadays and no doubt was in Gökalp's time too; whereas in political speeches it connotes the citizen body, the sovereign people, in common parlance it means the proletariat. Gökalp was certainly using it in the first sense, but the question is, what then did he mean by 'hanımlar'? Female res-idents of Istanbul, or Istanbul ladies as distinct from Istanbul women? We must assume the latter; at all events, his first principle was never put into effect. Nor was another of his pronouncements: 'İstanbul Türkçesinin savtiyatı, şekliyatı ve lûgaviyatı,[25] yeni Türkçenin temeli olduğundan, başka Türk lehçelerinden ne kelime, ne sıyga ne edat, ne de terkib kaideleri alınamaz' (As the basis of the new Turkish is the phonology, morphology, and lexicon of Istanbul Turkish, neither words nor moods and tenses nor suffixes nor rules of syntax may be taken from other Turkish dialects) (Gökalp 1339/1923: 122). While later reformers did not adopt moods and tenses or rules of syntax from other dialects, they adopted words and suffixes in full measure, as we shall see.

---

[24] Published in *Yeni Hayat* in 1918, reproduced in Levend (1972: 332–3).
[25] The three preceding nouns were coined by Gökalp from Arabic roots.

3

The New Alphabet

Turkish writers on *dil devrimi* (language reform) do not usually deal with the change of alphabet, which for them is a separate topic, *harf devrimi* (letter reform). A brief account of it is given here for the sake of completeness, since the two reforms are obviously linked, arising as they did from the same frame of mind. The purpose of the change of alphabet was to break Turkey's ties with the Islamic east and to facilitate communication domestically as well as with the Western world. One may imagine the difficulty of applying the Morse Code to telegraphing in Ottoman.

Its intrinsic beauty aside, there is nothing to be said in favour of the Arabo-Persian alphabet as a medium for writing Turkish.[1] All of its letters, including *alif*, the glottal stop, are consonants, some representing sounds not existing in Turkish and one, *k*, which may represent Turkish *g, k, n*, or *y*. The sound of *n* indicated by the Arabo-Persian *k* was originally /ng/, pronounced as in English *singer*; in scholarly transcriptions of old texts it is usually shown by *ñ*. It occurs in such Ottoman spellings as *kwkl* for *gönül* 'soul', and *dkz* or *dkyz* for *deniz* 'sea'. It is still heard in some Turks' pronunciation of *sonra* 'after'. With the addition of diacritics above or below the letters, the three vowels *a, i*, and *u* can be indicated, whereas Turkish needs to distinguish eight. The Arabic letters *alif*, *wāw*, and *yā* were employed in Arabic and Persian to show *ā, ū*, and *ī* respectively. In Turkish they were used to indicate *a/e*, *o/ö/u/ü*, and *i/ay/ey* respectively. An initial *a* or *e* was indicated by *alif* (henceforth shown as *ʔ*), medial or final *a* also by *alif*, and *e* by *h*, which is similar to the function of English *h* in 'Ah!' and 'Eh?': *kaynana* 'mother-in-law' was written *qynʔnʔ*, *yaparsa* 'if he does' as *yʔpʔrsh*, *ise* 'if it is' as *ʔysh*, *istemediğin* 'which you do not want' as *ʔsthmhdykk*.

Many equivocal readings were possible. Thus *ʔwlw* in an Ottoman text may be read as Turkish *ulu* 'great' or *ulu* [A] 'possessors', *ölü* 'dead', *evli* 'married', *avlu* 'courtyard', *avlı* 'stocked with game'; *dwl* may represent *döl* 'progeny', *dul* 'widowed', or *düvel* [A] 'States', while *kl* can be *gel* 'come', *gül* 'smile', *kel* 'scabby', *kel* [A] 'lassitude', *kül* 'ashes', *kül* [A] 'all', *gil* [P] 'clay', or *gül* [P] 'rose'. Only the context and a sufficient grasp of the vocabularies of Turkish, Persian, and Arabic can make clear which of the possible readings is intended. Problems often arise in Ottoman texts because scribes and printers were not always careful about word

---

[1] 'Arabo-Persian' rather than 'Arabic', because it includes three letters, *p, č*, and *j*, that were added to the Arabic alphabet in order to represent the three Persian sounds not occurring in Arabic.

divisions; the letters *bwsnh*, for example, could stand for *bu sene* 'this year' or *Bosna* 'Bosnia'.

In the article 'Turks' in the thirteenth edition of *Encyclopaedia Britannica* (1926), Sir Charles Eliot, after mentioning the ambiguities of this alphabet, shrewdly observes: 'The result is that pure Turkish words written in Arabic letters are often hardly intelligible even to Turks and it is usual to employ Arabic synonyms as much as possible because there is no doubt as to how they should be read.' An example of what he had in mind is shown by the words *mḥmd pʔš? ʔwldy*, which may be read as 'Mehmed paşa oldu' (Mehmed became a pasha) or 'Mehmed Paşa öldü' (Mehmed Pasha died). If you meant the former, you would resort to a circumlocution such as 'Mehmed was elevated to the rank of Pasha'. If you meant the latter, you would write 'Mehmed Pasha departed this world and journeyed to Paradise', 'Mehmed Pasha attained God's mercy', or at the very least 'Mehmed Pasha expired'.

The case for modifying the Arabo-Persian alphabet had been put forward as early as 1851, by Ahmed Cevdet, and thereafter various others tried their hands at the problem. In May 1862, in an address to the Ottoman Scientific Society (Cemiyet-i İlmiye-i Osmaniye), of which he was the founder, Antepli Münif Pasha blamed the paucity of literates on the deficiencies of the alphabet. He instanced the letters *ʔwn*, which could be read as *on* 'ten', *un* 'flour', or *ün* 'fame'. This last was properly written *ʔwk* (the *k* representing *ñ*); he could, therefore, also have cited *evin* 'of the house', as well as *ön* 'front', similarly written *ʔwk* but, like *ün*, popularly misspelt with *n* instead of *k*. He saw two possible solutions, the first being to write and print with full pointing, using the three diacritics inherited from Arabic and five newly devised as required by the phonology of Turkish. The second solution, which he favoured, was to stop joining the letters of words and to write or print them separately, with the necessary diacritics on the line rather than over or under it (Buluç 1981: 45–8, citing Münif Pasha 1974).

In 1863 the Azerbaijani dramatist and political scientist Feth-Ali Ahundzade came to Istanbul with a proposal for the addition of some new letters to indicate the vowels. He was well received and the Grand Vizier passed his proposal to the Ottoman Scientific Society for consideration. While they conceded its merits, their verdict was unfavourable, because of 'mücerred icrasında derkâr olan müşkilât-ı azîme' (the great difficulties which are evident simply in its implementation) and 'eski âsar-ı İslâmiyenin nisyanını da müeddi olacağından' (because it would conduce to the oblivion of ancient Islamic works) (Ülkütaşir 1973: 18–19).

In the Constitutional period, the time between 1908 and 1918, those intellectuals who saw modification as essential were agreed that the letters must be written, or at least printed, separately, so that students and compositors alike might be spared having to deal with three or four forms for each letter.[2] In the *Kamus*

---

[2] Most Arabo-Persian letters have three forms, depending on whether they are initial, medial, or final. Some have a fourth, used when the letter stands alone.

(1316/1901), Şemseddin Sami used three diacritics over the letter *wāw* to show the sounds of *o*, *ü*, and *ö*, while the bare letter denoted *u*.

The only scheme to be given a prolonged trial was the one sponsored by Enver Pasha from 1913 onwards, with the backing of his Ministry of War and, it is said, with strong-arm tactics to silence any critics. The principle was to use only the final forms of the letters, with no ligatures. The vowels were shown by variegated forms of *alif*, *wāw*, and *yā*, written on the line with the consonants. The result was far from pretty.[3] The system was variously known as *huruf-u munfasıla* (disjointed letters), *hatt-ı cedid* (new writing), *Enverpaşa yazısı* (Enver Pasha writing), and *ordu elifbası* (Army alphabet). Originally intended to simplify the work of military telegraphists, its use was extended to official correspondence within the ministry. There is some evidence (TTK 1981: 56–7) that the experiment was abandoned before the end of hostilities, though Enver published *Elifba*, a reading book to teach his system, as late as 1917. Ruşen Eşref [Ünaydın] (1954: 28–9) recalled that Kemal had spoken to him about it in late 1918 as being still in use:

İyi bir niyet; fakat yarım iş; hem de zamansız! . . . Harp zamanı harf zamanı değildir. Harp olurken harfle oynamak sırası mıdır? Ne yapmak için? Muhaverat ve muhaberat teshil için mi? Bu şimdiki şekil hem yazmayı, hem okumayı, hem de anlamayı ve binaenaleyh anlaşmayı eskisinden fazla geciktirir ve güçleştirir! Hız istiyen bir zamanda, böyle yavaşlatıcı, zihinleri yorup şaşırtıcı bir teşebbüse girişmenin maddî, amelî ve millî ne faydası var? . . . Sonra da mademki başladın, cesaret et; şunu tam yap; medenî bir şekil alsın, değil mi Efendim?

The intention is good, but it's a half-baked job as well as untimely. Wartime isn't letter time. When there's a war on, is it the occasion to play about with letters? What for? To facilitate dialogue and communications? The present system makes writing and reading and comprehension and consequently mutual understanding slower and harder than the old system. At a time when speed is of the essence, what material, practical, or national advantage is there in embarking on an enterprise like this, which slows things down and wearies and befuddles people's minds? Besides, once you've started, have courage; do the job properly so that it takes a civilized shape. Is that no so?

Atatürk's right-hand man İsmet [İnönü] later bore witness to the trouble caused during the war by Enver's experiment. It had fallen to him to talk the Deputy Chief of the General Staff out of insisting that documents presented for his approval must be in two copies, one in normal writing for him to read and one in Enver Pasha writing for him to sign (Arar 1981: 150–1).

Simultaneously with Enver's efforts to propagate his alphabet, a number of journalists and literary figures were urging the adoption of the Latin letters. It was a topic of conversation among Ottoman officers during the Gallipoli campaign.[4] This idea had a long past. Ahundzade had come round to it when his suggestion

---

[3] A sample will be found in Ülkütaşir (1973: 27).
[4] Verbal communication to the author in 1972 from Mr Taufiq Wahby.

for improving the Arabic script had been turned down.[5] The lexicographer Şemseddin Sami and his brother Abdül Bey devised an alphabet of thirty-six Latin and Greek letters for their native Albanian, a language to which the Arabic alphabet could do no more justice than it could to Turkish. It was called the A-be-ya after the names of its first three characters. On 29 January 1910 Hüseyin Cahit [Yalçın], a member of the Servet-i Fünun group and editor of the newspaper *Tanin*, published an article entitled 'Arnavut Hurufâtı' ('The Albanian Letters'), in which he commended their initiative and declared that the Turks would do well to follow it. A request from a group of Albanians for a *fetva*[6] on the subject elicited the response that it would be contrary to the Sacred Law for the Koran to be written in separated Arabic letters and for the Latin letters to be taught in Muslim schools (Levend 1972: 363–4).

In the spring of 1914 a series of five unsigned articles appeared in a short-lived weekly published by Kılıçzade Hakkı and dedicated to free thought, variously entitled *Hürriyet-i Fikriyye, Serbest Fikir*, and *Uluvvet-i Fikriyye*. These articles urged the gradual adoption of the Latin alphabet and prophesied that the change was bound to come. The writer propounded a problem, and invited a reply from the Şeyhülislâm or the Fetva Emini:[7]

Fransızlar İslâmiyetin esaslarını pek makul bularak milletçe ihtida etmek istiyorlar! Acaba onları Müslüman addedebilmek için o pek zarif dillerinin Arap harfleriyle yazılması şart-ı esasî mi ittihaz edilecek? 'Evet' cevabını beklemediğim halde alırsam kemal-i cesaretle 'Siz bu zihniyetle dünyayı Müslüman edemezsiniz' mukabelesinde bulunurum, 'Hayır, beis yok' cevabını alırsam: 'Biz Türklerin de Lâtin harflerini kullanmamıza müsaade bahş eder bir fetva veriniz' ricasını serdedeceğim. Hayır, Fransızlar ne kadar az Arap iseler, biz de o kadar az Arabız.

The French, finding the principles of our religion very reasonable, wish to convert *en masse* to Islam! Before they can be accepted as Muslims, will it be obligatory for that very elegant language of theirs to be written in the Arabic letters? I do not expect the answer to be 'Yes', but if it is I shall make so bold as to reply, 'With this mentality you cannot make the world Muslim.' If I am given the answer 'No, there is no harm in it' I shall make this request: 'Give a *fetva* permitting us Turks also to use the Latin letters.' No, we are no more Arab than the French are.

Kılıçzade Hakkı subsequently revealed that it was because of these articles that the Minister of the Interior closed the weekly down (Ülkütaşır 1973: 39–41.)

The subject had long interested Mustafa Kemal. Ruşen Eşref recalled his saying

---

[5] Levend (1972: 156) states that Ahundzade produced a Slav-based alphabet, but gives no details. Nor does Algar (1988), though he mentions his proposals for the reform of the alphabet and cites Muhammedzâde and Araslı, *Alefbâ-yı Cedid ve Mektûbât* (Baku, 1963), 3–39, 234–5, not available to the present writer.

[6] Arabic *fatwā*. In spite of the case of Salman Rushdie, which has familiarized the world with this word, it does not mean a sentence of death but a mufti's opinion on a point of law, with no executive force.

[7] These two officials were respectively the chief of the religious hierarchy and the head of the office that issued *fetva*s.

in 1918 that it had been a preoccupation of his between 1905 and 1907, when he was in Syria (Ünaydın 1954: 29.) Halide Edip Adıvar (1962: 264) remembered a conversation with him in June 1922 on the same theme, in which he spoke of the possibility of adopting the Latin letters, adding that it would require rigorous measures: 'Hattâ o gün, lâtin harflerini kabul imkânından bahsediyor, bunu yapmak için sıkı tedbirler gerektiğini de ilâve ediyordu.' Agop Dilâçar (1962: 41) tells of showing him, 'sometime between 1916 and 1918,' a copy of Németh's (1917), *Türkische Grammatik*, which printed the Turkish in a Latin transcription with *č* and *š* for what are now written *ç* and *ş*, the Greek γ for the sounds now represented by *ğ*, and χ for the Arabic and Persian *ḥ*. Kemal did not like it much.

While he was military attaché in Sofia just before the First World War, he corresponded with his friend Madame Corinne in Istanbul in Turkish, written phonetically with French spelling. Here is part of a letter dated 13 May 1914, followed by the same passage in modern orthography and the English of it:

Dunya inssanlar idjin bir dari imtihandir. Imtihan idilène inssanin hère çualé moutlaka pèke mouvafike djévabe vermessi mumqune olmaya bilire. Fékate duchunmélidir qui heuquume djévablarin héiéti oumoumiyéssindène hassil olan mouhassalaya gueuré virilir.[8]

Dünya insanlar için bir dar-ı imtihandır. İmtihan edilen insanın her suale mutlaka pek muvafık cevap vermesi mümkün olmayabilir. Fakat düşünmelidir ki, hüküm, cevapların heyet-i umumiyesinden hasıl olan muhassalaya göre verilir.

For human beings, the world is an examination hall. It may not be absolutely possible for the examinee to give a very appropriate answer to every question. But he must bear in mind that the verdict is given in accordance with the result deriving from the answers taken as a whole.

A comparison of the lengths of the first two paragraphs above reveals one reason for some people's antagonism to the idea of switching to the Latin alphabet: the French spelling takes up more room than the old letters (and the new). In those days, French was the European language most widely known among Turks and it was generally assumed that a new Latin alphabet would involve applying French orthography to Turkish words: the six letters of *gueuré* for the four of *kwrh* (göre), the nine of *tchodjouk* for the four of *čjwq* (çocuk), or the five of the alternative spelling *čwjwq*. The editor of *Resimli Gazete*, İbrahim Alâaddin [Gövsa], who was against change, generously published, on 22 September 1923, an article by Hüseyin Cahit, who was for it. İbrahim Alâaddin prefaced it with a response,[9] headed 'Latine houroufati ile Turkdje yazi yazmak mumkinmidir!' (Is it possible to write Turkish with Latin letters!). That took forty-seven characters, whereas the Arabo-Persian alphabet would have needed only thirty-nine: *l?tyn*

---

[8] The version given here is based on a collation of the texts in Özgü (1963: 25–6) and Korkmaz (1992: 6). Note the spellings *idilène*, *fékate*, *heuquume*, *virilir*, which reflect Kemal's own pronunciations: /idilen/ for *edilen*, /fekat/ for *fakat*, /höküm/ for *hüküm*, /virilir/ for *verilir*.

[9] For the texts of Hüseyin Cahit's article and İbrahim Alâaddin's response, see Ülkütaşır (1973: 45–52).

ḥrwfʔty ʔylh twrkčh yʔzy yʔzmq mmknmydr. (The new alphabet can do it in forty-three: Lâtin hurufatı ile Türkçe yazı yazmak mümkün müdür.)

A year before that, at a meeting with representatives of the Istanbul press in September 1922, Kemal had been asked by Hüseyin Cahit, 'Why don't we adopt Latin writing?' He replied, 'It's not yet time.' His answer is understandable if one remembers that this was the period of the first Grand National Assembly, some fifty members of which were *hocas*, professional men of religion, in addition to eight dervish sheikhs and five men who gave their occupation as 'tribal chief'.

At the Izmir Economic Congress in February–March 1923, three workers' delegates put forward a motion in favour of adopting the Latin letters. The chairman, General Kâzım [Karabekir], ruled it out of order as damaging to the unity of Islam, and went on to make a speech in which he said: 'derhal bütün Avrupa'nın eline güzel bir silâh vermiş olacağız, bunlar âlem-i İslâma karşı diyeceklerdir ki, Türkler ecnebî yazısını kabul etmişler ve Hıristiyan olmuşlardır. İşte düşmanlarımızın çalıştığı şeytanetkârane fikir budur' (we shall at once have placed a splendid weapon in the hands of all Europe; they will declare to the Islamic world that the Turks have acepted the foreign writing and turned Christian. The diabolical idea with which our enemies are working is precisely this).[10]

In an article in the journal *Hür Fikir* of 17 November 1926, Kılıçzade Hakkı made the point that the sacred nature of the Koran did not extend to the alphabet in which it is written. The title of the article sums up his argument very neatly: 'Arap Harflerini de Cebrail Getirmemişti ya' (Gabriel didn't bring the Arabic letters too, you know) (Levend 1972: 397). This argument was, however, a little disingenuous, in that it ignored one of the main worries of the defenders of the Arabo-Persian alphabet: if it were replaced by a Latin-based alphabet, the numer of Turks able to read the Koran—whether or not they understood it—would inevitably diminish, because one alphabet is as much as most people can be expected to learn in a lifetime.

On 20 May 1928 the Grand National Assembly voted to accept the international numerals.[11] During the debate, a member asked whether the international letters might be accepted as well. The Minister of Education replied that the government had been giving the matter its attention and that the question would naturally be resolved within the principles accepted by the civilized world, but that time was needed. 'Onun için bu işde biraz geç kalıyorsak, teşkil ettiğimiz komisyonun, encümenin faaliyetinin neticesine muntazır olduğumuzdandır' (So if we are a little late in this matter, it is because we are awaiting the result of the activity of the commission, the committee, we are forming). It is clear from the Minister's imprecision about the designation of the body he was talking about that at the time he spoke it did not yet exist.

---

[10] For the full text, collated from reports in three daily newspapers of 3 Mar. 1923, see Yorulmaz (1955: 90–3). See also Levend (1972: 392–3).

[11] By this was meant what we call the Arabic numerals and the Arabs call the Indian numerals.

Three days later, however, it did, when the Council of Ministers set up the Dil Encümeni, 'to think about the manner and feasibility of applying the Latin letters to our language'. Its nine members included Falih Rıfkı [Atay], Ruşen Eşref [Ünaydın], Yakup Kadri [Karaosmanoğlu], and Fazıl Ahmet [Aykaç]. The first act of the new body when it met on 26 June 1928 was to divide itself into two, one for the alphabet and one for grammar (Levend 1972: 400–1). Kemal attended the meetings of both whenever he had time.

The Alphabet Commission rejected in principle the idea of a transliteration alphabet, because they did not wish Arabic and Persian pronunciations (as in the story of the *softa* told in Chapter 2) to be perpetuated; they wanted them assimilated to Istanbul speech patterns. The longest discussions took place over the question of how to show the palatalized sounds of *k*, *g*, and *l* before back vowels. Before front vowels, as in *iki* 'two' and *gelmek* 'to come', this happens automatically.[12] Before back vowels there is no palatalization in native words[13] but there is in Arabic and Persian borrowings, as is seen in the English spelling *Kiazim* of the name appearing as *Kâzım* (/k^{y}āzım/) in modern Turkish spelling, and Byron's *Giaour* for what is now written *gâvur* (/g^{y}āvur/) 'infidel'. The Commission's proposal in its report, published early in August, was to write an *h* after the consonant, as in Portuguese (*velho*/vel^{y}u/, *Senhor*/sen^{y}or/), so *khatip* for what is now written *kâtip* 'clerk, secretary'. Another proposal was to use *q* to show the sound of palatalized *k*.[14] Many people preferred the latter alternative. Atay's (1969: 441) account of how it came to be quashed is so circumstantial that one feels it must be true:

Ben yeni yazı tasarısını getirdiğim günün akşamı Kâzım Paşa (Özalp) sofrada:
—Ben adımı nasıl yazacağım? 'Kü' harfi lâzım, diye tutturdu.
Atatürk de:
—Bir harften ne çıkar? Kabul edelim, dedi.
Böylece arap kelimesini türkçeleştirmekten alıkoymuş olacaktık. Sofrada ses çıkarmadım. Ertesi günü yanına gittiğimde meseleyi yeniden Ataya açtım. Atatürk el yazısı majüsküllerini bilmezdi. Küçük harfleri büyültmekle yetinirdi. Kâğıdı aldı, Kemal'in baş harfini küçük (kü) nün büyültülmüşü ile, sonra da (k) nın büyültülmüşü ile yazdı. Birincisi hiç hoşuna gitmedi. Bu yüzden (kü) harfinden kurtulduk. Bereket Atatürk (kü) nün majüskülünü bilmiyordu. Çünkü o (K)nın büyültülmüşünden daha gösterişli idi.

At table on the evening of the day when I brought the draft proposals for the new writing, Kâzım [Özalp] Pasha grumbled, 'How am I going to write my name? We must have a *q*.'

---

[12] See Lewis (1988: 3–4). In western Turkey the palatalization is audible though usually faint, the effect being the introduction of a *y*-sound after the *k*, *g*, or *l*; not so marked as in English *cure*, *angular*, and *British*, as distinct from American, *lurid*. The further east you go, the more distinct the palatalization. By the time you get to Erzurum you will hear *iki* sounding just like *içi*.

[13] For the exceptional *elâ*, see Ch. 4 n. 24.

[14] This may surprise Western orientalists, who regard *q* as the natural transliteration not of the Arabic letter *kāf*, pronounced like our *k*, but of *qāf* (sometimes transliterated as *ḳāf*), pronounced much like our *c* in *cough*. The explanation is to be sought in the name of the letter *q*, which Turks follow the French in calling *kü*, pronounced /k^{y}ü/. This letter, whose name had the requisite palatalized initial sound, seemed the ideal device for indicating /k^y/.

Atatürk said, 'What difference will one letter make? Let's have it.' Had we done so, we would have kept the Arabic word from being Turkicized. I didn't say anything at the table. When I went to see Atatürk next day I explained the problem to him again. He did not know the manuscript capitals; he simply wrote them like the small letters only bigger. He took a sheet of paper and wrote the initial letter of Kemal, first with an enlarged version of *q*, then with an enlarged version of *k*. He didn't like the first at all. So we were spared *q*. Thank goodness he didn't know the script capital *Q*, which was more flamboyant than *K*.

After Kemal's rejection of *q*, it was decided to use the Portuguese alternative, but it did not last long.

When Atay showed him the Commission's draft alphabet, Kemal asked whether they had thought about bringing it into use (Atay 1969: 440).

Bir on beş yıllık uzun, bir de beş yıllık kısa mühletli iki teklif var, dedim. Teklif sahiplerine göre ilk devirleri iki yazı bir arada öğretilecektir. Gazeteler yarım sütundan başlıyarak yavaş yavaş yeni yazılı kısmı artıracaklardır. Daireler ve yüksek mektepler için de tedrici bazı usuller düşünülmüştür.

Yüzüme baktı:—Bu ya üç ayda olur, ya hiç olmaz, dedi.

Hayli radikal bir inkılâpçı iken ben bile yüzüne bakakalmıştım.

—Çocuğum, dedi, gazetelerde yarım sütun eski yazı kaldığı zaman dahi herkes bu eski yazılı parçayı okuyacaktır. Arada bir harb bir iç buhran, bir terslik oldu mu, bizim yazı da Enver'in yazısına döner. Hemen terkolunuverir.

I told him there were two proposals, one long term, of fifteen years, the other short term, of five years. According to the proponents, in the first period of each the two systems of writing would be taught side by side. The newspapers would begin with half a column in the new letters, which would gradually be extended. He looked me full in the face and said, 'Either this will happen in three months or it won't happen at all.' I was a highly radical revolutionary but I found myself staring at him, open-mouthed. 'My boy,' he said, 'even when the newspapers are down to only half a column in the old writing, everyone will read that bit in the old writing. If anything goes wrong in the meantime, a war, a domestic crisis, our alphabet too will end up like Enver's; it will be dropped immediately.

As soon as the alphabet seemed satisfactory, Kemal introduced it to the vast crowds attending a Republican People's Party gala in Gülhane Park on the evening of 9 August 1928. Two days later lessons began in Dolmabahçe Palace, first for officials of the presidential staff and Deputies, then for university teachers and literary people. The latter session turned into a heated debate. At the end of five hours the following resolution was put to the meeting and adopted unanimously (Ülkütaşır 1973: 77):

Milleti cehaletten kurtarmak için kendi diline uymayan Arap harflerini terk edip, Latin esasından alınan Türk harflerini kabul etmekten başka çare yoktur. Komisyonun teklif ettiği alfabe, hakikaten Türk alfabesidir, kat'idir . . . Sarf ve imlâ kaideleri lisanın ıslahını, inkişafını, millî zevki takip ederek tekâmül edecektir.

To deliver the nation from ignorance, the only course open is to abandon the Arabic letters, which are not suited to the national language, and to accept the Turkish letters, based on the Latin. The alphabet proposed by the Commission is in truth the Turkish alphabet; that is definite . . . The laws of grammar and spelling will evolve in step with the improvement and development of the language and with the national taste.

That last sentence was soon proved true, as the ever-cautious İsmet, who framed the resolution, had foreseen. Equipped with a blackboard and easel, Kemal went on tour to teach huge crowds of villagers the new letters, which they called 'Gazi elifbası' (The Gazi alphabet).[15] Some weeks of this practical experience persuaded him that the use of a hyphen before the interrogative particle as laid down by the Alphabet Commission was unnecessary. From Sinop he telegraphed the Ministry of Education to say that the rule was abrogated. On his return to Ankara he addressed a directive to the Prime Minister's office (Ülkütaşır 1973: 122–3):

Encümen esasen yeni harfler ile yazıya başlanırken uzun kelimelerin hecelenmesini, seçilmesini kolaylaştıracak bir çare olmak üzere bağlamayı düşünmüş ve bağlamanın kaldırılmasını ileriye bırakmıştı.

Yeni harflerin kabulü ve taammümündeki sür'at, bu zamanın geldiğini gösteriyor . . . Bu sebeple ve halk içindeki müşahedelerime güvenerek âtideki esasları kabul etmek faydalı ve lâzım görülmüştür.

1. İstifham edatı olan mı, mi umumiyetle ayrı yazılır. Meselâ: Geldi mi? gibi. Fakat kendinden sonra gelen her türlü lâhikalarla beraber yazılır. Meselâ: Geliyor musunuz?, Ben miydim? gibi.
2. Râbıta edatı olan (ve, ki), dahi manasına olan (de, da) müstakil kelime olarak ayrı ayrı yazılır.
3. Türk gramerinde bağlama işareti olan - (tire) kalkmıştır. Binaenaleyh fiillerin tasriflerinden lâhikalar çizgi (-) ile ayrılmayarak beraber yazılır. Meselâ: Geliyorum, gideceksiniz, . . . güzeldir, demirdir. Kezalık (ile, ise, için, iken) kelimelerinin muhaffefleri olan (le, se, çin, ken) şekilleri kendinden evvelki kelimeye bitişik yazılır, çizgi ile ayrılmaz—Meselâ: Ahmetle, buysa, seninçin, giderken gibi . . .
4. Türkçede henüz mevcut olan farsça terkiplerde dahi bağlama çizgisi yoktur, terkip işareti olan sedalı harfler ilk kelimenin sonuna eklenir. Meselâ: hüsnü nazar gibi.

When writing with the new letters began, the Commission originally thought of hyphenation as a means of facilitating the spelling and recognition of long words, proposing to eliminate it at some future date.

The speed with which the new letters have been accepted and become current shows that that time has come . . . For this reason and on the basis of my observations among the people it is deemed advantageous and necessary to adopt the following principles:

1. The interrogative particle *mi* will generally be written separately, as in 'Geldi mi?' ['Has he come?'], but will be written together with any following suffix, as in 'Geliyor musunuz?' 'Ben miydim?' ['Are you coming?' 'Was it me?']
2. The conjunctions *ve* and *ki* ['and', 'that'], and *de/da* in the sense of *dahi* ['also'] will be written separately as independent words.
3. The hyphen marking a junction in Turkish grammar is abolished. In the conjugation of verbs the suffixes will therefore be written without being separated by hyphens:

---

[15] The Grand National Assembly had conferred the title of Gazi, 'Warrior for the Faith', on Mustafa Kemal in September 1921, after which he was generally referred to as Gazi Paşa. The picture of him with his blackboard is well known to stamp-collectors.

'geliyorum, gideceksiniz . . . güzeldir, demirdir' ['I am coming', 'you will go' . . . 'it is beautiful', 'it is iron']. Similarly the lightened forms of the words *ile, ise, için, iken* will be written contiguously with the preceding word and not separated by a hyphen: 'Ahmetle', 'buysa', 'seninçin', 'giderken' ['with Ahmet', 'if it is this', 'for you',[16] 'while going']. So too in the case of *ce/çe/ca/ça* and *ki*: 'mertçe', 'benimki', 'yarınki' ['manfully', 'mine', 'tomorrow's'].

4. Nor is there a hyphen in such Persian compounds as still exist in Turkish; the vowels which show the *izafet* are suffixed to the first word, as in 'hüsnü nazar' ['favourable consideration', literally 'goodness of view'].

Some years later the Language Society recommended the restoration of the hyphen in Persian izafet compounds, which certainly makes them easier to spot. From the fact that Kemal chose not to hyphenate them we may infer that he was not thinking at that time of speeding their demise by highlighting their alien nature; perhaps even that he was not then thinking of hastening the elimination of foreign borrowings except for technical terms. Hyphens tend not to be used in the few izafet compounds still surviving. *Türkçe Sözlük* shows *sukutu hayal*, not *sukut-u hayal*, for 'disappointment', and *sürcü lisan*, not *sürc-ü lisan*, for *lapsus linguae* (now usually replaced by *dil sürçmesi* 'slip of the tongue').

A few days after Kemal's directive, an announcement was made ending the use of *h* to show palatalization; instead, a circumflex would be placed on the vowel following the palatalized consonant (Ertop 1963: 66). This device was not totally satisfactory, because the circumflex retained its function of showing a long vowel. The resulting possibility of confusion becomes apparent when one considers, say, *mütalâa* 'observation', in which the first *a* is long and the *â* short: /mütāl'aa/. The 1977 edition of *Yeni Yazım Kılavuzu*, TDK's guide to spelling, restricted the use of the circumflex; *inter alia*, it would no longer be used on adjectives ending in *-î* [A]: *milli* 'national', not *millî*. The decision was reversed in the 1988 edition (the title of which, *İmlâ* [A] *Kılavuzu*, reflects the change in the Society's Council of Management in August 1983; see Chapter 12). By that time, however, the damage was done; fewer and fewer Turks were bothering to write or print the circumflex anyway. If *kâtip* is not totally supplanted by the neologism *yazman* or the French *sekreter*, it seems doomed to be pronounced /katip/ and not /k'ātip/.

Two other elements of the new alphabet, *ğ* and *ı*, are open to criticism. The *raison d'être* of *ğ* ('yumuşak ge') was to replace two characters in the old alphabet. The first was *ghayn*, the second was *kâf* where it had the sound of *y*, as in the words written *dkl* and *ckr* in the old letters, and *değil, ciğer* ('not', 'liver') in the new. Yumuşak ge now serves to lengthen a preceding back vowel, as in *kâğıt* 'paper' (Persian *kāğıḏ*), pronounced /k'āt/, and *ağa* 'master', pronounced /ā/; while between front vowels, as in *değil* and *ciğer*, it is pronounced like *y*. So *ğ* preserves some features of Ottoman spelling, but that was not the object of the exercise. At least two scholars in the 1930s felt uncomfortable with it. Ahmet Cevat Emre idiosyncratically used *ğ* for *ˤayn* in his writings on grammar, thus *fiğil* for *fiil* 'verb',

---

[16] The suffixed—Atatürk would have said 'lightened'—form *-çin* of *için* (for) is no longer in use.

Arabic *fī̆l*, while for *ghayn* he used *ġ*. It was doubtless the fact that *ġ* has two distinct functions that led him not to use it for *ghayn*. On the other hand, Ragıp Özdem (1939: 15) employed *ğ* for *ghayn* to show the pronunciation of French *programme* as *pğoğğam*, and *carte postale* as *kağt postâl*.

As for *ı*, when the Alphabet Commission hit on the idea of manufacturing it by removing the dot from *i*, they never stopped to ask themselves what the dot was doing there in the first place. The answer became apparent as soon as people began using the new alphabet: its function was to distinguish its bearer from the up- and downstrokes of *m*, *n*, and *u*.[17] To see this for oneself, one has only to compare *mınımum* with *minimum* in joined-up writing. A little brochure on the new alphabet (Necmi 1928), 'consisting in the lessons published in the newspaper *Milliyet*, revised according to the latest amendments', showed the handwritten form of *ı* as *ı* or *ĭ*. Atatürk always used the latter form in writing and also habitually wrote *u* as *ŭ*. Despite these imperfections, the Latin alphabet is undeniably the best that has ever been used for Turkish, and has played a large part in the rise of literacy; according to the official figures, from 9 per cent in 1924 to 65 per cent in 1975 and 82.3 per cent in 1995.

Commendation of it is found in an unexpected source, a book by the Director of the Media Laboratory of the Massachusetts Institute of Technology:

A speech synthesizer takes a stream of text . . . and follows certain rules to enunciate each word, one by one. Each language is different and varies in its difficulty to synthesize.

English is one of the hardest, because we write (right and rite) it in such an odd and seemingly illogical way (weigh and whey). Other languages, such as Turkish, are much easier. In fact, Turkish is very simple to synthesize because Atatürk moved that language from Arabic to Latin letters in 1929 [*sic*] and, in so doing, made a one-for-one correspondence between the sounds and the letters. You pronounce each letter: no silent letters or confusing diphthongs. Therefore, at the word level, Turkish is a dream come true for a computer speech synthesizer.   (Negroponte 1995: 145)

Provided that the synthesizer had been well programmed, the only word one can think of that it might fail to enunciate correctly is *ağabey* (elder brother), pronounced /ābī/, and a thorough programmer could take care of that.

Now briefly to complete the story of how the Latin alphabet was brought into use. Between 8 and 25 October 1928 all officials were examined for their competence in the new letters. It was only when Kemal had done all this that he sought the legal authority to do it. On 1 November the Grand National Assembly passed Law No. 1353, 'On the Adoption and Application of the New Turkish Letters', which came into effect two days later. It provided that documents in the new letters must be accepted and acted upon at once. The use of books printed in the old characters for instruction in schools was forbidden. No books were to be published in

---

[17] In some hands not only *m*, *n*, and *u* but *r* too can be a source of confusion. The author was gratified when he eventually deciphered, in a handwritten letter from Spain, what looked like *La Couuīa* but turned out to be *La Coruña*.

the old letters after the end of the year. All correspondence between private citizens and government departments would have to be in the new letters from 1 June 1929. Those Deputies who were ignorant of the Latin alphabet suddenly found that Article 12 of the Constitution had taken on a sinister importance for them: among those it excluded from membership of the Grand National Assembly were 'Türkçe okuyup yazmak bilmiyenler' (those who do not know how to read and write Turkish). They hastened to emerge from the state of illiteracy into which they had thrown themselves. One small concession: the 'old Arabic letters' could be used in official and private records as shorthand—'stenografi makamında'—until 1 June 1930.

Kemal was not given to procrastinating once his mind was made up. So why the delay of three months between the unveiling of the new alphabet in Gülhane Park and its legitimation? The obvious answer is that he did not want the details of the new letters to be the subject of endless wrangling in the Assembly; far better to present the Deputies with a *fait accompli*. There is also evidence that İsmet, mindful of how much of the General Staff's time had been wasted by Enver's new alphabet during the First World War, argued against the change because he was uneasy about the chaos that would surely set in while the old and new alphabets were in use side by side. He was no doubt placated and relieved by the speed with which the new letters were left in undisputed command of the field. And, despite his initial disapproval, once the reform had happened he never used the old letters again.

On 31 August 1928 *The Times* of London devoted a well-informed and sympathetic editorial to the new alphabet:

The advantages of the change can scarcely be appreciated by those who have not struggled with the difficulties presented to the student of Turkish by the Arabic letters . . . No alphabet is less fitted to express the melodious Turkish speech, which has relatively few consonants and an astonishing wealth of vowels and diphthongs . . . Conservatism, the religious associations of Arabic which gave a sanctity to the letters in which the Koran was written, and the oriental delusion that writing should not be made too intelligible in content or in form explain the long domination of the Arabic letters over the Turks . . .

By this step the Turks, who for centuries were regarded as a strange and isolated people by Europe, have drawn closer than ever to the West. It is a great reform, worthy of the remarkable chief to whom the Turkish people has entrusted its destinies.

Memories, however, can be short, even the corporate memory of a newspaper of record. Twenty-one years later, on 10 August 1949, *The Times* devoted a leading article to the proposed admission of Greece, Turkey, and Iceland to the Council of Europe:

To have any chance of success a federal union would have to start with nations either adjoining each other or separated by no barrier more formidable than the English Channel . . . They could not share a common language but at least it would be an advantage if the different languages were written in the same script . . . Muslim in tradition, with an Asiatic language in an Arabic script, it is not easy to see how Turkey could take her place easily in a United States of Western Europe.

The author of that egregious howler could have mentioned that the Greeks have a different script from other Europeans, but he did not. Nor was there any evidence of remorse in his subsequent reference to it:

On another occasion I wrote a leader on Turkey's claim to be a member of any united European federation. (This was before the days of the Treaty of Rome and the Common Market.) I ridiculed this proposal and pointed out that it would be difficult enough to form a European Federation without adding a country which was neither European nor Christian and which did not even use the Roman alphabet. Alas! I was wrong, Turkey had changed from arabic [sic] letters to Roman letters in 1928. Well, one should not make mistakes in *The Times*—or anywhere else for that matter—but the fuss! The Turkish Government sent for the British Ambassador and reprimanded him severely. The Foreign Office sent for the Foreign Editor and reprimanded *him* severely. And Iverach McDonald [the Foreign Editor] did his best to reprimand *me* severely (he was a very kind man). All this because of the absurd myth, which had not been true for many years, that *The Times* spoke for the British Foreign Office and always reflected British foreign policy. It was a disastrous burden for my newspaper to carry.   (Pringle 1973: 81)

To quote Yunus Emre, Turkey's greatest folk-poet, 'Bilmeyen ne bilsin bizin?[18] Bilenlere selâm olsun' (What should the ignorant know of us? To those who know, greetings).

[18] Yunus's *bizin* instead of *bizi* is for the sake of the rhyme (vowel plus *n*).

4

Atatürk and the Language Reform until 1936

The scattered local movements of resistance to the Allied armies that invaded Anatolia after the 1918 Armistice could never have liberated the country without the boundless energy and organizing genius of Mustafa Kemal. In the same way, it was he who gave effect to the desires of the many intellectuals who wanted to make their language more truly Turkish. I specify intellectuals because in those days four-fifths of the population were peasants, who would no more have thought of tampering with the language than of changing the alternation of the seasons. Above all he wanted to turn his people's face westwards. He resented the dominance of the Arabic and Persian elements in the language and believed that the intelligent use of its native resources could make the use of foreign borrowings unnecessary.

An indication of how such a feeling could arise in a Turk of his generation is seen in a reminiscence of Hasan Reşit Tankut's (1963: 113):

Ben liseyi Şamda okudum. Hürriyetin ilânlandığı[1] günlerde son sınıfta idik. Araplar birdenbire ulusçuluğa başladılar. Türkçe ile alay ediyorlardı. Bir gün, sınıfta kara tahtada tebeşirle yazılmış beş on satır gördük. Bunun başında Türk dili nedir? yazılı idi. Yazıyı içimizden okuduk. Bunda, tek bir Türkçe kelime yoktu. Osmanlı üslûbuna ve kurallarına uydurularak yazılmıştı. Bu yazının sonu 'dır' ile bitiyordu. Araplar, bu dil edatını beş on defa tekrarlamışlar ve bu *dırdırların* altını çizmişler ve önüne de Türkçe budur. Yani (dırdır)dır yazmışlardı. O gün, biz 4–5 Türk öğrenci bütün bir sınıfla âdeta boğuştuk ve o günden başlıyarak Türkçeci olduk.

I received my secondary education in Damascus and was in my final year at the time of the proclamation of freedom [the restoration in 1908 of the 1876 Constitution]. The Arabs suddenly started on nationalism and took to making fun of Turkish. One day in the classroom we saw half a dozen or so lines written on the blackboard, headed 'What is the Turkish language?' We read the writing to ourselves; it contained not a single word of Turkish. Written in conformity with the style and rules of Ottoman, it ended with -*dır*. The Arabs had repeated this suffix several times, underlining this string of -*dır*s and writing in front of it 'Turkish is this. That is to say, it's *dırdır* [tedious babble]'. That day we four or five Turkish pupils very nearly came to blows with a whole class, and became devotees of Turkish from that day on.

As early as August 1923, a proposal was introduced into the Grand National Assembly by the writer Tunalı Hilmi for a new law, the *Türkçe Kanunu*,

---

[1] The text has 'alanlandığı', but *alanlanmak* is an obsolete neologism for 'to give ground'. What Tankut intended must have been a Turkicization of 'ilân [A] edildiği'.

providing for the creation in the Ministry of Education of a Commission for the Turkish Language. Technical terms would be Turkicized, school books, official documents, and new laws would be prepared in accordance with the rules of Turkish, and no newspaper or journal breaching these rules would be licensed. Opinion in and out of the Assembly was not yet ready for such a proposal and it was not accepted (İmer 1976: 87). The story of an early, perhaps the earliest, official attempt at simplifying the language was told by H. E. Erkilet (1952), who towards the end of 1924 was appointed to head Talim ve Terbiye, the Army's Directorate of Training. Eleven years of almost incessant wars had allowed no time for revising the training manuals. 'Sözün kısası, ordu kitapsızdı' (To put it briefly, the Army had no books). With the backing of the Chief of the General Staff, Fevzi [Çakmak], and his deputy, Kâzım [Orbay], he ordered that the language of the new manuals should be intelligible to conscripts, with no Arabic or Persian constructions that could be avoided or words for which Turkish equivalents were available. *Tarassut* [A] 'observation' became *gözetleme*, *pişdar* [P] 'vanguard' became *öncü*, *esliha-i hafife* [A] 'light weapons' became *hafif silâhlar*. *Şura-yı Âli-i Askerî* [A] 'Supreme Military Council' became *Yüksek Askerî Şura*. Some changes were not as radical as they could have been: *Erkân-i Harbiye-i Umumiye* 'General Staff' became *Büyük Erkâni-i Harbiye*; on the other hand, *Erkân-i Harbiye Mektebi* 'Staff College' was simplified to *Harp Akademisi*. A good effort, ahead of its time.

The first years of the Republic were not easy for the Turks. They were buoyed up by the pride of being the only people on the losing side in the First World War who had successfully resisted the victors' territorial demands and won their independence. But the economic situation was parlous[2] and the ranks of the commercial and professional classes had been depleted by the departure, one way or another, of many members of the Christian minorities in the course of the First World War and the War of Independence. In addition, the exchange of populations arranged at Lausanne in January 1923 had brought about the displacement of 1.3 million ethnic Greeks from their native Turkey to the 'homeland' that few of them had ever seen, and the arrival from Greece of half a million ethnic Turks in a similar state. There was a pressing need to raise morale, to make the people see themselves as a nation with a great past and a great destiny, who would one day take their place among the civilized nations of the West. Turks must have no feeling of inferiority *vis-à-vis* Europe; they were not outsiders. For the moment they might be poor relations, but relations they were. To this end, history teaching in the country's schools was based on the postulate that all the famous peoples

---

[2] Money was very short indeed. As Falih Rıfkı Atay put it, there was never a limited company worth mentioning that was founded with so little capital as that state in Ankara. He tells a story he heard from Osmanzade Hamdi, co-editor of *Yeni Gün*, a newspaper that though nominally independent could not survive without its government subsidy. At the end of a frantic day spent in trying to placate the paper's creditors, Hamdi rushed round to the tea garden where the Minister of Finance was accustomed to sit for a while after office hours, and caught him just as he was mounting his horse to go home. Hamdi said, 'For heaven's sake give me some money!', to which the Minister of Finance replied, 'I've left the safe open. If you can find anything in it you're welcome' (Atay 1969: 515).

of antiquity were either Turks themselves or had been civilized by Turks.[3] In the same spirit, it was thought desirable to show that the Turkish language was not out on a limb but had affiliations with all the great languages of the world.

Atatürk's first concern, as we have seen, was to change from the Arabo-Persian alphabet to the Latin. Already on 3 February 1928 it was ordered that the Friday sermon in the mosques must be delivered in Turkish. Two years later he contributed a short foreword to a book on the history and potentialities of the language (Arsal [1930]), in which he included these two sentences: 'Türk dili, dillerin en zenginlerindendir; yeter ki bu dil, şuurla işlensin. Ülkesini, yüksek istiklâlini korumasını bilen Türk milleti, dilini de yabancı diller boyunduruğundan kurtarmalıdır' (Turkish is one of the richest of languages; it needs only to be used with discrimination. The Turkish nation, which is well able to protect its territory and its sublime independence, must also liberate its language from the yoke of foreign languages). The second sentence unleashed the language reform. If more people had heeded the first, the success of the reform could have been unqualified.

Atatürk practised what he preached. In August 1930 he dictated a list of topics that he wanted historians to address. One of them was 'Beşeriyet menşe ve mebdei' (The source and origin of humankind), all four words being of Arabic origin. When the typescript was brought to him he amended this to 'İnsanların nereden ve nasıl geldikleri' (Where humans came from and how they came), three of the five words being Turkish (*Tarih Vesikalari* (Jan. 1958), opposive p. 192). The key to understanding the course taken by the reform in its early years is that language was his hobby. In the draft bill creating the first faculty of Ankara University, which opened on 9 January 1936, its name was shown as Tarih-Coğrafya Fakültesi (Faculty of History and Geography), and it took a directive from Atatürk to add language to its name and its responsibilities—Dil Tarih-Coğrafya Fakültesi—before the bill became law.

The usual setting for his discussions on language, as on everything, was his table, *sofra*, in the special sense of a *rakı sofrası*, a dining-table laden with *rakı* and *meze* (*hors d'œuvre*), theoretically a prelude to dinner but commonly a substitute for it. This institution is well described by Atay:

For anyone who knew him, the name Atatürk conjures up memories of sessions round his table. His custom was to bring his friends together of an evening and talk into the small hours. We never knew in advance whether we would be there just for fun, for a command conference to prepare an attack, or for a meeting that would decide the most involved affairs of State, though we might hazard a guess when we saw who the guests were.

The sessions that were just for fun were very rare, and when they did occur it was like having a free period at school. Generally we would debate, read, or write on the most serious topics. Atatürk seemed never to tire. He would talk and listen. His prime concern

---

[3] In this connection we may mention Vecihe Hatiboğlu's statement (1986: 97): 'Türkçe dünyanın en eski yazılı dilidir' (Turkish is the world's oldest written language). Someone in the language business should have heard of Ancient Egyptian, if not Linear A; perhaps she was subsuming those languages in Turkish.

was not to tell us what he was thinking but to learn what we thought, to hear the country's various voices. He had a genius for synthesizing. After hours of rambling conversation which darted from one topic to another, he would bring together and arrange what had been said, and produce a logical, clear, and well organized work of cogitation.

His guests were always a varied bunch, and he had a perfect tolerance of criticism from those he liked and whom he knew to share his beliefs. I estimate that the problems of Turkish language and history took up as much time round his table as they would have done at a university seminar. Facing him was a blackboard and chalk. All of us, ministers, professors, deputies, were expected to take up the chalk and perform. All of us except him would grow weary and, to be honest with you, a little bored.[4]

Atatürk's personal library, part of which is on display at his mausoleum, the Anıt-Kabir in Ankara, included many works on language, among them Jespersen's *Essentials of English Grammar* and *The Philosophy of Language*, Fowler's *The King's English*, and some less common items such as Chambers and Daunt's *London English 1384–1425*. Ernest Weekley's etymological writings are well represented on the shelves. Nevertheless, in indulging his passion for etymology Atatürk was more enthusiastic than scientific. He saw *asker* [A] 'soldier' (originally the Latin *exercitus*) as a conflation of the Turkish words *asık* 'profit' and *er* 'man', and explained it as meaning 'a man useful to the country, the State, the nation' (Korkmaz 1992; Özgü 1963: 31–2). He equated the first two syllables of *merinos* 'merino' with the Yakut *ibri* 'fine', and merino wool is indeed fine. He wondered whether the word might have travelled to Spain with the Iber Turks,[5] in which case the names not only of the merino sheep and its wool but of the Iberian peninsula too would be of Turkish origin. He is reputed also to have proposed Turkish etymologies for *Niagara* and *Amazon*: *Ne yaygara* 'What tumult!' and *Ama uzun* 'But it's long!'

Admiral Necdet Uran describes in his memoirs an occasion during a cruise in the Mediterranean in 1937, when Atatürk came into the chart-room and, having studied the chart for a moment, pointed to the *rota*, the line indicating the ship's course. 'What's this?' he asked and, without waiting for an answer, went on, 'You're going to tell me it's English, Italian, French, that sort of thing, but what I was asking was the origin of the word.' The Admiral hesitated. Atatürk took a scrap of paper and wrote on it the word *yürütmek* ('to cause to walk, to set in motion'). Below it he wrote the same word divided into syllables: *yü-rüt-mek*. 'The origin of the word is that *rüt*,' he said, 'and its origin is Turkish. The Italians took it and called it *rota*. The Germans have said it another way. So have the French. But that's its origin' (Özgü 1963: 31).

The trouble was that, although Atatürk liked nothing better than a good argument, none of his intimates had the guts to say 'Very amusing as an after-dinner game, Pasha, but we mustn't take it too seriously, must we?' On the contrary, they

---

[4] Collated from various passages in Atay (1969), principally on p. 507.
[5] According to E. Blochet (1915: 305–8), the Iber were a Tunguz people, whom he equates with the Juan-juan of the Chinese chronicles. The relationship of the Tunguz with the Turks, however, is far from certain.

played the same game. This being long before the age of political correctness, Samih Rifat, the president of TDK, found the origin of the Western word *academy* in the Turkish *ak* 'white' and *adam* [A] 'man'. He also thought that the French *demeure, domicile,* and *domestique* were derived from the Turkish *dam* 'roof' and was not ashamed to say so in a public lecture ('Relations between Turkish and Other Languages') at the Turkish Historical Society's first Congress, which took place on 2–11 July 1932. The tone was thereby set for many a subsequent lecture and article. *Tarama Dergisi* marks with an asterisk 'words in use in our language which, although shown in ancient dictionaries as foreign, have emerged in the latest studies as Turkish or are firmly held to be Turkish'. Among the words so marked are *köşe* 'corner' and *tac* 'crown', both of them borrowings from the Persian (*gūše, tāj*), and *kıral* 'king', ultimately from Carl, the given name of the Emperor Charlemagne. Another was *kültür*, with the comment 'Keltirmek mastarının kökünden kurulmuş olduğundan ana kaynağı türkçe görünür' (As it is based on the root of the verb *keltirmek*, its original source seems to be Turkish). It is not clear why *kültür* 'culture' should come from an ancient verb meaning 'to bring', but it should be noted that this wild etymology could have been made to look a fraction less wild if *keltür-*, the proper ancient form, had been cited.

Here a general observation must be made, in view of the several allusions in this book to the unscholarliness of some of those who shaped the new Turkish. One should not be shocked at the apparent disingenuousness or self-deception that still allows some Turks to look one in the eye and insist that all the neologisms are entirely home-grown and uninfluenced by the foreign words that have manifestly inspired them; to swear, for example, that the resemblance between *okul* 'school' and the French *école* is fortuitous. One's first thought is, who do you think you're fooling? But when anyone except the most unregenerate of reformers says such a thing, it means no more than 'But it *could* have a Turkish etymology, couldn't it?'

In the several neologisms whose consonants resemble those of the Arabic words they were intended to replace, there is a reflection of their inventors' belief that they were restoring the original Turkish forms of these Arabic words: *ilgi* for *alâka* 'interest', *varsay-* for *farz* 'to suppose', *sömurme* for *istismar* 'exploitation', *kutsal* for *kudsî* 'holy', *sapta-* for *tespit* 'to establish'. All these are current.

Had the reformers happened to know the English *ashlar,* 'dressed stone for building or paving' (ultimately the Latin *axillaris*), they would surely have claimed it as derived from their *taşlar* 'stones'. Similarly they would have claimed the suffix of our *kingdom* and *Christendom* as borrowed from the suffix of Turkish *erdem* 'manly virtue' (compare *er* 'man'). Nor can they have come across Clauson's (1972: p. xliii) mention of *tanığma* as meaning 'riddle', or they would have hailed it as the etymon of *enigma*.[6] The disappearance of the initial *ts* of *taşlar* and *tanığma*

---

[6] Clauson, p. xliii. One assumes that by 'riddle' Clauson meant 'enigma' rather than 'sieve'. He seldom made mistakes, but neither meaning is right for *tanığma*, which in the body of the dictionary he shows as meaning 'denial'. His subconscious must have been brooding on the resemblance between *tanığma* and *enigma*.

would not have bothered them, for they would certainly have agreed with Müller's (1910: 30) dictum 'The change of a consonant is a mere trifle, for in etymology vowels are worth but little, and consonants almost nothing.'[7] And can it be that nobody noticed the resemblance between *illet* [A] and its English equivalent *illness*? Or the suffix *-ebil-* and English *able*? Had they come across the nineteenth-century attempt to establish a Polynesian etymology for *taboo* as from *ta* 'to mark' and *pu*, an adverb of intensity,[8] they would have been delighted by this proof that the influence of Turkish had reached the other side of the world. For *tapu* is Turkish for 'title deed', and what is a title deed if not an intensive marking, a legally cogent proof of ownership? The reader may think that what I am trying to say is that etymology is not a game for amateurs, but that is exactly what it is, whereas for others it is a science.[9]

To come back to the Dil Encümeni, which we met in Chapter 3: it had not been idle; in 1929 it had resumed the word-collecting begun by the Ministry of Education in 1920. By mid-1932, however, it was judged to be dormant, for on 25 June the Minister of Education told the Grand National Assembly that an allocation of just one lira had been made to it in the budget (Korkmaz 1992: 252–3). He explained, 'Dil Heyeti, Dil Encümeni, Dil Cemiyeti vesair namlarla her halde böyle bir heyetin . . . lüzumunu Hükûmet kabul etmiştir . . . Bunun için bir lira koyduk. (Kâfi sesleri)' (The Government has accepted the necessity for some such body . . . whether under the name of Language Committee, Language Council, Language Society or some other name . . . That is why we have put down one lira. (Cries of 'Enough!')). It is not apparent whether members' lack of enthusiasm at the prospect of perpetuating the existence of the moribund body was just because it was moribund or because they did not favour the language reform; in view of the general fervour for reform at that time, the former reason is the more likely.

Having founded Türk Tarihi Tetkik Cemiyeti (the Turkish Society for the Study of History, later Türk Tarih Kurumu), on 15 April 1931, on 12 July 1932 Mustafa Kemal established the Turkish Society for the Study of Language, Türk Dili Tetkik Cemiyeti, the name of which was changed four years later to Türk Dil Kurumu, after a brief period when *tetkik* [A] was replaced by *araştırma*.[10] The Society's creation is said to have been at the suggestion of four men: Samih Rifat, Ruşen

[7] Not the great nineteenth-century Oxford philologist Max Müller but his cousin, George A. Müller.

[8] 'The compound word *tapu*, therefore, means no more than "marked thoroughly" . . . because sacred things and places were commonly marked in a peculiar manner in order that everyone might know that they were sacred' (Shortland 1851: 81, quoted in Steiner 1967: 32).

[9] The author vividly recalls learning this fact in his youth from listening to one of the regulars at Speakers' Corner in London, a woman who preached the necessity of atheism and tried to prove it by explaining away the pagan deities as personifications of natural forces. The god Thor, for example, was the force that ended the winter, his name being identical with the English *thaw*. See also Lewis (1991).

[10] Already in September 1934 Atatürk was referring to the Society as Türk Dili Araştırma Kurumu. Two numbers of the Society's journal *Türk Dili* appeared in June 1935. In the first, no. 11, as in its predecessors, the subtitle was *Türk Dili Tetkik Cemiyeti Bülteni*; in the second, no. 12, it had become *Türk Dili Araştırma Kurumu Bülteni*.

Eşref, Celâl Sahir, and Yakup Kadri, who became its first board of management, with Samih Rifat as its first president (Doğan 1984: 25). In the forefront of this new organization were the purifiers (*tasfiyeciler*, a term soon replaced by *özleştirmeciler*). One of its first tasks was to draw up a list of philosophical and scientific terms, of which the Ottoman and French ones were sent to the universities and various private scholars, with a request that they produce Turkish replacements for them. The replies, after scrutiny by the Society, were sent to the Ministry of Education, which authorized their use in school textbooks. Not all of them were new; some were long-established Arabic borrowings or coinages from Arabic, some were of Greek or Latin origin.

On 21 November 1932 the Directorate of Religious Affairs instructed all 'cami ve mescid hademeleri' (servants of congregational and other mosques) to prepare themselves to recite the *ezan*, the call to prayer, not in Arabic but in Turkish, though this did not happen all over the country at once, because it took time for all muezzins to master the new version. A gramophone record made by Hafız Sadettin, the chief muezzin of the Sultan Ahmed mosque, was distributed to muezzins as the model to follow. This was the prescribed text:

> Tanrı[11] uludur!
> Şübhesiz bilirim bildiririm
> Tanrıdan başka yoktur tapacak.
> Şübhesiz bilirim bildiririm
> Tanrının elçisidir Muhammed.
> Haydin namaza!
> Haydin felâha!
> (Namaz uykudan hayırlıdır.)
> Tanrı uludur!
> Tanrıdan başka yoktur tapacak.

> (Jäschke 1951: 75)

> God is great!
> I know without doubt and I declare:
> There is none to be worshipped but God;
> I know without doubt and I declare:
> Muhammad is the envoy of God.
> Come to prayer!
> Come to felicity!
> (Prayer is better than sleep.)
> God is great!
> There is none to be worshipped but God.

The line in parentheses is recited only for the dawn prayer.

On 9 July 1933, when it had become obvious that it was not going to be easy to

---

[11] *Tanrı*, anciently *teñri*, originally meant 'sky' and then 'God'; Clauson (1972: 523–4) describes it as 'a very old word, prob. pre-Turkish, which can be traced back to the language of the Hsiung-nu, III B.C., if not earlier'.

find native equivalents for all the doomed Arabic and Persian words, *Hakimiyet-i Milliye* announced that words current among the people, whatever their origin, were to be regarded as Turkish. This sensible provision could have made little impression on the reformers, or they would not have wasted so much time trying to devise Turkish etymologies for Arabic words. Everyone had a go at the etymology game.

Birinci Türk Dili Kurultayı (the First Turkish Language Congress)[12] was held between 26 September and 5 October 1932, in the great ceremonial hall of Dolmabahçe Palace in Istanbul. Of some thirty papers read to the Kurultay, nine dealt with relationships between Turkish and other languages, one speaker going so far as to entitle his contribution 'Turkish Philology: Turkish is an Indo-European Language' (Dilemre 1933). A Philology and Linguistics Division was created, with responsibility for making comparisons between Turkish 'and the most ancient Turkish languages, such as Sumerian and Hittite, and the languages called Indo-European and Semitic'.

Many people threw themselves enthusiastically into this task. In 1934, if we may get a little ahead of the chronological account, Saim Ali (Dilemre 1935) presented to the Second Kurultay a paper in which he sought to establish a connection between Turkish and the West European languages. He equated the *bi-* of *bicarbonate* and *bilingual* with the *bi* of *bile* 'together' and *binmek* 'to mount', and the prefix *ex-* with the *eks* of *eksik* 'lacking' and *eksitmek* 'to reduce'. Even more bizarre was his identification of Latin *ab* 'as in *abjure* and *abandon*' (although the *ab* in the latter word is not in fact the Latin *ab*) with the first syllable of *abaki* 'scarecrow' and *abacı*, which he explained as 'kaşkarlıların ummacısı' (the Kashghars' bogyman),[13] the connection being that scarecrows and bogymen are frightening and turn birds and people *ab*, 'away'.

Other products of the same frame of mind were displayed at that Second Kurultay.[14] Naim Hâzım delivered himself of a paper (Onat 1935) on the relationship between Turkish and the Semitic languages, having previously published an article entitled 'Türk kökleri Arap dilini nasıl doğurmuş' ('How Turkish Roots Gave Birth to Arabic' (*Hakimiyet-i Milliye*, 4 Mar. 1933; Levend 1972: 430)). At the

---

[12] The title of the third and subsequent congresses was Türk Dil Kurultayı—i.e. not Turkish-Language Congress but Turkish Language-Congress, indicating a greater breadth of interest. The title on bound volumes of the proceedings of the second congress is Türk Dil Kurultayı, but the term used throughout the text is Türk Dili Kurultayı.

[13] The normal spelling of the word translated 'bogyman' is *umacı* with a single *m*. Abaki does not seem to be recorded elsewhere. The common Anatolian word for scarecrow is *abak*; see Koşay and Işıtman (1932: 1). As for the kaşkarlılar (*sic*): 'The Kashgharians are a people living in Kulja and the western part of Chinese Turkestan' (Czaplicka 1918: 58). 'Kashgartsy, Kashgarlyki: local designation of an Uyghur population of the Kashgar oasis (Western China). The Kashgars in Central Asia are a group of Uyghurs who resettled from the Kashgar oasis to the Ferghana valley in the 1840's; at the present time they are fused with the Uzbeks' (Krueger 1963: 197-a). So far as one can tell in the absence of an index, they are not mentioned in Bainbridge (1993).

[14] And after it: an article by Dilemre, entitled 'Türk–Kelt dil karşılaştırmaları' ('Linguistic Comparisons between Turkish and Celtic'), appeared in *Türk Dili*, 15 (1936), 1–97. The proceedings of the Second Kurultay were published in numbers 9–14 (Sept. 1934 to Dec. 1935) of the journal.

Third Kurultay, in 1936, he returned specifically to the relationship with Arabic, this time in the light of the Sun-Language Theory (Onat 1937). Years later he published a two-volume work on the same theme (Onat 1944–9), though the second volume did not go beyond one fascicle. The kindest comment one can make is that he could scarcely be blamed for failing to prove his thesis.

Yusuf Ziya Özer, a lawyer, not a language man, found the origin of *Aphrodite* in *avrat* 'woman' ('*awrāt* [A]). He spoke at the Second Kurultay on the relationship between Turkish and the Ural-Altaic languages, including Finnish:

Fin dili son zamanlarda indo-avrupayi [*sic*] sayılmak için bir meyelan vardır. Bu bir fali hayırdır, çünki fin dilinin indo-avrupaî zümresine girmesi uralo-altay lehçeleri üzerinde yapılacak lisanî tetkikatı genişletecek ve sonunda bu lehçelerin de aynı membadan geldiği anlaşılarak türkçenin ana dil olduğu hakikatini meydana koymaya vesile olacaktır.   (*Türk Dili*, 12 (1935), 55)

There has been a tendency recently for Finnish to be counted as Indo-European.[15] This bodes well, since the entry of Finnish among the Indo-European languages will broaden linguistic studies on the Ural-Altaic dialects, and eventually the realization that these dialects also come from the same origin will be the occasion to bring to light the truth that Turkish is the mother language.

This same Yusuf Ziya figures in a reminiscence of the constitutional lawyer Ali Fuad Başgil:

Hiç unutmam, 1935 yazında, bir gün, Ada vapurunda, rahmetli Eskişehir Mebusu Yusuf Ziya hoca ile buluştuktu. Ankara'dan geldiğini ve beş yüz sahfelik [*sic*] bir eser hazırlamakta olduğunu söyledi. Neye dair diye sordum. Arapça'nın Türkçe'den çıkma olduğuna dairmiş . . . Bir de misâl verdi, meselâ Firavun kelimesi Arapça sanılır, halbuki Türkçedir ve 'Burun' kelimesinden çıkmadır. Burun, insanın önünde, çıkıntı yapan bir uzuvdur. Hükümdar da cemyetin [*sic*] önünde giden bir şahsiyet olduğu için, Mısır'da buna burun denilmiş, kelime zamanlar içinde kullanılarak nihayet Firavun olmuş . . . Üstad hakikaten uydurmacılık hastalığından kurtulamıyarak Allahın rahmetine kavuştu.   (Erer 1973: 186–7)

I shall never forget; on the Islands steamer one day in the summer of 1935, I met the late Professor Yusuf Ziya, the Deputy for Eskişehir. He told me he had come from Ankara and was preparing a work of five hundred pages. I asked what it was about. It emerged that it was on the Turkish origins of Arabic. And he gave an example: for instance the word *Firavun* 'Pharaoh' is thought to be Arabic, whereas it is Turkish, being derived from *burun* 'nose', an organ protruding in front of a person. As the sovereign is a personage going in front of the society, in Egypt he was called The Nose. In the course of time, this word *burun* became altered to *Firavun* . . . The Professor in fact attained God's mercy without managing to escape from the disease of fakery.

To revert to 1932: the Society's by-laws, accepted by the First Kurultay, set out two aims (Kurultay 1932: 437): 'Türk dilinin öz güzelliğini ve zenginliğini meydana çıkarmak; Türk dilini dünya dilleri arasında değerine yaraşır yüksekliğine

---

[15] This looks like a moonbeam from the larger lunacy, but one cannot confidently assert that there never was such a tendency.

eriştirmek' (To bring to light the particular beauty and richness of the Turkish language and to raise it to the level it merits among the languages of the world). The Central General Committee elected by the Kurultay issued the following directive on the tasks to be given priority:

(1) Halk dilinde ve eski kitaplarda bulunan Türk dili hazinelerini toplayıp ortaya koyma; (2) Türkçede söz yaratma yollarını belli etmek ve bunları işleterek Türk köklerinden türlü sözler çıkarmak; (3) Türkçede, hele yazı dilinde, çok kullanılan yabancı kökten sözler yerine konabilecek öz Türkçe sözleri ortaya koymak ve bunları yaymak. (*Söz Derleme Dergisi* (1939–52): i. 7–8)

(1) Collecting and publishing the treasures of the Turkish language existing in the popular language and old books; (2) clarifying the methods of word-creation in Turkish and employing them to extract various words from Turkish roots; (3) uncovering and publicizing pure Turkish words which may be substituted for words of foreign roots widely used in Turkish, especially in the written language.

On the evening after the close of that First Kurultay there was great euphoria round Atatürk's table. He himself was saying, 'We are going to defeat Ottoman. Turkish is going to be a language as free and as independent as the Turkish nation, and with it we shall enter the world of civilization at one go' (Tankut 1963: 116–17).[16] Then there began *söz derleme seferberliği* (the word-collection mobilization).

'Mobilization' was not an empty metaphor; those called upon included army officers, teachers, tax, agriculture, and forestry officials, and government doctors, whose duties brought them into regular contact with the people. The central committee of the Language Society distributed to every part of the country a booklet explaining how the work was to be carried out, together with slips on which to enter the words collected. In the capital of every province (*vilayet*) a 'collection committee' of mayors, military commanders, and head teachers was set up, chaired by the provincial governor (*Vali*), with a branch committee chaired by the sub-governor (*Kaymakam*) in the chief town of every sub-province (*kaza*); the duty of these committees was to organize the collection of words in use among the people. Within a year, a total of 125,988 slips had been returned, from which, after checking and the elimination of repetitions, 35,357 words were left. To these were added 765 words collected by private individuals and gleaned from folk-poetry and various books, including the first ever Turkish dialect dictionary: Hamit Zübeyr [Koşay] and İshak Refet [Işıtman], *Anadilden Derlemeler* (1932),[17] a scholarly work containing the results not only of its authors' own investigations but also of the 1920 inquiry mentioned in Chapter 2. In addition, there was a number of words from *Türkmence* (Turcoman), and *Azerice*, the dialect of Azerbaijan (Kurultay 1934 (= *Türk Dili*, 8 (1934), 12)).

---

[16] Tankut does not quote Atatürk's actual words. His version of them runs 'Osmanlıcayı yeneceğiz. Türk dili Türk ulusu gibi özgür ve başına buyruk bir dil olacak ve biz onunla uygarlık acununa birden ve toptan gireceğiz.' But *özgür*, for example, was not invented until twenty years after the First Kurultay.

[17] Twenty years later a second volume appeared: Koşay and Aydın 1952.

A Commission of Inquiry was created and from March to July 1933 *Hakimiyet-i Milliye* published daily lists of a dozen or so Arabic and Persian words under the heading 'Türk okur yazarları! Büyük dil anketi seferberliği başladı. İş başına!' (Literate Turks! Mobilization for the great language inquiry has begun. To work!). Other newspapers and radio stations were invited to cooperate and readers' suggestions for Turkish replacements were published as they came in. (There is anecdotal evidence that suggestions were paid for at the rate of TL6 a word.) When it became apparent that different contributors had different ideas about what sort of replacements were acceptable, belatedly on 9 July *Hakimiyet-i Milliye* stated two principles: (*a*) words current among the people, whatever their origin, were to be counted as Turkish, and (*b*) replacements must be *Öztürkçe* (see note 25, p. 56): while *kalem* [A] 'pen', for example, would not be discarded, *yazak* would also be used and whichever proved the more popular would survive. This exercise was not very productive: the number of words in the daily lists totalled 1,382. Of the replacements suggested, 640 were accepted.

Meanwhile, scholars had been combing through dictionaries of Turkic languages and more than 150 old texts in search of words that had fallen out of use or had never been in use in Turkey; these totalled close on 90,000. After a very brief process of checking, mostly by middle-school teachers, the results of both researches were embodied in *Tarama Dergisi* (1934). Although the compilers had conscientiously put question marks against some words of which they were not sure, and warned that this huge mass of material was undigested, enthusiasts did not feel inhibited from using any word found in it, and for a while Babel set in. If you wanted to express 'pen' without using the normal *kalem*, you looked up *kalem* and made your choice from among *yağuş* or *yazgaç*, shown as recorded at Bandırma and İzmir respectively, or the Karaim *cizgiç* or *sızgıç*, or the Tatar *kavrı*, or *kamış* from the *Kamus*[18] or *yuvuş* from Pavet de Courteille (1870). For *hikâye* 'story' there were twenty-two possibilities, including *erteği*, *höçek*, *ötkünç*, and *sürçek*, but not *öykü*, which eventually supplanted it. For *hediye* 'gift' you could pick your favourite from a list of seventy-seven words ranging from *açı* through *ertüt* and *tanşu* to *yarlığaş* and *zını*.

Agop Dilâçar notes (Korkmaz 1992: 363) that for *akıl* 'intelligence' there were twenty-six equivalents, from *an* to *zerey*. He describes a visit he paid some time in 1934 to Necmettin Sadak, editor-in-chief of the newspaper *Akşam*:

Sadak, gazetenin başyazısını yazmıştı, Osmanlıca. Zile bastı, gelen odacıya yazıyı vererek 'bunu ikameciye götür' dedi. Karşı odadaki ikameci *Tarama Dergisi*'ni açtı ve yazının sözdizimine hiç bakmadan, Osmanlıca sözcüklerin yerine bu dergiden beğendiği Türkçe karşılıkları 'ikame' etti. Başka bir gazete bürosunda başka bir 'ikameci' aynı

---

[18] What the *Kamus* (1316/1901: ii. 1039) actually gives under *kamış* 'reed' is 'kalem kamışı: yontularak yazı yazmağa yarayan kamış cinsi . . .' (pen-reed: a type of reed which on being trimmed serves for writing . . .). 'Reed pen' is *kamış kalem*; the two words are not synonymous.

Osmanlıca sözcüklere başka karşılıkları seçmiş olabilirdi. İşte Atatürk'ün ilk bunalımı bu kargaşadan doğdu.

Sadak had written the editorial, in Ottoman. He rang the bell, gave the text to the messenger who arrived, and said 'Take this to the substitutor.' The substitutor, in the room across the corridor, opened *Tarama Dergisi* and, paying no regard to the structure of the passage, 'substituted' for the Ottoman words the Turkish equivalents he liked from that book. In another newspaper office another 'substitutor' might have chosen other equivalents for the same Ottoman words.

The author had some first-hand experience of the rite of 'substitution' in 1984, when he spent a memorable evening in Istanbul with a group of members of the Faculty of Political Science who were organizing a symposium on the *Tanzimat*, the nineteenth-century reforms. Their chairman, a venerable retired professor, was composing his opening address, which, for the sake of the many young students who were expected, he wanted to couch in the most up-to-date language. So in his own archaic and courtly Turkish he told the company what he wanted to say and we suggested the appropriate neologisms. There was much discussion about how to say 'modern'. He knew *asrî* was too old-fashioned but he did not know the new word. One or two people suggested *çağdaş*, but we agreed that that was the neologism for *muasır* 'contemporary'. The eventual consensus was that he should use *modern*, which he did.

It was around 1934 that a Turkish writer, when asked how many languages he knew, is said to have replied that it was as much as he could do to keep up with Turkish. The situation is well summed up by Heyd (1954: 31):[19]

Now any Turkish word found in the vernacular of a remote Anatolian village, in the speech of an even more remote Turkish tribe in Siberia or in the manuscript of an eleventh century Turkish–Arabic dictionary was regarded as a possible addition to the modern Turkish vocabulary. On the other hand, practically every word of Arabic or Persian origin was considered outlawed and condemned to suppression as soon as a Turkish equivalent was found.

An undated leaflet, published by TDK and distributed to the participants at one of the early Kurultays, deserves to be rescued from oblivion. It is entitled *Kurultay Marşı* ('Congress March'), words by Dr Hilmi Oytaç, Deputy for Malatya, music by Maestro Karlo d'Alpino Kapoçelli. The presence of the surnames Atatürk and Oytaç shows it could not have been before 1934, as does Dr Oytaç's manifest indebtedness to *Tarama Dergisi* of 1934: *buşgut, tolunay, cankı* [M], and so on. The translation offered here is in parts tentative; the rendering 'respect' for *okkay*, for example, which is not found in *Tarama Dergisi*, is based on the possibly far-fetched assumption that it is a back-formation from *okkalı* (from *okka* 'oke', a measure of weight), first meaning 'weighty' and then 'worthy of respect', with the *y* added for the sake of the rhyme.

---

[19] This book is immensely useful for details of the Society's history, as is Brendemoen (1990: 454–93).

Gözün aydın Türk oğlu açıldı benlik yolu
Ey bu yolun yolcusu artık sana ne mutlu
Atatürk çocukları diline el bastırmaz
Kurultay buşgutları diline dil kattırmaz
　　Selâm sana Kurultay yeni doğan tolunay
　　Selâm sana Atatürk, bizden sana bin okkay
Bil ki tarih ile dil benliğin damgasıdır
İçi dışı gösteren bir kılık aynasıdır
Bu cankıdan doğacak öz Türklüğe yom olcay
Özge dilden öz dili kurtaracak Kurultay
　　Selâm sana Kurultay yeni doğan tolunay
　　Selâm sana Atatürk, bizden sana bin okkay

Joy to you, son of Turks, the road to identity has been opened
O traveller on this road, how happy you are at last.
The children of Atatürk let no stranger encroach on their language
The disciples of the Kurultay let no language adulterate their language
　　Salutations to you, Kurultay, full moon newly rising
　　Salutations to you, Atatürk, a thousand respects from us to you
Know that history and language are the mark of identity
A full-length mirror showing the inside and the outside
From this council blessings and felicity will be born for pure Turkdom
The Kurultay will save the pure language from other languages.

İbrahim Necmi displayed some cheerful ignorance in his speech on the occasion of the second *Dil Bayramı* (Language Festival), in which he spoke of *Tarama Dergisi*:

Dergideki sözler, öz dilimizin hem zenginliğini, hem de başka dillere kaynaklığını gösterecek değerdedir. Bir örnek verelim. Bugün herkesin söylediği 'psikoloji' sözünün kökü aranacak olursa bunun 'psikoz' dan çıktığı görülür. Etimoloji kitapları bunu da 'nefes' diye anlatırlar. Yaşamanın nefes almakla bir olduğunu düşünen eskilerin 'nefes' le 'ruh' u bir tutmaları kolay anlaşılır bir iştir. Şimdi Dergide 'nefes' sözüne bakarsanız 'Pıs' diye bir söz görürsünüz ki 'psikoz' sözünün de, 'nefes' lakırdısının da hep bu ana kaynaktan kaynamış olduğunu anlamak pek kolay olur. . . .   (*Turk Dili*, 10 (1934), 23–4)

The words in the *Dergi* are capable of showing both the richness of our language and the fact that it is the source for other languages. Let me give an example. If one looks for the root of the word *psikoloji*, which today is on everyone's lips, it will be seen that it comes from *psikoz*. The etymology books explain this as *nefes* [A] 'breath'. It is easily understandable that the ancients, reflecting that living was one with breathing, took 'breath' and 'soul' as one and the same. Now if you look up the word *nefes* in the *Dergi* you will see a word *pıs*, and it will be very easy to understand that *psikoz* and *nefes* have both welled up from this ultimate source.

He then gave another example, *tünel* (familiar to Istanbul people as the name of the underground railway going down from the lower end of İstiklâl Caddesi to the Golden Horn), 'which everyone knows we borrowed from the French'. Having said that a recent French etymological dictionary explained the word as a French borrowing from the English *tonnel* (*sic*), of obscure origin, he continues: 'Şimdi

Dergiyi açınız: "Tün" sözünün "gece, karanlık" demeye geldiğini görürsünüz. Buna "Kural, kaval, çakal, sakal, güzel . . ." sözlerinin sonunda görülen "al-el" ekini katarsanız "Tünel" in "karanlık yer" demeye gelen öz Türkçe bir söz olduğu ortaya çıkar' (Now open the *Dergi* and you will see that *tün* means 'night, darkness'. If you add to this word the suffix appearing at the end of words such as *kural* ['rule'],[20] *kaval* ['shepherd's pipe'], *çakal* ['jackal'], *sakal* ['beard'], *güzel* ['beautiful'], and so on, it becomes apparent that *tünel* is a pure Turkish word meaning 'dark place'). That last paragraph, together with his confusion of *psikoz* 'psychosis' and *psyché*, and his equating the second syllable of the Arabic *nefes* with *pıs* (according to *Tarama Dergisi* (1934), a Kirghiz word for 'weak breath'),[21] may be thought to show a deficiency of philological competence. Although he taught literature and from 1935 was a member of the Grand National Assembly, by training he was a lawyer, but that did not harm his career in the Language Society, of which he was Secretary-General from 1934 to 1945.

It was during the period of linguistic chaos following the publication of *Tarama Dergisi* (1934) that Atatürk said to Atay something on these lines:[22] 'Çocuğum beni dinle, dedi. Türkçenin hiçbir yabancı kelimeye ihtiyacı olmadığını söyleyenlerin iddiasını tecrübe ettik. Bir çıkmaza girmişizdir. Dili bu çıkmazda bırakırlar mı? Bırakmazlar. Biz de çıkmazdan kurtarma şerefini başkalarına bırakamayız' ('Listen to me, my boy,' he said. 'We have put to the test the claim of those who say that Turkish has no need of any foreign word. We really have got into a dead end. Will they leave the language in this dead end? They won't. But we can't leave to others the honour of saving it from the dead end'). Atay's next words are of greater significance: 'Fakat bir noktada ısrar etti. Türkçede kalacak kelimelerin aslında Türkçe olduğu izah edilmeli idi' (But on one point he was insistent: it had to be explained that the words which were to remain in Turkish were Turkish in origin).

Atay gives us an insight into the method used to avoid branding as foreign any essential word for which no native equivalent could be found. He tells of a discussion on the Dictionary Commission about possible replacements for *hüküm* [A] 'judgement':

Naim Hâzim Hoca was sitting on my right, Yusuf Ziya on my left. I said, 'There's no equivalent for it. Let's keep it.' They both said, 'Impossible!' I turned to my right and said, 'Professor, you say that the origin of Arabic is Turkish. You claim as originally Turkish any word we cite from the Koran.' I turned to my left. 'And you, Professor, maintain that all languages derive from Turkish. You resort to all kinds of dodges to show that the French *chambre* is

[20] *Kural* 'rule' is a neologism of dubious ancestry. In the real world it occurs in the sense of 'instrument, tool' in most Central Asian dialects.

[21] *Pıs*, which looks onomatopoeic, is not to be found in Taymas (1945–8), the Turkish translation of Yudakhin, *Kirgizsko-Russkiy Slovar* (1940).

[22] The reason for the *Russkiy Slovar* uncertainty is that this version, from Atay (1951), is one of his three versions of the same reminiscence. It has been selected as being the oldest and, one therefore hopes, the nearest to what Atatürk actually said. There is yet another version in Akbal (1984), obviously quoted from memory: 'Atatürk "öz Türkçe işi çıkmaza girdi, vazgeçelim bundan" diyesi imiş!' (Lewis 1988: 115) (A. is supposed to have said, 'The pure Turkish business has got into a dead end; let's drop it'.)

derived from *oda*. And now, when it comes to a word like *hüküm* which has become part of village speech, the two of you dig your toes in.' We had quite an argument. After the meeting, my friend Abdülkadir came up to me in the upper corridor of Dolmabahçe Palace. He it was who had once said to me, 'I know most of the dialects of the Asian Turks. I also understand the dialect spoken by you and people like Yakup Kadri. If there's one dialect I can't make head or tail of, it's the dialect of the Turkish Language Society.' On this occasion he said, 'You look worried. Tell me what words are bothering you and I'll find Turkish origins for them.' 'Well,' I replied, 'there's this word *hüküm*.' 'Don't worry,' he said, 'tomorrow we'll make *hüküm* Turkish.' Next day he quietly put into my hand a slip of paper on which he had noted that some dialects had a word *ök* meaning 'intellect', which in several of them took the form *ük*. I had myself discovered that in Yakut there was a word-building suffix *-üm*. The rest was easy: *ük* plus *üm* had in the course of time become *hüküm*. When the meeting began, I said, 'The word *hüküm* is Turkish,' and gave a full account of what I had learned, which reduced the two professors to silence. We had laid the foundations of the science of—I shan't say fakery, but flim-flam. ['Uydurma' demiyeyim de 'yakıştırmacılık' ilminin temelini atmıştık.'] That evening I reported to Atatürk on the Commission's proceedings and he was very pleased that we had won so important a word by this fabrication. What he wanted us to do was to leave as many words in the language as possible, so long as we could demonstrate that they were Turkish.[23]

Atay of course knew that *hüküm* was borrowed from the Arabic *ḥukm* but he offers no justification for his conduct; if taxed with dishonesty he would no doubt have pleaded that what he had told the Commission and Atatürk was a white lie intended to save the life of a word that had served the Turks well for centuries. Atatürk, who was no doubt equally aware of the origin of *hüküm*, was satisfied that it could be reprieved now that it had been provided with a Turkish pedigree.

A remarkable revelation of the Language Society's way with words is to be seen in an unsigned article entitled 'Cep Kılavuzları ne kadar Sözü Karşılamıştır?':

Şimdiye kadar lûgatlerde arapça farsça . . . gibi Türkçeden başka sanılan dillere mensup diye gösterilmiş olan, fakat Kılavuz araştırmaları arasında gerek kökünün Türkçe olduğu anlaşılması ve gerek yaygınlığı ve dilin ihtiyacı olması bakımından Türk kökünden geldiği tesbit edilen sözlerin sayısı (583)tür. (*Türk Dili*, 16 (1936), 22–3)

Up to now, 583 words have been shown in the dictionaries as belonging to languages thought to be different from Turkish, such as Arabic, Persian etc., but their derivation from Turkish roots has been established, in view of the facts that it has become clear in the course of researching the *Guide* that their roots are Turkish, that they are widely used, and that the language needs them.

One may wonder why, once it had become clear that the roots of the words in question were Turkish, further evidence was required that their derivation from Turkish roots had been established. In so far as it betokens an uneasy conscience on the anonymous writer's part, let us not condemn him.

Atatürk was far too intelligent to be deluded by those who maintained that all languages derived from Turkish. The logical consequence of such a belief would

---

[23] Atay's story is here pieced together from his two divergent accounts, one in Atay (1969: 478), the other in Atay (1965).

have been to retain all the Arabic and Persian elements in the language, which at that time was the exact opposite of his intention. So, for a limited period, he seized on the *Öztürkçe* words produced by the reformers and used them in his speeches and letters.

In February 1935 he dropped his given names, Mustafa and Kemal, both being irremediably Arabic, and for a little while took to signing himself as Kamâl. The origin of this novel name was explained in a communiqué from Anadolu Ajansı, the official news agency:

İstihbaratımıza nazaran Atatürk'ün taşıdığı 'Kamâl' adı Arapça bir kelime olmadığı gibi Arapça 'Kemal' (olgunluk) kelimesinin delâlet ettiği mânâda değildir.

Atatürk'ün muhafaza edilen öz adı, Türkçe 'ordu ve kale' mânâsına olan 'Kamâl' dir. Son 'a' üstündeki tahfif işareti 'l' harfini yumuşattığı için telaffuz hemen hemen Arapça 'Kemal' telaffuzuna yaklaşır. Benzeyiş bundan ibarettir. (*Cumhuriyet*, 5 Feb. 1935, quoted in Bozgeyik 1995: 15)

In the light of our information, the name 'Kamâl' that Atatürk bears is not an Arabic word, nor does it have the meaning indicated by the Arabic word *kemal* ['maturity', 'perfection'].

Atatürk's personal name, which is being retained, is 'Kamâl', the Turkish meaning of which is army and fortification. As the circumflex accent on the final *a* softens the *l*, the pronunciation closely approximates that of the Arabic 'Kemal'. That is the full extent of the resemblance.

Tarama Dergisi (1934) gives *kamal* as meaning fortification, castle, army, shield. That, however, is of no relevance, because *kamâl* (/kamal^y/) is not *kamal* (Lewis 1988: 6–7).[24] Apart from the improbable final syllable, the substitution of *a* for the *e* of *Kemal* would alter the sound of the initial consonant, from /k^y/ to /k/. But clearly the purpose of the change was not to affect the pronunciation of the name but only to make its written form look less Arabic. In fact he did not persist with 'Kamâl' but habitually signed himself K. Atatürk.

In the spring of 1935 the newspapers began to publish lists of proposed replacements for Arabic and Persian words, on which readers were invited to comment. Later that year the results were presented to the public in a little 'Pocket Guide from Ottoman to Turkish' (*Cep Kılavuzu* (1935)), as planned at the Second Kurultay in August 1934. The speed with which the plan had been implemented was due to the active interest of Atatürk himself, but it is a pity the editors did not have more time to spend on it. Two examples: the new word they offered for 'education' was *eğitim*, which was supposed to be a noun derived from an ancient verb *eğitmek* 'to educate'. But there never was a verb *eğitmek*; it was a misreading of *igidmek* 'to feed (people or animals)'. For *millet* 'nation' *Tarama Dergisi* had come up with eight possibilities, among them *uluş* and *ulus*. The compilers of *Cep Kılavuzu* backed the wrong horse and chose the latter, which represented the Mongolian pronunciation of Turkish *uluş* 'country', an early borrowing by the

---

[24] There is a Turkish word containing a back vowel and a clear *l*, the somewhat mysterious *elâ* (/el^{y}ā/) 'hazel' (of eyes). Agop Dilâçar's new surname 'language-opener' (he was born Martayan) was given to him by Atatürk; the circumflex shows that the *l* is clear.

Mongols, used by them for 'a confederation of peoples' (Clauson 1972: 152). By the fourteenth century the Turks had borrowed it back, and it was in its Mongolian form *ulus* that they used it until the seventeenth century and use it again now.

The end product was to be *Öz Türkçe*[25] (Pure Turkish), a term said to derive from a favourite expression of Atatürk's, 'öz Türk dilimiz' (our own Turkish language), *öz* meaning 'pure' as well as 'own'. The new words were circulated to schools by the Ministry of Education, and publicized and used in the newspapers.

Atatürk had already gone a long way in the use of *Öztürkçe*; he took it to the limit in the speech he made on 3 October 1934, at a banquet in honour of the Swedish Crown Prince and Princess. Turks refer to it as 'baysal utkulu nutuk' (the speech characterized by 'baysal utkusu'), this expression standing out as the oddest of all. It contains three French words, *Altes*, *Ruvayâl*, and *Prenses*, and only two words of Arabic origin, *tarih* 'history' and *tüm* 'all'.[26] It also contains some startling neologisms. Here is a sample (full text and glossary in Levend 1972: 424–6): 'Avrupanın iki bitim ucunda yerlerini berkiten uluslarımız, ataç özlük-lerinin tüm ıssıları olarak baysak, önürme, uygunluk kıldacıları olmuş bulunu-yorlar; onlar, bugün, en güzel utkuyu kazanmıya anıklanıyorlar: baysal utkusu' (Our nations, which hold firm their places at the two extremities of Europe, in full possession of their ancestral qualities have become the agents of tranquillity, progress and harmony; today they are preparing to win the most beautiful victory of all: the victory of peace). Tankut (1963: 125) says that the speech was composed in Ottoman and the Arabic words were then replaced by neologisms. He says too that Mustafa Kemal delivered it 'okumaya yeni başlamış öğrencilerin acemiliğiyle' (with the awkwardness of schoolchildren who have just begun to read).

This self-inflicted injury must have caused him great irritation, for he was a proud man and a master of his own language. He had the rare gift of being able to extemporize, in Ottoman, lengthy periods of the kind that others might strug-gle for hours to compose, while he was equally at home with the straightforward and often racy colloquial he used in conversation and when addressing informal meetings. His address opening the new session of the Grand National Assembly on 1 November 1934 contained a fair number of *Öztürkçe* words,[27] though they were nothing like so numerous or so outlandish as those that must have tried the skill of the Swedish Crown Prince's interpreter a month earlier unless he had been given a sight of the original Ottoman text.

Towards the end of 1935, Atatürk seems to have decided that he would no longer deny himself the full use of the instrument he wielded so well; this is evident from the language of his subsequent public utterances, as we shall see. One can only imagine his mortification after all the effort he had invested in the language reform. And then, in what must have been a time of great chagrin and heart-searching for him, there appeared a *deus ex machina*: along came Kvergić.

[25] Now generally written as one word, a practice which henceforth is followed in this book.
[26] It is not totally certain that *tüm* is originally Arabic, but there is no evidence that it is not.
[27] Text in *Atatürk'ün Söylev ve Demeçleri* (1945: i. 362–4).

5

The Sun-Language Theory and After

Sometime in 1935 Atatürk received a forty-seven-page typescript in French, entitled 'La Psychologie de quelques éléments des langues turques', by a Dr Hermann F. Kvergić of Vienna. The theme was that man first realized his own identity when he conceived the idea of establishing what the external objects surrounding him were. Language first consisted of gestures, to which some significant sounds were then added. Kvergić saw evidence for his view in the Turkish pronouns. *M* indicates oneself, as in *men*, the ancient form of *ben* 'I', and *elim* 'my hand'. *N* indicates what is near oneself, as in *sen* 'you' and *elin* 'your hand'. *Z* indicates a broader area, as in *biz* 'we' and *siz* 'you'. Further, Kvergić considered that Turkish was the first human language to take shape. Nothing could have been more timely.

Two months before, a copy of the paper had been sent to Ahmet Cevat Emre, the chairman of the grammar section of the Language Society, who after a cursory examination dismissed it as unsubstantiated and worthless. Atatürk was more impressed, partly because, having discussed it with Emre, he suspected that the latter's rejection of it was due to his seeing in Kvergić a potential rival. 'To me,' he said, 'the psychological analyses look important.' He thought that primitive man might well have given vent to exclamations such as 'Aa!' and 'Oo!' and that language could have emerged from utterances of this kind. He passed the paper on to İbrahim Necmi Dilmen, the secretary-general of the Language Society, and said, 'It looks important; let it be examined carefully.' Dilmen talked it over with Hasan Reşit Tankut, Naim Hâzım Onat, and Abdülkadir İnan, who saw merit in the psychological analyses (Emre 1960: 342–6).

The result of Atatürk's subsequent lucubrations, aided by these and others of the staff of the Society, was *Güneş-Dil Teorisi* (the Sun-Language Theory), which saw the beginning of language as the moment when primitive man looked up at the sun and said 'Aa!'. As it was concerned only with the beginning and not the development of language, it cannot be reproached for omitting to explain how mankind progressed from that primeval 'Aa!' to the sublimity of 'Faith, hope and charity, these three things', or Virgil's 'sunt lacrimae rerum' or even to so commonplace an utterance as 'Let's go for a walk in the park.'

Here is a brief summary of the theory, which came equipped with a battery of rules for its application. That 'Aa', *ağ* in Turkish spelling, was the first-degree radical of the Turkish language. Its original meaning was sun, then sunlight, warmth, fire, height, bigness, power, God, master, motion, time, distance, life, colour, water, earth, voice. As man's vocal mechanisms developed, other vowels and consonants became available, each with its own shade of meaning. Because the primeval exclamation was shouted, and it is obviously easier to begin a shout with a vowel than with a consonant, any word now beginning with a consonant originally began with a vowel, since abraded. The words *yağmur* 'rain', *çamur* 'mud', and *hamur* 'dough', for example, are compounded of *ağmur* 'flowing water' preceded by *ay* 'high', *aç* 'earth', and *ah* 'food' respectively. The reader is urged not to waste time looking for the last four 'Turkish' words in the dictionary.

There is a cryptic foreshadowing of the theory in Dilmen's preface to *Türkçe-den Osmanlıcaya Cep Kılavuzu*. After asserting that it was becoming daily more certain that 'the languages termed non-Turkish are equally of Turkish origin', he says, 'There can be no doubt that the great truth we are referring to will soon reveal itself with the brightness of the sun.' The authorship of the theory is archly hinted at by the anonymous writer of 'Güneş-Dil Teorisinin Esaslarına Kısa bir Bakış',[1] which speaks of it as a product of 'Türk jenisi' (the Turkish genius).

The Third Kurultay, in 1936, was dominated by what Heyd (1954: 34), with admirable restraint, refers to as 'this amazing theory'. So does Brendemoen (1990: 456), who with less restraint also calls it 'infamous'. Atatürk's responsibility for the theory is not disputed, though clearly he did not do all the donkey work. Dilâçar (1963: 50) says in so many words that the paper on the application of the analytical method of the theory, described in the agenda as the work of İsmail Müştak Mayakon, who read it to the Congress on 27 August 1936, was wholly due to Atatürk. So was the anonymous and undated little brochure *Etimoloji Morfoloji ve Fonetik Bakımından Türk Dili* ('The Turkish Language Etymologically, Morphologically and Phonetically Considered'), a condensed version of which was given away with the issue of *Ulus*, 14 November 1935. Between 2 and 21 November of that year, half of the front page of the newspaper was devoted to a series of unsigned 'Dil Yazıları', articles purporting to demonstrate the Turkish origin of some sixty words, mostly Arabic borrowings, on the basis of the Sun-Language Theory. The fact that *Ulus* gave up half its front page day after day to these articles is a pointer to the identity of their writer, but Atatürk's authorship of them was not known for sure until the publication in 1994 of an article that established with documentary evidence (Ercilasun 1994: 89) what had long been generally assumed.

This is how the first section of the brochure began:

Etimoloji, morfoloji ve fonetik bakımından Türk dili' hakkındaki şu notların ifade ettiği fikirler . . . Birinci Dil Kurultayından beri geçen üç sene içinde, Türk Dil üzerinde ve bu münasebetle diğer dillerde yapılan tetkik ve araştırmalardan ve dille alâkadar olan filozofi,

---

[1] Originally serialized in *Ulus* from the beginning of November 1935 onwards, reprinted in *Türk Dili*, 16 (1936), 33–123.

psikoloji, sosyoloji bahislerinin gözden geçirilmesinden doğmuştur. Bu doğuş, filolojide yeni bir teori olarak görülebilir. Bu teorinin temeli, insana benliğini güneşin tanıtmış olması fikridir.

The ideas set out in these notes on 'The Turkish Language Etymologically, Morphologically and Phonetically Considered' have emerged in the three years since the First Language Congress . . . They grew from studies and research conducted during that time on Turkish and other languages and from a review of topics in philosophy, psychology, and sociology that have a bearing on language. This outcome may be seen as a new philological theory, based on the concept that what made man aware of his identity was the sun.

Having cited several works in which he had found confirmation for his theory— by Carra de Vaux on Etruscan, and Hilaire de Barenton on the derivation of languages from Sumerian—Atatürk continues:

Dil bu buluşla, tamamen câmit olmaktan kurtulamamıştır. Ona can ve hareket vermek lâzımdır. İşte bu nokta üzerinde düşünmeğe ve tetkike başladık . . . Türk diline ait lûgat kitaplarını önümüze aldık. Bu kitaplardaki tam ve belli anlamlar ifade eden sözleri ve bu sözlerde ek olarak köke yapışmış konsonları birer birer gözönünde tutarak, bunların kökte yaptıkları mana nüanslarını etüt ettilk . . . Bu sırada Dr. Phil. Orient. H. F. Kvergitch'in 'Psychologie de quelques éléments des langues turques' adlı basılmamış kıymetli bir eserini okuduk. Türk dilindeki süfikslerin gösterici manalarını bulmak için Dr. Kvergitch'in bu nazariyesini Türk Dil Kurumunun ekler hakkındaki geniş ve çok misalli çalışmaları sayesinde anlıyabildik ve istifade ettik.

This discovery could do nothing to save the language from being totally lifeless. It had to be given soul and activity. It was on this point that I began to concentrate my thinking and investigation . . . I sat down with the Turkish dictionaries in front of me. Scrutinizing one by one the words in them that expressed complete and clear meanings, and the consonants suffixed to the root of each word, I studied the shades of meaning these made in the root . . . About this time I read a valuable unpublished work, Dr. Phil. Orient. H. F. Kvergić's 'Psychologie de quelques éléments des langues turques'. To find out the demonstrative senses of the Turkish suffixes, thanks to TDK's extensive labours on the suffixes, with abundant examples, I was able to understand this theory of Dr Kvergić's and I made use of it.

The first hint of what was coming was in a paper entitled 'The Sun, from the Point of View of Religion and Civilization', presented on the first day of the Congress by Yusuf Ziya Özer. The theory was mentioned only at the very end:

Beşerî kültür üzerinde bu kadar mühim rol yapan Güneşin . . . dil üzerinde de aynı tesiri ve aynı rolü yapmış olması gayet tabiî görülmek lâzım gelir. Binaenaleyh Güneş-Dil Teorisi'nin de Guneşe bu kadar ezelî surette merbut olan Türk ilmi telâkkiyatının bir eseri olarak meydana konmuş olması iftihara lâyıktır.   (Kurultay 1936: 48)

It must be seen as quite natural that the Sun, which plays so important a part in human culture, has . . . exercised the same influence on, and played the same part in, language too. We should therefore take pride in the fact that the Sun-Language Theory has been propounded as a product of the outlook of Turkish science, which has been linked to the Sun since time immemorial.

Dilmen began the next day with a lengthy outline of the theory, in which he proved, among other things, the identity of English *god*, German *Gott*, and Turkish *kut* 'luck'. The proof was simple enough: *Gott* is oğ + ot, *god* is oğ + od, *kut* is uk + ut. By spelling *Gott* with only one *t*, he spared himself the necessity of explaining its second *t*. Similar moonshine was delivered on that second day and the three following days, the sixth day being given over to the foreign scholars. Dilmen used the theory to show the identity of the Uyghur *yaltrık* 'gleam, shining', and *electric* (*Türk Dili*, 19 (1936), 47–9). An article in the *Wall Street Journal* of 16 March 1985 on the language reform states that a headline in *Cumhuriyet* of 31 January 1936 ran: 'Electric is a Turkish word!'.

Space does not permit a full examination of the material presented to the Congress, much as one would like to go into the content of papers with such intriguing titles as Tankut's 'Palaeosociological Language Studies with Panchronic Methods according to the Sun-Language Theory' and Dilâçar's 'Sun-Language Anthropology'. Emre's contribution, however, deserves a word, because Zürcher (1985: 85) describes him as 'l'un des rares linguistes un peu sérieux de la Société'. Emre, who had expressed his contempt for Kvergić's paper, which was not devoid of sense, went overboard on the Sun-Language Theory.

Here is a summary of his lengthy presentation (Kurultay 1936: 190–201) on the origin of the French borrowings *filozofi* 'philosophy', *filozof* 'philosopher', and *filozofik* 'philosophic(al)', commonly supposed to be from the Greek *phil-* 'to love' and *sophía* 'wisdom'. Having learned that the etymology of Greek *phil-* was doubtful, he decided that the word was his to do with as he would, to the following effect. As the Sun-Language Theory shows, no word originally began with a consonant, so the first syllable of *filozof* was *if* or *ef*, and in its original form *ip* or *ep*. Now *ip* or *ep* in Turkish meant 'reasoning power' (this was no better founded than his preceding assertions). Further, the Greek *phil-* is generally supposed to mean 'to love' or 'to kiss', but he rejected the first sense on the grounds that Aristotle used *sophía* alone for 'philosophy', so the *philo-* could only be an intensifying prefix, having nothing to do with love. On the other hand, he accepted the second sense, because *ip*, besides meaning 'reasoning power', was clearly the same as the Turkish *öp-* 'to kiss'. Next, the original form of *philo-* was *ipil-*, the function of the *il* being 'to broaden the basic meaning of the *ip*', and this was obviously the same word as the Turkish *bil-* 'to know'. As for *sophía*, that did indeed mean wisdom; compare *sağ* 'sound, intelligent' and *sav* 'word, saying'. In short, *filozofi*, *filozof*, and *filozofik* were Turkish, so there was no need to create replacements for them.[2] Emre concluded his contribution with a verse 'from one of our poets', the second line of which indicates that Atatürk's proprietorial interest in the theory, if not common knowledge, was at least an open secret:

---

[2] Clement of Alexandria would have put this differently. He is quoted by Peter Berresford Ellis (1994: 67) as saying, 'It was from the Greeks that philosophy took its rise: its very name refuses to be translated into foreign speech.'

Atatürk, Atatürk antlıyız sana
Güneşinden içtik hep kana kana.

Atatürk, Atatürk, we are pledged to you,
We have all drunk deep of your sun.

The impact of the theory on books and articles published during its brief reign is easily recognized. Turning the pages of Abdülkadir İnan's (1936) *Türkoloji Ders Hülasaları* for example, you see it to be a compendium of notes on the history of the language and on its dialects, particularly that of the Kirghiz (Kırgız). Then, after a discussion of various views on the etymology of the name, you come across Fig. 5.1 and know you have left the realm of scholarship for the land of the Sun-Language Theory.

	(1)	(2)	(3)	(4)
kırgıy	(*ık* +	*ır* +	*ıg* +	*ıy*)
Kırgız	(*ık* +	*ır* +	*ıg* +	*ız*)

FIG. 5.1. A typical 'etymological analysis' according to the Sun-Language Theory
Source: İnan (1936: 52).

This figure purports to show the components of the words *kırgıy* and *Kırgız*, the former being the Kazakh-Kirghiz word for falcon, a bird which may have been the Kirghiz tribal totem. Then comes the analysis. *Ik* is the first-degree principal root, representing abrupt motion, *ır* expresses the confirmation of the root meaning, *ıg* is the object or subject over which the abrupt motion recurs, while *ıy* is the expression and nominalization of this. The first three elements of *kırgıy* and *Kırgız* are identical in form and meaning, but one of the final elements ends in *y*, the other in *z*. The explanation is that the function of *ıy* was to turn the word into a noun. In the totemistic period all surrounding subjects and objects were the same, but once the concepts of distance and the individual had emerged, all such subjects and objects, starting from the centre, the ego, were expressed by the element *z*. Here İnan, to his credit, loses interest in the Sun-Language Theory and goes on to talk about his experiences among the Kirghiz.

Another sample of the application of the theory will be found in the first volume (1937) of *Belleten*, the journal of Türk Tarih Kurumu (the Turkish Historical Society). Its name looks like the present participle of *belletmek* and its apparent meaning is 'causing to learn by heart', which is perhaps just possible as the title of a learned journal.[3] The earlier and later word for 'bulletin' is *bülten*, correctly shown in *Türkçe Sözlük* (1988) and other dictionaries as from the French *bulletin*. On pages

---

[3] *Belleten* is indeed a learned journal, with a high international reputation; the accident that it was given its name during the heyday of the Sun-Language Theory must not be held against it.

311–16 of the first volume of the journal, however, will be found an analysis in French of *belleten* and *bulletin*, from which we learn that the two are phonetically identical and that, Turkish being the oldest of languages, the French word is derived from the Turkish, and not, as some may have supposed, *vice versa*.

In defence of *belleten*, Doğan Aksan (1976: 25) writes:

Bu sözcük, dilimize Fransızcadan gelen *bülten*'in (Fr. *Bulletin*) etkisiyle, daha doğrusu, onu Türkçeleştirme amacıyle türetilmiştir. Ancak türetme, Türkçenin kurallarına uygundur (*belle-*, *bellet-*, *bellet-en*). Ayrıca, dile, yeni bir kavramı karşılayan yeni bir sözcük kazandırılmış olmaktadır. *Belleten*'i, *bülten*'in bozulmuş biçimi değil, yeni bir sözcük saymak gerekir.

This word has been derived under the influence of *bülten* (French *bulletin*), which comes into our language from French; to be more precise, with the purpose of Turkicizing it. But the derivation is in accordance with the rules of Turkish . . . Moreover, a new word covering a new concept has thereby been won for the language. *Belleten* must be regarded not as a corrupted form of *bülten* but as a new word.

Atatürk's faith in his theory must have been shaken by the reactions of the foreign guests at the 1936 Congress, a group of distinguished scholars including Alessio Bombaci, Jean Deny, Friedrich Giese, Julius Németh, Sir Denison Ross, and Ananiasz Zayączkowski. One, variously referred to as Bartalini, Baltarini, and Balter, and variously described as Lector and Professor in Latin and Italian at Istanbul University, mentioned it tactfully in the course of a graceful tribute to Atatürk and the new Turkey: 'La théorie de la langue-Soleil, par son caractère universel, est une preuve nouvelle de la volonté de la Turquie de s'identifier toujours davantage avec la grande famille humaine.' Four of them did not mention it at all in their addresses to the Congress or subsequent discussion. Two thought it 'interesting'. Hilaire de Barenton agreed that all human speech had a common origin, but saw that origin in Sumerian rather than Turkish. Two wanted more time to think about it. The only foreign guest to swallow it whole was Kvergić, who volunteered the following etymology of *unutmak* 'to forget':

Its earliest form was *uğ* + *un* + *ut* + *um* + *ak*. Uğ, 'discriminating spirit, intelligence', is the mother-root. The *n* of *un* shows that the significance of the mother-root emerges into exterior space. The *t/d* of *ut* is always a dynamic factor; its role here is to shift the discriminating spirit into exterior space. The *m* of *um* is the element which manifests and embodies in itself the concept of the preceding *uğ-un-ut*, while *ak* completes the meaning of the word it follows and gives it its full formulation. After phonetic coalescence, the word takes its final morphological shape, *unutmak*, which expresses the transference of the discriminating spirit out of the head into the exterior field surrounding the head; this is indeed the meaning the word conveys.   (Kurultay 1936: 333)

Yet Atatürk did not immediately drop the theory; for this we have, *inter alia*, the testimony of Âkil Muhtar Özden, a highly respected medical man who served in 1937 on the Language Commission (Dil Komisyonu), over which Atatürk presided, and who attended sessions on the technical terms of geometry, physics, chemistry, mechanics, and geology. He kept notes, mostly on individual words and tantalizingly brief. After listing the names of those present at a session on 8 March 1937, he recorded:

Kara tahta geldi. Atatürk hemen terim meselesi ile meşgul olmaya başladı. Benden ne yaptığımızı sordu. Gösterdikleri istikamette giderek çalıştığımızı söyledim. Güneş-Dil tatbikatında abstrait (soyut) kelimeler için zahmet çektiğimizi söyledim. Bir misal istedi. Aklıma muvazi kelimesi geldi. Hemen analiz başladı. *Parallel* kelimesinin Türkçe olduğu ispat edildi. (Tevfikoğlu 1994: 99)

The blackboard arrived. Atatürk at once began to deal with the question of technical terms. He asked me what I had been doing, and I told him I was working on the lines he had indicated. I told him I was having difficulty in applying Sun-Language to abstract words. He asked for an example. The word *muvazi* ['parallel'] came to mind. The analysis started immediately. It was proved that *parallel* was Turkish.

Others of his notes read: 'atom (Türkçe)', with no explanation, and 'Geometri (Türkçe)', followed by a terse 'ge = gen = geniş'; i.e. the *ge of geometri* is not the Greek *gē* 'earth' but the Turkish *gen* 'wide'. On *polygon* be made two notes: 'Poligon Türkçe/Pol = bol/gen = en', and 'gen = geniş/poligon (genişliği çok)'. These can be expanded as follows: *Poligon* is Turkish. *Pol* is *bol* 'abundant', *gen* is *en* 'width', and *geniş* 'wide'; *poligon* means 'of much width'. Later on comes an analysis of *likid* 'liquid' according to the Sun-Language Theory: 'Likid (Türkçe) Yg-il-ik-id-ēy Yg = Katı İl = Bunu namütenahiye kadar uzaklaştıran, yani yok eden ek. (İlik Türkçe katı olmayan bir şey demektir.)' In other words, *liquid* is Turkish, its original form being *ygilikidēy. Yg* means 'hard'. *İl* is the suffix removing it to infinity, i.e. annihilating it. (*İlik* ('marrow') is Turkish, meaning a thing which is not hard.)

These instances of the application of the theory are not cited just for their inherent fun. They also demonstrate the unscholarliness of the officers of the Language Society (as well as of Dr Kvergić), who unblushingly delivered themselves of such drivel in public. And these people and others like them were largely responsible for the creation of *Öztürkçe*, a fact which helps to explain why so much of it violates the rules of the language.

About Atatürk's motive in launching the theory, opinions differ. Did he deliberately take up Kvergić's idea of the antiquity of Turkish and enlarge on it in order to justify ending the purge of words of Arabic and Persian origin? A footnote to the article on *Cep Kılavuzları* (1935) cited in Chapter 4, while not suggesting that this was Atatürk's purpose, indicates that it was the result of the theory:

Kılavuzun neşrinden sonra Türk dehasından fışkıran 'Güneş-Dil Teorisi' yalnız bu Kılavuza alınan sözlerin değil, daha pek çoklarının Türkçeden üremiş sözler olduğunu ortaya çıkarmıştır. Kılavuz araştırmaları arasında yalnız benzerliklere ve klâsik etimoloji bilgilerine göre elde edilebilen neticeler, 'Güneş-Dil Teorisi' nin yüksek ışığı altında çok daha esaslı ve muayyen bir şekilde genişlemiştir. Bu genişleme bir derecededir ki dilimizin ihtiyacı olan ve halk arasında manası bilinen kelimelerden hiç birini atmağa ve yerini yeniden bilinmeyen bir kelime koymağa ihtiyaç kalmamıştır.   (*Türk Dili*, 16 (1936), 22–3)

The Sun-Language Theory, which welled up from the Turkish genius after the publication of *Cep Kılavuzu*, has revealed that not only the words included in *Cep Kılavuzu* but a great many more are of Turkish derivation. The results that could be obtained in the course of the research for *Cep Kılavuzu*, going by resemblances and the findings of classical etymology alone, have broadened far more fundamentally and definitely under the sublime light of the Sun-Language Theory. Such is the extent of this broadening that there is no longer any necessity to discard a single one of the words that our language needs and whose meanings are known among the people, and to start from scratch to replace them with words that are not known.

Karaosmanoğlu (1963: 110) saw in the theory 'dil konusundaki tutumuna yeni bir biçim, bir orta yol arama endişesi' (a concern with seeking a new shape, a middle way, for his attitude to language). Hatiboğlu (1963: 20) is more explicit: Atatürk put the theory forward to end the impossible situation in which satisfactory replacements could not be found for words that were being expelled from the language. Nihad Sâmi Banarlı (1972: 317), an inveterate opponent of the reform, is of the same opinion:

öztürkçeyi denemiş ve bu yoldaki çalışmalara bizzat iştirâk etmiştir. Fakat, aynı Atatürk, tecrübeler ilerledikçe, işi yar şa döküp soysuzlaştıranların elinde Türk dilinin ve Türk kültürünün nasıl bir çıkmaza sürüklendiğini de derhal ve çok iyi görmüştür. Neticede, Atatürk, bu durumu düzeltme vazifesini de üzerine almış ve yine dâhiyâne bir taktikle Güneş-Dil teorisinden faydalanarak öztürkçe tecrübesinden vazgeçmiştir.

[Atatürk] tried *Öztürkçe* and took a personal part in the efforts in this direction. As the experiment advanced, however, this same Atatürk saw instantly and clearly what sort of impasse the Turkish language and Turkish culture had been dragged into by people vying with each other to bastardize the whole thing. Eventually he took upon himself the duty of rectifying this situation too and, again by a stroke of tactical genius, availed himself of the Sun-Language Theory to drop the *Öztürkçe* experiment.

So is Ercilasun (1994: 89):

Atatürk'ün kaleme aldığı bütün bu broşür ve dil yazılarından çıkan sonuç şudur: Güneş-Dil Teorisini ortaya atarken Atatürk'ün amaçlarından biri de aşırı özleştirmecilikten vazgeçmek, 'millet, devir, hâdise, mühim, hâtıra, ümit, kuvvet' vb. [ve başkaları 'and others'] kelimelerin dilde kalmasını sağlamaktı.

The conclusion emerging from all these brochures and articles on language penned by Atatürk is this: one of his aims when launching the Sun-Language Theory was to give up excessive purification and to ensure the survival in the language of the words *millet* ['nation'], *devir* ['period'], *hâdise* ['event'], *mühim* ['important'], *hâtıra* ['memory'], *ümit* ['hope'], *kuvvet* ['strength'], and others.

Ertop's (1963: 89) view is quite different:

Atatürk tarafından dildeki özleştirmeciliği sınırlamak amacıyle kullanıldığını ileri sürenler, Atatürk'ün kişiliğini de gözden uzak tutmaktadırlar. Atatürk ulusun iyiliğine dokunacağına inandığı hiçbir konuda kesin, köklü davranıştan kaçınmamıştır . . . Atatürk Güneş-Dil Kuramını bir geriye dönüş aracı olarak kullanmamıştır. Böyle bir davranışın gerektiğine inansaydı düşüncesini açık, kesin yoldan doğrudan doğruya belli ederdi.

Those who assert that the Sun-Language Theory was used by Atatürk in order to limit the purification are overlooking Atatürk's personality. He never refrained from acting decisively and radically in any matter which he believed would affect the good of the nation . . . He did not use the theory as a means of turning the clock back; had he believed in the necessity for such a move, he would have made his thinking plain, candidly, positively, and directly.

The argument has some force, but it is harder to accept Ertop's subsequent remarks, which reflect the views of the many adherents of the pre-1983 Language Society who refuse to believe that Atatürk abandoned the campaign to 'purify' everyday speech. He goes on to offer what he calls clear proof that the theory was not advanced with the aim of slowing the pace of language reform: work on the reform went on after the theory was propounded, technical terminology continued to be put into pure Turkish, and Atatürk busied himself with linguistic concerns almost until his death. While all three statements are accurate, they are irrelevant to the question of whether or not Atatürk, having tired of the campaign to purge the general vocabulary, concocted the Sun-Language Theory to justify abandoning it. The basis of all three items of 'proof' is the fact that, while at one time he had tried his hand at finding *Öztürkçe* equivalents for items of general vocabulary, his enduring concern was with technical terms.

However much lovers of the old language may regret some of the consequences of the language reform, they cannot deny that something had to be done about scientific terminology. This was almost entirely Arabic; what was not Arabic was Persian. English technical terms, though mostly of Greek or Latin origin, have long been Anglicized; we say ecology not oikología, hygiene not hygieiné. In Turkish, however, there had been no naturalization of Arabic and Persian terms; they remained in their original forms. Atatürk decided to tackle the problem in person.

In the winter of 1936–7 he wrote *Geometri*, a little book on the elements of geometry, which was published anonymously. The title-page bears the legend 'Geometri öğretenlerle, bu konuda kitap yazacaklara kılavuz olarak Kültür Bakanlığınca neşredilmiştir' (Published by the Ministry of Education as a guide to those teaching geometry and those who will write books on this subject).

In it he employed many words now in regular use, though not all were of his own invention; some are discussed in later chapters. They included *açı* 'angle', *alan* 'area', *boyut* 'dimension', *dikey* 'perpendicular', *düşey* 'vertical', *düzey* 'level', *gerekçe* 'corollary', *kesit* 'section', *köşegen* 'diagonal', *orantı* 'proportion', *teğet* 'tangent', *türev* 'derivative', *uzay* 'space', *yanal* 'lateral', *yatay* 'horizontal', *yöndeş* 'corresponding', *yüzey* 'surface'. He created the terms *artı*, *eksi*, *çarpı*, *bölü*, for 'plus', 'minus', 'multiplied by', and 'divided by', and *izdüşümü* ('trace-fall') 'projection'.

Of these, *eksi* is an example of *uydurma*; the others are made from the appropriate verb-stems, whereas *eksi* is formed analogously with them but solecistically, from the adjective *eksik* 'deficient'. He also devised new names for the plane figures, which until then had been called by their Arabic names, his method being to add an invariable *-gen* to the appropriate numeral. *Müselles* 'triangle' became *üçgen*, while *müseddes* 'hexagon' became *altıgen*, and *kesirüladlâ* 'polygon' became *çokgen*.[4]

In *Sinekli Bakkal* (1936), Halide Edib describes Sabit Beyağabey, the local bully, as standing with his arms at his sides like jug-handles, each making a right angle. And for 'right angle' she says 'zaviye-i kaime', two Arabic words joined by the Persian izafet. That is because until 1937 Turkish children were still being taught geometry with the Ottoman technical terms. When Halide Edib learned geometry, this is how she was taught that the area of a triangle is equal to the base times half the height: 'Bir müsellesin mesaha-i sathiyesi, kaidesinin irtifaına hasıl-ı zarbinin nısfına müsavidir.' Largely through the personal effort of Atatürk, this has now become: 'Bir üçgenin yüzölçümü, tabanının yüksekliğine çarpımının yarısına eşittir', which contains no Arabic or Persian. This achievement may be said to justify much of what has been done in the name of language reform. It is true that the pedigree of *-gen* is attained, owing more to the *-gon* [G] of *pentagon* than to the ancient and provincial Turkish *gen* 'wide'. But the new terms of geometry must be numbered among Atatürk's greatest gifts to his people. A Turk would have to be a pretty rabid enemy of change to persist in calling interior opposite angles 'zāviyetān-ı mütekābiletān-ı dāhiletān' rather than 'içters açılar'.

A related topic that may conveniently be discussed here is the much debated question of whether Atatürk, while adhering to the new technical terms, many of which he himself devised, gave up the use of neologisms for everyday concepts.

There is no shortage of misrepresentations of his attitude; here is one specimen, by Gültekin (1983: 72):

1936'dan sonra, özleşme çalışmalarındaki aşırı yönleri görmüş ve bunları düzeltmiştir. Ama bundan, Atatürk'ün 1932'de başlattığı dil hareketinden döndüğü çıkarılabilir mi? Böyle bir iddia, gerçekleri tersyüz edip, olmsını istediğimizi gerçekmiş gibi göstermektir. Atatürk, 1932 yılı öncesi dile dönmemiştir. Bilindiği üzere, 1937 yılında özellikle bilim dilinin özleşmesi doğrultusunda kendi çalışmaları vardır. Gene mirasından Türk Dil Kurumu'na pay bırakması, 1932'de başlattığı dil çalışmalarının devam etmesini istediğini gösterir.

After 1936, [Atatürk] saw the extremist aspects of the purification campaign and he corrected them. But can one deduce from this that he turned away from the language movement which he initiated in 1932? To make such a claim is to stand the facts on their head, to show as fact that which we want to be fact. Atatürk did not return to pre-1932 Turkish.

---

[4] Not to be confused with the variable *-gen* seen in *unutkan* 'forgetful' and *döğüşken* 'quarrelsome' (see Lewis 1988: 223). *-gen/gan* was once the suffix of the present participle, as it still is in many Central Asian dialects: Kazakh *kelgen* = *gelen* 'coming', Tatar *bilmägän* = *bilmeyen* 'not knowing', Uyghur *alğan* = *alan* 'taking'.

It is well known that in 1937 he himself worked especially on the purification of scientific language. Again, his bequest of a share in his estate to TDK shows that he wanted the work on language, which he initiated in 1932, to continue.

And another, by Yücel (1982: 36):

Burada raslantıdan söz edilebilirse, ilginç bir raslantıyla, 'Türk Dili Tetkik Cemiyeti' adının 'Türk Dil Kurumu'na dönüştürüldüğü yıl, kimilerinin sık sık sürdükleri bir görüşe göre, Atatürk'ün böyle bir girişimin çıkar yol olmadığını, yani *yanıldığını* anlayarak özleştirme etkinliklerini durdurttuğu yıldır. Atatürk'ün Türk Dil Kurumu çalışmalarıyla yaşamının sonuna değin çok yakından ilgilendiği, daha da önemlisi, bu çalışmaları kendi görüşleri doğrultusunda yönlendirdiği göz önüne alınacak olursa, kesinlikle özleştirme doğrultusunda olan bu ad değiştirmenin onun bilgisi dışında yapılmış olmasına olanak bulunmadığını, onun bilgisi dışında yapılmış olmasına olanak bulunmadığı için de, böyle bir değişikliğe izin vermekle Atatürk'ün çelişkiye düştüğünü kesinlemek gerekir.

If one may speak here of coincidence, it is by an interesting coincidence that the year [1936] in which the name Türk Dili Tetkik Cemiyeti was changed to Türk Dil Kurumu was, according to a view frequently advanced by some, the year in which Atatürk realized that this kind of undertaking was a dead end, i.e. *that he had made a mistake*, and put a stop to the purification exercise. If one keeps before one's eyes that until the end of his life Atatürk was very closely involved in TDK's endeavours and, more important, that he directed these endeavours along the lines of his own views, one is bound to state categorically that this change of name, which was definitely on the lines of purification, could not possibly have been made without his knowledge and that, because this change of name could not possibly have been made without his knowledge, in allowing such a change Atatürk fell into an inconsistency.

The italics, which are Yücel's, must be intended to point to the enormity of the implication. Atatürk was in fact never afraid to admit that he was fallible, but idolatry, by definition, denies the humanity of its object. In italicizing these words, Yücel seems to be rejecting the possibility not only of Atatürk's making a mistake but of his realizing that he had done so.

A dispassionate examination of the evidence leads to the following conclusion. When Atatürk launched the theory, it was not with the express intention of justifying a change of course. He had decided that a change of course was due, because he had appreciated the futility of trying to make the mass of the people give up their ancestral vocabulary. On the other hand, he could not abandon his declared purpose of freeing Turkish from the yoke of foreign languages. He loved playing at etymology and had persuaded himself that Turkish origins could be found for the ostensibly non-Turkish elements in the language. He had already been toying with the notion that what made man aware of his identity was the sun before he read Kvergić's paper, which asserted the antiquity of Turkish (but did not mention the sun). The elements of the Sun-Language Theory all came together in his mind and he published it. It was not an excuse to justify a change of policy but a systematization of his ideas. He launched the theory because he genuinely believed in it; he started to abandon it when he saw that foreign scholars thought it nonsensical. Intelligent as he was, he must have sensed that the best native opinion too, though scarcely outspoken, was on their side.

To disprove the common assertion that he never returned to pre-1932 Turkish, we need do no more than examine the proof-texts, his own speeches and writings. While in general exhibiting a desire to avoid using words of Arabic origin if Turkish synonyms—or synonyms he believed to be Turkish—existed, they show that he was no longer going out of his way to give up the words he had used all his life in favour of unnecessary neologisms. From 1933 on, 26 September had been celebrated as *Dil Bayramı* (the Language Festival). The vocabulary of his telegrams to the Language Society on this occasion is worthy of study. Those he had sent in 1934 and 1935 were couched in *Öztürkçe* throughout,[5] including the words *kutunbitikler* 'messages of congratulation', *orunlar* 'official bodies', and *genelözek* 'general headquarters', none of which proved viable. The 1936 telegram contained four words of Arabic origin: *mesai* 'endeavours', *teşekkür* 'thanks', *tebrik* 'congratulations', and *muvaffakıyet* 'success': 'Dil Bayramını mesai arkadaşlarınızla birlikte kutluladığınızı bildiren telgrafı teşekkürle aldım. Ben de size tebrik eder ve Türk Dil Kurumuna bundan sonraki çalışmalarına da muvaffakıyetler dilerim' (I have received with thanks the telegram telling me that you and your colleagues who share in your endeavours offer congratulations on the occasion of the Language Festival. For my part I congratulate you and wish the TDK success in its subsequent endeavours too).

The 1937 telegram contained six: *münasebet* 'occasion', the *hakk* of *hakkımdaki* 'about me', *mütehassis* 'moved', *teşekkür* and *muvaffakıyet* again, and *temâdi* 'continuation': 'Dil bayramı münasebetiyle, Türk Dil Kurumu'nun hakkımdaki duygularını bildiren telgraflarınızdan çok mütehassis oldum. Teşekkür eder, değerli çalışmanızda muvaffakıyetinizin temâdisini dilerim' (I have been greatly moved by your telegrams conveying your feelings about me on the occasion of the Language Festival. I thank you and wish that your success in your valuable labours may continue).

But of no less significance than the old words he used are the new words that he also used; the inference is not that he had abandoned the language reform— *birlikte* 'together', *duygu* 'sentiment', *bildiren* 'conveying', *değerli* 'valuable'; had he been simply rejecting the reform he would have said *beraber, his, tebliğ eden,* and *kıymetli* or even *zikıymet*. What he was doing was adhering to the wholly praiseworthy aspect of the reform: making full use of the existing resources of the language. His use of *kutlulamak* 'to congratulate' as well as *tebrik etmek* 'to felicitate' in the 1936 telegram is a perfect example, reflecting the stylist's desire to avoid repeating a word if a synonym could be found.

On 1 November 1936 he delivered his annual speech opening the new session of the Grand National Assembly. It too was peppered with words of Arabic origin, including *sene* not *yıl* for 'year', *maarif* not *eğitim* for 'education', *tetkik*

---

[5] The text of the 1933 telegram does not seem to be available. The texts of the later telegrams were published in the September issues of *Türk Dili* (1934–7).

not *araştırma* for 'research', and *millet* and *memleket* rather than *ulus* and *yurt* for 'nation' and 'country'. He did use *Kamutay* for 'Assembly', however, and not *Meclis*.

The language and content of his last message to the Language Society is highly significant. It consists of two sentences of the speech read for him by the Prime Minister, Celâl Bayar, at the opening of the new session of the Assembly on 1 November 1938, nine days before he died. It is worth quoting, because it has often been used as evidence that the Society never ceased to enjoy Atatürk's total support for its campaign to eliminate everyday pre-reform words from the language. The contents of the message (Özgü 1963: 37), however, no less than its language, give the lie to that claim (words of Arabic origin are italicized):

Dil Kurumu en güzel *ve feyiz*li bir iş olarak türlü *ilim*lere *ait* Türkçe terimleri *tespit* etmiş ve bu *suret*le dilimiz yabancı dillerin *tesir*inden kurtulma yolunda *esas*lı adımını atmıştır. Bu yıl okullarımızda *tedrisat*ın Türkçe terimlerle yazılmış *kitap*larla başlamış olmasını kültür *hayat*ımız için *mühim* bir *hâdise* olarak *kayd*etmek isterim.

The Language Society, in a most excellent *and fruit*ful endeavour, has *establish*ed Turkish technical terms *pertaining* to the various *science*s, and our language has *thus* taken its *essential* step on the road to liberation from the *influence* of foreign languages. I should like to place it *on record*, as an *important event* for our cultural *life*, that *teaching* has begun this year in our schools from *books* written with Turkish technical terms.

The partisans of 'purification' will not give Atatürk credit for saying what he meant. Those words are regularly cited as praise for the Society's 'sürdürülen özleştirme çabaları' (continued exertions towards purification) (e.g. Yücel 1982: 38). Aksoy, too honest a man not to concede that there was precious little *Öztürkçe* in that speech, could still write (1982: 146–7): 'Büyük Millet Meclisi açılırken okunan söylevinde öz Türkçe sözcükler kullanmamış olmakla birlikte, özleştirmeden duyduğu mutluluğu belirtmiyor mu?' (Although he did not use pure Turkish words in his speech at the opening of the Grand National Assembly, does he not make clear the happiness he felt in the purification?). No, he does not. All he does is to praise the Society for its work on technical terms, and for nothing else. In fact those words reflect his disillusionment with the people who sat round his table night after night, drinking his *rakı* and enthusiastically applauding his views without ever having the honesty—even if they had the knowledge—to tell him that some of the ideas he came out with could not be taken seriously.

Anyone who pictures him as a typical 1930s dictator may suppose that nobody could be blamed for pretending to agree with him. In fact one of the things he liked best in the world was a good argument. An observation by Falih Rıfkı Atay (1969: 474), who knew him better than most, is worth quoting in this context. Having described a heated discussion at Atatürk's table, he says, 'Sakın bu tartışmalarda bulunmağı cesarete vermeyiniz . . . Atatürk'ün sofrasında fikirlerini söylemek bir cesaret değildi. Söylememek, aksini söylemek lüzumsuz bir "müdahane", yahut çıkar bekleyen bir dalkavukluktu' (You must not think that it called for courage to take part in this kind of argument . . . To speak one's mind at Atatürk's table was not an act of courage. Not to say what one thought, or to say the opposite of what one thought, was an act of unnecessary sycophancy, or toadying in the expectation of personal gain).

Melâhat Özgü (1963: 37) notes, 'Atatürk bu söylevinde henüz pek aykırı gelmiyen: *feyizli, tesir, tedrisat, mühim*, ve *hâdise* gibi yabancı sözleri kullanmıştır' (In this speech [his last message to TDK], Atatürk used such foreign words as *feyizli, tesir, tedrisat, mühim*, and *hâdise*, which did not yet sound incongruous). She sanctimoniously continues: 'Yeni kuşak, bugün, Atatürk'ten aldığı esin ve buyrukla daha ileridedir' (The new generation today is further advanced, thanks to the inspiration and the command it has received from Atatürk). Instead of singling out five of the fourteen 'foreign words' he used in those two sentences, she could have been better employed in noticing that he used only two of the new words, *terim* rather than *ıstılah* for 'technical term' and *okul* rather than *mektep* for 'school'. His use of them is understandable: *terim* was the new technical term *par excellence*, which he himself had originated, while *okul* did not have the pre-Republican connotations of *mektep* and was partly his work.

In the face of Atatürk's clear indication of his opinion, why did the Language Society continue to introduce not just technical terms, as he wanted it to do, but also replacements for normal items of standard Turkish? Many otherwise reasonable Turks will tell you it was all a communist plot to destabilize the country by impoverishing the language, widening the generation gap, and demoralizing the people by cutting them off from the records of their great past. Comparisons were drawn between the Society's ceaseless undermining of the language and the Trotskyite doctrine of permanent revolution. Tekin Erer (1973: 61) said: 'Türkiyemizde solcuları tefrik etmek için basit bir usûl vardır: Bir insanın ne derece solcu olduğunu anlamak için yazdığı ve konuştuğu kelimelere dikkat edeceksiniz. Eğer hiç anlıyamıyacağınız kadar uydurma kelimelerle konuşuyorsa, ona tereddütsüz Komünist diyebilirsiniz' (There is a simple method of distinguishing the leftists in our country. To ascertain how far to the left a person is, look at the words he uses in writing and speech. If the fake words he employs when speaking are too numerous for you to be able to understand, you may unhesitatingly call him a communist).

Turkish communists, on the other hand, saw the language reform as a bourgeois movement aimed at widening the gulf between the official and literary language and the language of the people. It is worth remembering that the poet and playwright Nazım Hikmet (1902–63), the most distinguished of all Turkish communists, did not use *Öztürkçe* but followed Atay in making full use of the language as it stood.

The extremists of the right regarded the Language Society as a subversive organization whose mission was to decrease mutual understanding between the Turks of Turkey and the Turks of the then Soviet Union, whom they hoped some day to liberate. In this they were overlooking the high degree of mutual unintelligibility that existed even before the reform began, due only in part to the influx of Russian words into the Central Asian dialects, most of which use, for example, the Russian names of the months.[6]

This point is worth a digression. A vivid illustration of how the meanings of words may vary from one dialect to another was given by Nermin Neftçi, a former Minister of Culture, at the 1992 meeting of the Standing Congress on the Turkish Language:

Af buyurun, 'kıç' bizde başka manaya gelir, ama Kerkük Türkçesinde 'kıç' bacaktır. Ben Kerkük'e gittiğim zaman eşimin süt ninesi 'ay ay' diye ağlıyordu 'kıçım kırıldı, sümüğüm yazıya çıktı' diyordu. Allah aşkınıza bu ne diyor diye sordum. Meğer 'bacağım kırıldı, kemiğim dışarı çıktı' demek istiyormuş.   (*Sürekli Türk Dili Kurultayı* 1992: 169)

The word *kıç*, if you will pardon the expression, means something else to us [backside'], but in the Turkish of Kerkuk it's 'leg'. When I visited Kerkuk, my husband's foster-mother was sobbing bitterly and saying, 'My backside is broken and my mucus has gone up to the writing.' 'For goodness' sake, what is she talking about?' I asked. It emerged that she meant, 'My leg is broken and my bone is sticking out.'

The national motto of Uzbekistan is 'Müstäkıllık, Tinçlik, Hämkàrlik' (Independence, Peace, Cooperation). The first and third words would be intelligible to anyone old enough to remember when *müstakil* was the Turkish for 'independent' (now *bağımsız*), and *kâr* was 'work'. The second would convey only 'vigour'.

To resume: it was neither left-wing nor right-wing ideology that motivated those who were not content to follow Atatürk's lead and confine their creative urge to technical terms. They began with a genuine desire to close the gap between the official and the popular language, or at least to comply with his desire to do so. When he decided that things had gone too far, and reverted to his natural mode of expression, they allowed a decent interval for him to depart from the scene and then resumed their work, having developed a taste for inventing words, which for many of them had become a profession. So they continued to invent, for which one should not blame them too harshly; after all, Atatürk's withdrawal from the wilder shores of *Öztürkçe* was based on a personal decision which he did not seek to impose on anyone else. But while continuing to invent, they persisted—and this was their unpardonable offence—in claiming to be following in the footsteps of Atatürk.

Their frequent line of argument is to adduce the fact that Atatürk wrote his little book on geometry with his own hand in the winter of 1936–7; would he

---

[6] Kirghiz and Uyghur are partial exceptions. In Kirghiz both the Russian and the following names are used: *Üçtün ayı, Birdin ayı, Calğan Kuran, Çın Kuran, Bugu, Kulca, Teke, Baş öna, Ayak öna, Toguzdun ayı, Cetinin ayı, Beştin ayı*. In Uyghur, as well as the Russian names, the months are called 'First Month' etc., from *Birinçi Ay* to *Onikkinçi Ay*. The Kazakh months are: *Kañtar, Akpan, Navrız, Kökek, Mamır, Mavsım, Şilde, Tamız, Kırküyek, Kazan, Karaşa, Celtoksan*. None of the Kirghiz or Kazakh names would be understood in Turkey, where indeed *Tamız* 'August' would be mistaken for *Temmuz* 'July'.

have done so if he had turned against the language reform? The answer, as we have seen, is that it was only the creation of technical terms that continued to interest him.

For a defence of their position, Ömer Asım Aksoy's (1982: 144–5) would be hard to beat, depending as it does on his coolly equating the Language Society with the nation:

Tutalım ki, Güneş-Dil Teorisini biz yanlış yorumluyoruz ve Atatürk iki üç yıl özleştiricilik yaptıktan sonra Güneş-Dil Teorisi ile eski dile dönmüştü. Bunu kabul etmek neyi değiştirir? 1932'de başlayan özleşme akımı durmuş mudur, gittikçe genişleyip güçlenmemiş midir? Denilmek isteniyor mu ki 'Atatürk özleştiricilikten vazgeçtiğine göre bizim de vazgeçmemiz gerekir'? Gerekseydi, buna 'vazgeçme' (!) tarihinde uyulamaz mıydı? Böyle bir dönüşün olmaması, özleşmenin sürüp gelmesi neyi kanıtlar? Atatürk'e karşın ulusun özleştirme eyleminde direndiğini mi, yoksa Atatürk'ün özleştirmeden vazgeçtiği savının yanlışlığını mı? Elbette ikincisini. Çünkü ulus, hiç bir zaman Atatürk'e ters düşmediği gibi Atatürk de hiç bir zaman ulusçuluk, halkçılık ve bağımsızlık ilkelerine ters düşen bir yol tutmamıştır.

Let us suppose that we have been misinterpreting the Sun-Language Theory and that Atatürk, after practising purism for two or three years, used the theory as a way of reverting to the old language. If we accept this, what does it change? Has the current of purification which began in 1932 stopped? Has it not gradually broadened and gained strength? Is what is meant that since Atatürk abandoned purism, we must do so too? If that were the case, would people not have complied at the time of the 'abandonment'? The fact that there was no such reversion and that the purification kept on going; what does that prove? Is it that the nation persisted in the purification activity in spite of Atatürk, or that the allegation that he abandoned purification is wrong? Certainly the latter, for never has the nation been at variance with Atatürk, nor did Atatürk ever take a course at variance with the principles of nationalism, populism, and independence.

All that is proved by the fact that the purification went on is that the Language Society—not the nation, which was not consulted—persisted in the purification although Atatürk had abandoned it.

Whether that persistence was justified is another matter. Had the Society not persisted, Atatürk's goal of liberating the language from the Arabic and Persian yoke would not have been achieved. But one may recognize this without insisting that he himself never gave up purification, because he indubitably did, and to deny it is to falsify history.

Heyd's (1954: 36) statement that the Sun-Language Theory gradually faded out after Atatürk's death needs to be modified; the theory had already begun to fade out during his lifetime, and interest in it evaporated the moment he died. Tankut (1963: 125) says the theory was carried to excess by people out to make a name for themselves, 'and Atatürk eventually abandoned it'. There are several pieces of evidence that he was still interested in it in 1937 and perhaps even in the following year. One is Âkil Muhtar's testimony that the topic was still alive in March 1937, another is that Atatürk was still corresponding with Kvergić in September of that year. A third is that in the first week of that month the seventeenth session of the

Congrès International d'Anthropologie was to be held in Bucharest, and Atatürk decided that a Turkish delegation should be there to present the theory to the participants. A few days before the congress opened, he gave Tankut a pile of his own handwritten notes on the theory and said, 'Produce a thesis out of these and go to Bucharest.' Tankut produced his paper in two days and in another two days it was translated into French 'again at Atatürk's table and in his presence'. On their arrival in Bucharest they found that no one had been aware that they were coming, but an opening was made for Tankut on the last morning of the congress. According to the report subsequently presented to Atatürk by Dilmen, his paper was well received, but as the proceedings of the congress were never published this cannot be confirmed.

There is one scrap of evidence that Atatürk may have maintained his interest in the theory into 1938. On 1 June of that year, when he was very ill indeed, he was moved from the heat of Istanbul to his yacht, the *Savarona*, in the port of Istanbul. 'Bununla ilgili haberi verirken, *Cumhuriyet* gazetesi, yata Güneş-dil adı verilmesi olasılığı bulunduğunu ekliyordu' (In presenting the news of this, the newspaper *Cumhuriyet* added that there was a possibility that the yacht might be given the name *Güneş-Dil*) (Derin 1995: 130). Although the possibility never materialized, this at least suggests that somebody thought it would please him.

Dilmen, who had been giving a series of lectures on the Sun-Language Theory at Ankara University, cancelled the course when Atatürk died. When his students asked him why, he replied, 'Güneş öldükten sonra, onun teorisi mi kalır?' (After the sun has died, does its/his theory survive?) (Banarlı 1972: 317). It was not mentioned, for good or ill, at the 1942 Kurultay. Atatürk never publicly repudiated it; why did he not 'make his ideas plain, openly and directly', on this matter? A sophistic answer could be that as he had never put his name to it he could fairly have claimed that it was not his business to disown it. But the simple truth is that, although his belief in it had been shaken by the reception given to it by the foreign guests at the 1936 Kurultay, he still clung to it because he saw it as his contribution to scholarship.

One can well understand his reluctance to engage in a public debate that might have entailed a public retreat, and not just because it would have hurt his pride to do so. In those years there were more pressing calls than the Sun-Language Theory on the time and energy of a Head of State, particularly one in poor health. Five months before the theory was first aired, Hitler occupied the Rhineland. Three months before, Mussolini annexed Ethiopia. Two months before, the Spanish Civil War began. Three days before, Germany introduced compulsory military service. In addition, during 1937 and until a matter of months before his death on 10 November 1938, Atatürk was spending much of his waning strength—successfully—on coercing France into ceding Hatay, the former Sanjak of Alexandretta, to Turkey. The Sun-Language Theory must have recurred to haunt him while he was trying to concentrate on matters of high policy. What began as a harmless after-dinner game had ended up as an incubus.

On 27 September 1941, İsmet İnönü, who had succeeded Atatürk as President of the Republic, gave an address to mark the ninth Language Festival. It included these words: 'Büyük Atatürk'ün, Türk dili uğrunda harcadığı emekler boşa git-memiştir ve aslâ boşa gitmiyecektir' (The efforts which the great Atatürk expended for the sake of the Turkish language have not gone to waste and never shall). (*Türk Dili*, 2nd ser., 11–12 (1941), 2). But who suggested that they had? Could there have been any reason for İnönü to say this other than his awareness of a general feeling that the Sun-Language Theory had been a fiasco?

It is recorded (Şehsuvaroğlu 1981: 260, cited in Tevfikoğlu 1994) that during the evening of 16 October 1938, when Atatürk lay on his deathbed, he said again and again in delirium 'Aman dil . . . Aman dil . . . Dil efendim.' Some interpret this as 'For pity's sake, the language', and explain it, according to their point of view, either as 'Don't let them stop the language reform' or as 'Don't let them go on ruining the language'. Others cite the well-known fact that he habitually pro-nounced *değil* in the Rumelian fashion, as /dīl/, and prefer 'For pity's sake . . . It isn't . . .' What he really meant is unknown, save only to God.

6

Atay, Ataç, Sayılı

Two people besides Atatürk made significant contributions to the vocabulary of modern Turkish: Falih Rıfkı Atay and Nurullah Ataç. The third subject of this chapter, Aydın Sayılı, did not, but his efforts to do so deserve to be commemorated.

Atay and Ataç both believed that the language had to be modernized and both saw the futility of merely producing lists of neologisms; the new words had to be used in the sort of newspaper and magazine that ordinary people read. As Atay was fond of saying, the neologisms were dead butterflies pinned into collections; what they needed was the life and colour they could be given by stylists. On how the new words were to be arrived at, however, the two men's views could not have been more different.

Atay (1894–1971), having graduated from Istanbul University, spent most of his working life before and after the First World War as journalist, editor, and newspaper proprietor. From 1922 he was the friend and confidant of Atatürk, until the latter's death in 1938. He had a fine feeling for language and shared Atatürk's conviction that the intelligent use of the native resources of Turkish, with its enormous capacity for word building, could reduce dependence on foreign borrowings. The underground railway in Istanbul, on which work began in the 1980s, is called the Metro, as it was when planned at the beginning of the century. Atay would never have used this name for it; in 1946, when speaking of an underground train he had taken in the course of his travels abroad, he called it just that: 'yeraltı treni' (Atay 1946, cited in Özön 1961b: 42).

Here, in his own words (Atay 1969: 477) is how he set about 'purifying' the Turkish vocabulary:

Anadolu kulübünde 'Cep kılavuzu' denen Osmanlıcadan–Türkçeye lûgatı hazırlamağa başladık. Usulümüz pek sade idi: Bir Türkçesi olan yabancı kelimeleri tasfiye ediyorduk. Kullanılır Türkçesi olmayanları Türkçe olarak alıkoyuyorduk. Artık Türkçe kelimeler yapılma devrine girmiş olduğumuzdan, şivemizdeki ek ve köklerden yeni kelimeler üretiyorduk.

At the Anatolia Club we began preparing *Cep Kılavuzu*, the dictionary from Ottoman into Turkish. Our method was very simple: we were purging the language of foreign words which had a Turkish equivalent. Words with no current Turkish equivalent we retained as being Turkish. Because by now we had entered the era of making Turkish words, we were producing new words from the suffixes and roots existing in our dialect.

His contribution is the subject of a lengthy article by M. Nihat Özön (1961b). On running an eye over the six hundred or so items in it and noticing, say, *cinsdaş* (1956)[1] 'member of the same race' (the Ottoman *hemcins*), one wonders why credit should be given to Atay for this regularly constructed word. Surely somebody before Atay must have added that suffix to that noun? The answer is that somebody may well have done so in conversation; somebody indeed may have used it in writing and not been lucky enough for it to be noted by an Özön.

Özön includes among Atay's words *vurgunculuk* 'profiteering' (1945), derived from the expression *vurgun vurmak* 'to pull off a shrewd stroke of business'. It does not occur in the *Kamus* or Redhouse (1890). Redhouse (1968), on the other hand, by showing it in the old letters as well as the new, indicates that it was used in Ottoman, so what we have here may be that rarity, an error in a work bearing the name of Redhouse, in which case the word is post-Ottoman and may well be due to Atay.

One of his successes was to popularize *içtenlik*, literally 'from-within-ness', for 'sincerity', now well on the way to supplanting *samimiyet*.[2] From the expression *mırın kırın etmek* 'to shilly-shally, to find excuses not to do something', he made *mırın kırıncı* to describe the sort of person who does that sort of thing (1950). He refers to the chart at the bed-end of a patient suffering from fever as 'indili çıktılı grafik' (1951), using *-li* to make adjectives from *indi* 'it went down' and *çıktı* 'it went up': 'the graph with its ups and downs'. He contrasts *yapılamazcılık* with *olurculuk* (1956), the first being the quality (*-lık*) of the defeatist who says *yapılamaz* 'it can't be done', the second that of the sanguine person who says *olur* 'it will happen'.

In 1946 he suggested a new use for an old word, *ufantı* 'fragment', as a replacement for *teferruat* [A] 'details': 'Ufantı kelimesi dilimizde vardır ve pek güzel "teferruat" yerine kullanılabilir' (We have the word *ufantı* in our language and it may very well be used in place of *teferruat*). But *ayrıntı*, from *Cep Kılavuzu* (1935), has carried the day, except with those who prefer the French *detay*.

In 1951 he wrote, 'Bursa benim için bile bir dinlenti yeri' (Bursa, even for me, is a place of repose). This *dinlenti* 'rest, repose' has an *Öztürkçe* look about it, but is a respectable formation, from *dinlenmek* 'to rest' with the same deverbal noun-suffix *-ti* as in *ufantı*, only no one seems to have used it before or since; *dinlenme* is the usual word.

Others of his are: *operetleştirmek* 'to make into a light opera' (1932), i.e. to turn something serious into something frivolous; *yazı kalfaları* 'hacks' (lit. 'writing-journeymen', 1945); *yapım* 'manufacture' (1946); *yıkıcılık* 'destructiveness' (1951); *kesik* for 'newspaper cutting/clipping' (1951), previously *kupür* [F] or *gazete maktuası* [A]; *oycu* 'vote-catcher' (1951); *politikasızlaştırılmalıdır* 'must be

---

[1] In what follows, dates in parentheses after individual words indicate the first recorded use of these words.

[2] It is not known whether Atay was the first to use *içtenlik*. *Tarama Dergisi* (1934), in the production of which he was closely involved, gives *içten* for *samimî* 'sincere', attributing it to the *Kamus*, in which work the present writer has failed to find it.

depoliticized' (1952); *yaranıcı* 'smarmy, ingratiating', from *yaranmak* 'to curry favour' (1954); *yasaksızlık* 'policy of *laissez-faire*' (1954); *nutukçu* 'speechifier' (1956); *oydaş* 'holding the same opinion' (1956).

His *danışçılık* (1961) for 'consultancy' is at first sight surprising, as one would have expected him to know better than to use a verb-stem (*danış-* 'to consult') as a noun.[3] But in the Ottoman Turkish that was his mother tongue *danış* was a noun, the Persian borrowing *dāniš* 'knowledge, learning'. Its connection with the verb *danışmak*, in use since the fourteenth century, is unclear; there may have been a confusion with *tanışmak* 'to become acquainted'. Atay's *danışçı* was not taken up; the neologism for 'consultant, counsellor' is *danışman*, ostensibly derived from *danış-* and the spurious suffix *-men/man* making nouns of agent, but in fact a corruption of the Persian *dānišmand* 'learned'.

His *uçum* for 'flight' (1946), as in 'Bir uçum ötede kıta' (the continent which is a flight away), fell by the wayside; *uçuş* is the current word. Using *uçum* in this sense was an uncharacteristic oversight on his part, as it existed already for what in English is termed the fly—i.e. the end of a flag furthest from the flagstaff.[4]

In 1951 he created *eyim* from *eyi*, a by-form of *iyi* 'good', and *kötüm* from *kötü* 'bad', for 'approval' and 'disapproval' respectively, which one might think a heavy load to impose on the unassuming suffix *-m*. From these two words, someone manufactured the verbs *iyimsemek* and *kötümsemek*, 'to be optimistic' and 'to be pessimistic', neither much used except for their aorist participles *iyimser* and *kötümser*, 'optimistic' and 'pessimistic', which have totally replaced the Persian *nikbin* and *bedbin*.

To judge by a passage from his study of Atatürk (Atay 1969: 476), Atay deserves credit for assuring the survival of *şey* 'thing'. The resurrected *nesne* has won limited currency but will never replace *şey*, a word without which many Turks would find difficulty in conversing, for it is what comes automatically to their lips when groping for a word or a name, or thinking what to say next. It is used much like the English 'what-d'you-call-it' or the French *chose* and, as a sentence opening, like 'Well now' or 'I'll tell you what', or 'Il-y-a une autre chose qui est celle-ci'. Atatürk wanted it abandoned, as it was a borrowing from Arabic. (Had that happened, an English analogy would be the inhibiting effect of a ban on 'y'know' or 'basically'.)

beni her toplantıda bulundurup tenkidlerimi dinlemeğe tahammül göstermekte idi:

—Yapmayınız Paşam, diyordum, bir mucize olsa da Anadolu'da ne kadar ölmüş Türk varsa hepsinin aynı anda dirilmesi mümkün olsa, hepsinin beraber ilk ağızlarından çıkacak kelime 'şey'dir. 'Sey' o kadar Türkçedir.

Hiç unutmam. Atatürk, dil meselesine sarıldığından beri kendi dairesinin işleri ile uğraşmamasına pek sevinen vekil ile aynı arabaya binmiştim. Bana dönerek:

---

[3] Only a handful of pre-reform nouns are also verb-stems, such as *göç* 'migration', *göç-* 'to migrate', *boya* 'paint', *boya-* 'to paint'. See Lewis (1988: 227).

[4] *Uçum* is so defined in Kurtoğlu (1938), the definitive work on Turkish flags, which is not mentioned in Eren (1990). *Okyanus* (Tuğlacı 1971–4), a comprehensive dictionary marred by many misprints, gives the correct definition of *uçum* but under the headword *uçun*. So did *Türkçe Sözlük* before the 1988 edition, but has since got it right.

—Falih'ciğim, sen de 'şey' gibi koyu Arapçaların Türkçe olduğunu iddia edecek kadar ileri varma! demesin mi?

Bu vekilin dili de zevki de eskinin eskisi idi.

he had me present at every meeting and was indulgent enough to listen to my criticisms. 'Don't do it, Pasha!' I was saying, 'If a miracle were to occur and all the dead Turks in Anatolia could suddenly be resurrected, the first word to come out of their mouths in unison would be *şey*. That's how Turkish *şey* is.'

I shall never forget; I had got into the same car as the Minister, who was delighted that Atatürk had not been concerning himself with the business of his Ministry since he had become engrossed in the language problem. He turned to me and, would you believe it, he said, 'My dear Falih, don't go so far as to claim that genuine Arabic words like *şey* are Turkish.'

This Minister's language and his taste were the oldest of the old.

Özön does not distinguish between words Atay originated and words he merely used. He credits him with several neologisms proposed in *Cep Kılavuzu* (1935), such as *kurtarıcı* 'saviour' and *uyanık* 'wide-awake', as well as several words in use in the nineteenth century and earlier—for example, *bulantı* 'feeling of nausea', *ölüm-kalım* (*savaşı*) 'life-and-death (struggle)', and *yapıcı* 'builder, constructive'. But the credit is deserved, if not for creating these and other words, then for giving them new leases of life and inspiring others to explore the existing resources of the language before resorting to invention.

Nurullah Ataç (1898–1957) was a late convert to the cause of *Öztürkçe*, which he had long opposed. The autobiographical note on the jacket of his *Karalama Defteri* (1952) reads:

1898de İstanbul'da doğmuş. 1909da üç sınıflık iptidai mektebinden çıkmıştır. Sonra bir iki okula gitmişse de hiçbirini bitirememiştir. İmtihana girerek fransızca öğretmeni olmuş edebiyat dersleri de vermiştir. Bazı dairelerde mütercimlik etmiştir. Şairliğe, hikâyeciliğe özenmişse de becerememiş işi eleştirmeciliğe dökmüştür. Son yıllarda türkçeyi—kend-ince—özleştirmeye çalışmaktadır. Birkaç kitabı dilimize çevirmiştir . . .

Born 1898 in Istanbul.[5] Left three-year primary school 1909. Subsequently attended a school or two but failed to finish any of them. Went in for an exam and became a teacher of French and also taught literature. Worked as a translator in some government departments. Longed to be a story-teller and poet but could not make it. Turned to criticism. In recent years has been trying to purify—as he sees it—Turkish. Has translated several books into our language . . .[6]

He was a prolific essayist, whose work appeared regularly in a number of newspapers and journals. For some twenty years his interests were literary, but in the early 1940s his attention was increasingly directed towards language reform. He explained this change of heart as due to a realization that, in a country

---

[5] His father was Mehmet Ata, who translated von Hammer's *Geschichte des osmanischen Reiches* into Turkish.

[6] They number over sixty, the authors ranging from Balzac to Simenon.

where Latin and Greek were not taught (earlier he had advocated their inclusion in the school syllabus and he continued to stress, rather wistfully, the desirability of knowing them), the only rational course was 'to go to the pure language' (Ataç 1954: 11). In other words, he rejected Ziya Gökalp's view that Turks should go back to Arabic and Persian when creating new words for new concepts, in the way that West Europeans resorted to Greek and Latin. As he saw it, the Turks had to exploit the resources of their own language. Incidentally, by Ataç's time Ziya Gökalp's view could never have prevailed anyway, the Ministry of Education having removed Arabic and Persian from the school syllabus on 1 September 1929.

Ataç's place in the language reform is that he was the great inventor of words. He was no language expert, nor did he profess to be; indeed he is said to have remarked, 'My ignorance is boundless and at my age it cannot be eradicated.' He had, however, a passionate love of language. He detested the habit some intellectuals had of using Western words as clichés without understanding their origins. He came out strongly against those who maintained that language can only develop naturally and that no individual or group of individuals can bring about linguistic change. He took to task a writer, whom he does not name, for saying in a newspaper article: 'bir milletin dilini heyetler düzenleyemez. O kendi kendine gelişir. Ve en doğru tabirler halkın sağduyusundan doğar' (A nation's language cannot be regulated by committees. It develops by itself, and the most authentic forms of expression are born of the common sense of the people). He points out that the words used by the writer for 'regulate', 'develop', and 'common sense'—*düzenlemek, gelişmek, sağduyu*—were not words he had grown up with but were products of the language reform: 'Sorun kendisine: Bunlar halkın sağduyusundan mı doğmuş? Bir kurul, bir kurum yapmamış mı onları? Ne yaptığını bilmeden söylüyor: Kendisi bir kurulun çıkardığı sözleri kullanıyor, sonra da kurulların dil yapamayacağını söylüyor' (Ask him: were they born of the common sense of the people? Weren't they the work of a committee, a society? He speaks without knowing what he is doing: he uses words produced by a committee, then he says that committees could never create language!).[7]

As has been said, he shared Atay's belief that it was futile to produce new words unless they were brought to public attention by being used, preferably in newspaper articles that would be widely read. He declared his philosophy in an article in *Ulus* of 8 March 1948 in which he spoke of his last conversation with Kemalettin Kamu, a recently deceased member of TDK's central committee: '"Sizin Dil Kurumu'nda yaptığınız doğru değildir, birtakım yabancı sözlere karşılık arıyorsunuz; ancak onları birer yazıda kullanacağınıza sözlük yapmağa kalkıyorsunuz. Tilcikler sözlüklerde ölüdür, yazılarda dirilir" gibi sözler söyledim' (I said something on these lines: 'What you're doing in the Dil Kurumu isn't right. You're looking for equivalents for a lot of foreign words but instead of using each

---

[7] *Cep Kılavuzu* (1935) gives *gelişmek* as the replacement for *inkişaf etmek* 'to develop'. The word existed long before, but in pre-reform days it meant 'to grow, improve'.

of them in a piece of writing you set about making dictionaries. Words are dead in dictionaries; they come to life in writing').

The popularity he enjoyed with his readers enabled him to familiarize them with existing *Öztürkçe* and to make known his own neologisms, adding in parentheses the words they were intended to replace, usually with no explanation of how he had derived them. Here is a typical example: 'Dörüt yapıtlarında (*sanat eserlerinde*) ancak biçime bakılır, konunun bir önemi yoktur derler. Bu söz, ezgiciler (*bestekârlar*), bedizciler (*ressamlar*) için kesin olarak doğrudur belki; öykücüler (*hikâyeciler*), oyun-yazanlar için de bilmem öyle midir?' (They say that in works of art one looks only at the form; the subject has no importance. This may be absolutely true for composers and painters; I wonder if it is so for storytellers and playwrights) (Ataç 1964: 187).

His many opponents called him an extremist. One of his friends said in his defence that you cannot adopt a balanced position until you have been to the far end, a not unreasonable remark but hardly applicable to Ataç who, when it came to *Öztürkçe*, never aspired to being anything but extreme.

I met him in Ankara in 1953 and found him to be not the irascible Antichrist my linguistically conservative friends had told me to expect but an amiable and enthusiastic man of high intelligence. As we strolled up and down the Atatürk Boulevard, stopping every now and then for coffee, his good humour and his doggedness were amply displayed. He spoke of the problem that was currently exercising him: finding a Turkish replacement for *rağmen* [A] 'in spite of'. He had invented and had for some years been using *tapa*, but was not satisfied with it.[8] He said, 'I don't feel at all proprietorial about my ideas for new words. If people like them and use them, of course I'm pleased; if they don't, I tell them to have a go themselves and I think of some more.' At one point he shyly mentioned that he had tried his hand at writing poetry in English, but had got no further than a single couplet. He wrote it down on a scrap of paper, treasured by the author to this day:

> O Lord! give me the power of a song-creator,
> For the joyful love I would sing!

He devised a game, described by Aksoy at a memorial meeting held on the tenth anniversary of Ataç's death. The idea was to find meanings for Ottoman words of Arabic origin on the assumption that their consonants were not those of Arabic triliteral roots but those of a more familiar Turkish or Western word.

Birgün odama gelmiş, 'meşruta' ne demek, diye sormuştu. Ben 'hükûmet-i meşruta', 'evkaf-ı meşruta' gibi örneklere göre açıklama yaparken o kıs kıs gülüyor;
—Yorulmayın, bilemezsiniz, diyordu.
Bu sözlerini ciddiye aldığımı görünce hemen açıklamıştı:

---

[8] Where he got *tapa* from is not evident; *tap-* means 'to worship'. The modern replacement for *rağmen* is *karşın*, another of his inventions, based on *karşı* 'against', though he used it not for *rağmen* 'in spite of' but for *muhalif* [A] 'opposed to'.

—Meşruta 'şort giymiş kadın' demek.

Bu kez gülme sırası bana gelmişti.

O zaman karşı karşıya oturup birçok sözcüklerin bu biçim anlamlarını bulmuştuk: 'Tereddi' radyo dinlemek, 'tebenni' banyo yapmak, 'terakki' rakı içmek demekti, 'mezun' Özen pastahanesinde oturan kimseye denirdi. 'Tekellüm'ün birkaç anlamı vardı: Kilim satın almak, kelem yani lahana yemek ve KLM uçağı ile uçmak.   (Aksoy 1968: 18)

He came to my room one day and asked me the meaning of *meşruta*. While I was trying to explain it on the basis of examples such as *hükûmet-i meşruta* ['constitutional government'] and *evkaf-ı meşruta* ['pious foundations subject to conditions'], he was chuckling and saying, 'Don't wear yourself out, you'll never guess.' Seeing that I was taking what he said seriously, he explained. '*Meşruta* means a woman wearing shorts.' This time it was my turn to laugh. Thereafter we sat down together and invented this kind of meaning for a number of words. *Tereddi* meant 'listening to the radio', *tebenni* 'to take a bath', *terakki* 'to drink *rakı*'. *Mezun* was an habitué of Özen's patisserie.[9] *Tekellüm* had several meanings: 'to buy kilims', 'to eat the sort of cabbage known as "kelem"', 'to fly KLM'.

Readers who have seen the point need not bother with the rest of this paragraph. *Meşruta* is the feminine of *meşrut* 'bound by conditions', Arabic *mašrūṭ*, the triliteral root of which is $Š–R–Ṭ$ (whence *šarṭ* 'condition'). Ataç was pretending that the root was $Š–R–T$, the consonants of Turkish *şort*, English *shorts*. The Arabic root of *tereddi* 'degeneration' is $R–D–Y$ 'fall', not $R–D–Y$ as in Turkish *radyo*, English *radio*. *Tebenni* 'adoption' is from Arabic $B–N–Y$, not from the three consonants of Turkish *banyo* (Italian *bagnio*) 'bath'. *Terakki* 'progress' is from Arabic $R–Ḳ–Y$ 'ascent', not from *rakı* 'arrack'. *Mezun* 'authorized, graduate' is from Arabic $ʔ–D–N$ 'permission', not from the name of a Turkish pastry-cook. The root of *tekellüm* 'speaking' is Arabic $K–L–M$, not Turkish *kilim* 'woven rug' (Persian *gelim*) or the Turkish dialect word *kelem* 'cabbage' or the Dutch abbreviation KLM.

In 1947 he was using *keleci* [M] (Mongolian *kele-* 'to speak') for *kelime* [A] 'word'. *Keleci* is found in written Turkish of the fourteenth to eighteenth centuries in the sense not of 'word' but of 'words, discourse',[10] just like Turkish *söz*. Even if it had been of impeccably Turkish parentage, it would have stood little chance of general acceptance, because the final *-ci* makes it look like a noun of agent, specifically *kelleci*, 'dealer in sheeps' heads'. Yet that fact did not seem to bother him, as is evident from the explanation he gave in *Ulus* (9 February 1948) for dropping *keleci*: 'Şimdiye dek *kelime* yerine *keleci* diyordum, pek de beğenmiyordum; çünkü *keleci*, *kelime* değil, söz demektir; bundan böyle *tilcik*, belki *tilce* diyeceğim. *Til*, *dil* lûgat demektir, *tilcik*, *tilce* de "küçük til" demek olur' (Until now I've been saying *keleci* instead of *kelime* but I didn't like it much, because *keleci* doesn't mean *kelime* but *söz*. From now on I shall say *tilcik*, perhaps *tilce*. *Til*, *dil* means speech, so *tilcik* or *tilce* would mean 'speechlet'). What he was doing was adding a diminutive suffix to a word he alleged to mean 'speech', as if *speechlet* meant 'unit of

---

[9] Özen Pastahanesi on the Atatürk Boulevard, a favourite haunt of Ankara intellectuals.

[10] It is recorded for 'agreement' in the spoken language of the vilayet of Tokat (*Derleme Sözlüğü* 1963–82: viii. 2726).

speech' and so 'word'; a good example of the cavalier attitude that shocked the language specialists. And why *til*? Because *dil* 'tongue' already had a diminutive, *dilcik*, a botanical term for 'ligule' and a physiological term for 'clitoris'. It was not, however, as his wording suggests, an alternative to *dil*, but an older form of it that had been obsolete for centuries, its initial *t* having followed the normal course and become *d*. *Tilcik* was used by hardly anyone but its inventor. The neologism that carried the day was *sözcük*, invented by Melih Cevdet Anday in 1958 on the same lines as Ataç's *tilcik* but based on *söz*, which really did mean 'speech'. Here is Anday's note on it: 'Dağlarca, "kelime" karşılığı olarak "sözcük"ü değil, "tilcik"i benimsemiş. Ben, "tilcik"e karşı "sözcük" ü önerirken, bunun, yeni sözcük yapma kurallarına daha uygun olduğunu düşünmüştüm: elden geldiğince canlı kökler-den, canlı eklerden yararlanarak . . .' (As the replacement for *kelime*, [the poet Fazıl Hüsnü] Dağlarca has adopted not *sözcük* but *tilcik*. When I proposed *sözcük* instead of *tilcik*, I had reflected that it was more consistent with the rules for building new words: making use as far as possible of living roots and living suffixes . . .) (Anday 1960, cited in Kudret 1966: 61).

There is a critical study of Ataç's contribution to the new Turkish in Talât Tekin's (1958) paper 'Ataç'ın Dilciliği ve Tilcikleri' ('Ataç as Language Expert, and his Speechlets', the use of Ataç's own *tilcik* being ironic.

Tekin lists the *tilcik*s in three groups, though the first and second sometimes overlap: (1) Anatolian dialect words found in *Tarama Dergisi* (1934) and *Söz Derleme Dergisi* (1939–52); (2) OT words, most of them from *Dīwān Luġāt al-Turk* (*DLT*),[11] the rest from *Tarama Sözlüğü* (1963–77) or *Tarama Dergisi*; (3) words of Ataç's own coining. Some examples of each group are now discussed; all the words Ataç hoped his proposals might replace are Arabic unless otherwise indicated.

Group 1: *ayak* for *kafiye* 'rhyme'; *gerçek* for *hakikî* 'true, real' and *hakikat* 'truth'; *kez* for *defa* 'time, occasion'; *kural* for *kaide* 'rule'; *küşüm* for *şüphe* 'doubt'; *öğseyin* for *elbette* 'certainly'; *sin* for *mezar* 'tomb'; *töre* for *ahlâk* 'customs, ethics'; *tüm* for *kül* 'whole, totality'; *umut* for *ümit* [P] 'hope', *ürün* for *mahsul* 'crop, product'; *yazak* for *kalem* 'pen'; *yımızık* for *çirkin* [P] 'ugly', *yitirmek* for *kaybetmek* 'to lose'.

Tekin remarks that, in spite of all Ataç's efforts, a large number of the words in Group 1 had not become part of the written language and never would, because the words they were meant to replace were so widely known. Time has proved him wrong; the majority of them—all but *küşüm*, *öğseyin*, *yazak*, and *yımızık*— are in everyday use. While *ayak* has not superseded *kafiye* for 'rhyme', it has always been a technical term of folk-poetry, applied to the rhyming refrain between verses. For rhyme in general, from 1949 onwards Ataç himself used *uyak*,

---

[11] Mahmud Kaşgarî's dictionary of Turkish, written in Arabic and completed probably in 1079. See References under *DLT*. A Turkish translation of the unique manuscript and a facsimile of it were available to Ataç (Atalay 1939–41).

obviously based on *ayak* but having as its first syllable the stem *uy-* 'to fit, to conform', and *uyak* is well on its way to ousting *kafiye* among the younger generation of poets. For *sin*, see pages 6 and 82.

As for *şüphe*, which Tekin thought assured of survival, though still common in speech it is rarely seen in writing, being rapidly edged out not by Ataç's *küşüm* but by *kuşku*, proposed in *Cep Kılavuzu* (1935) as a replacement for *vehim* 'groundless fear' and *vesvese* 'Satanic prompting, morbid suspicion'. Ataç rightly objected to it, as he said in an article in *Ulus* of 21 February 1957: 'Çünkü *kuşku, doute* demek değil, olsa olsa *soupçon* demektir. *Kuşku* bir türlü güvensizlik gösterir. Ben bu sözden kuşkulandım demek, bunun altında bir kötülük, başka bir dilek sezdim demektir' (For *kuşku* does not mean *doute* but, if anything, *soupçon*. *Kuşku* indicates a kind of lack of confidence. To say 'I felt *kuşku* about this remark' means that behind it I sensed some evil, some *arrière pensée*). He was not wedded to his own suggestion, *küşüm*:

Konya'da öyle derlermiş de onun için. Sonra *küşüm* tilciğinin başka yerlerde başka anlamlarda kullanıldığını öğrendim. Kökünü bilmiyorum. Konya'da *şüküm* dedikleri de olurmuş. Arapça *şek*'in bozması olacak. Bunun için şimdi *sizin* diyorum. Onu da pek beğenmediğim için daha iyisini arıyorum.

That's how they're reported to say it in Konya, that's why [I proposed it]. Later I learned it was used elsewhere in other senses. I don't know its root. It seems that sometimes in Konya they also say *şüküm*. That will be a corruption of the Arabic *şek*. So now I use *sizin*. As I don't like that much either, I'm looking for a better word for it.

Tarama Dergisi records *küşüm* as being in colloquial use for 'doubt' or 'worry' in nine vilayets besides Konya, but it has not achieved literary status. *Şüküm*, not in *Derleme Sözlüğü* (1963–82) or *Tarama Dergisi*, may well have been a metathesis of *küşüm* under the influence of *şek* (the Arabic *šakk*), to which Ataç refers. As for *sizin*, which he first used for 'doubt' in 1956, it sank without trace; given that *sizin* is the Turkish for 'of you', it was clearly a non-starter.[12]

Ürün, an Anatolian word for 'produce' that has now almost totally supplanted *mahsul*, is probably a Turkicization of *üren* [M] 'seed, fruit, progeny' (Clauson 1972: 233). If so, while Ataç may not have been aware of its non-Turkish origin, he would not have cared anyway, considering as he did that anything was preferable to an Arabic word.

Group 2: *betik* for *kitap* 'book'; *köğ* for *vezin* 'metre' (of verse); *tin* for *ruh* 'soul, spirit'; *netek* for *nasıl* 'how'; *ozan* for *şair* 'poet'; *tamu* for *cehennem* 'hell'; *tükeli* for *tamamiyle* 'wholly'; *tüp* for *asıl* 'origin, original'; *uçmak* for *cennet* 'paradise'; *yanıt* for *cevap* 'answer'; *yavuz* for *kötü* 'bad'.

Tekin includes *çevre* 'surroundings', now 'environment', in this group, which is

[12] Ataç may have come across and misread *sezik*, which in the old alphabet was written identically with *sizin*. *Tarama Sözlüğü* (1963–77) gives two citations, from the fifteenth and sixteenth centuries, with the meanings *sezgi, zan, tahmin*: 'perception, supposition, estimation'.

an error, as the word has never totally lost currency since the thirteenth century. He may have confused it with *çevren*, manufactured by Ataç from *çevre* to replace *ufuk* [A] 'horizon' but scarcely known nowadays even to intellectuals. *Tamu* and *uçmak* for 'hell' and 'paradise' did not catch on; they would scarcely have helped the ethnic cleansing, as they were not Turkish but Sogdian. Some items in this group were taken in a form consistent with the phonetic development of modern Turkish—for example, *yanıt*, anciently *yanut*. The changes Ataç made in others were contrary to the laws of phonology. Tekin tells how in 1949, while still an undergraduate, he wrote to Ataç to point out that *netek* (properly *neteg*) was the ancient form of a word that, had it survived into modern Turkish, would have become *nite*. Ataç accepted the correction and used *nite* thereafter. *Betik* has won some currency but it was a mistake for *bitig*, the natural development of which, *biti*, was in use as late as the eighteenth century for 'letter, document'. *Tin* too is flawed; its ancient form was *tın* 'breath, spirit'. Tekin, comparing its derived verb *dinlenmek* 'to rest', originally 'to draw breath', notes that its modern form would have been *din*. Even if Ataç had known that, however, he would have been unwise to chose the latter form, since a homograph and so near a homophone of *din* [A] 'religion' (in which the *i* is long) would have been unlikely to gain favour,[13] whereas *tin* and its adjective *tinsel* 'spiritual' are nowadays not without their devotees. *Tükeli* (in the older language not 'wholly' but 'perfect') would have become *dükeli* if it had survived into the modern language. *Tüp* did in fact survive, as *dip* 'bottom, base'.

He took *yavuz* for 'bad', the opposite of its most usual modern sense. Tekin notes that, although 'bad' was its ancient meaning, it is used in dialect for 'good, beautiful'. He could have added that it is also used in dialect for 'generous, manly, capable'. And for 'bad'. In view of its ambiguity, in a country where Yavuz is a common male name it could never have won acceptance as a replacement for *fena* [A] 'bad', much less for *kötü*, which being pure Turkish stood in no need of a replacement.[14] As the appellation of Sultan Selim II, *Yavuz* is rendered 'Grim' by English-speaking historians.[15] but 'Steadfast' is closer to what it meant to those who applied it to the ruler who added Egypt and Syria to the Ottoman dominions.[16]

It is a pity that many modern writers have followed Ataç in using *ozan* in place of *şair* for 'poet', because its old meaning was 'bard, minstrel'. Those who know—a large category, including as it does every Turk with an interest in folk-poetry—preserve the distinction.

---

[13] In the light of his toying with *sizin* for 'doubt', that consideration might not have deterred him.

[14] Not that that is much to go on, as the impeccably Turkish *bütün* for 'all, whole' has for years been fighting for life against *tüm*, of whose Arabic origin there is little doubt. The two words, however, are not synonymous. While the sophisticated may use *tüm elmalar* for 'all the apples', to the people who grow them it means whole apples, as distinct from sliced apples. Even *istemek* 'to want' is looked on with disfavour, the in-word being *dilemek* 'to wish for'.

[15] Some old Turkey hands refer to him affectionately as Grim Slim.

[16] The use of *wicked* as a term of approbation by English and American schoolchildren is worth mentioning in this context but, as with *yavuz*, should not be cited as evidence of moral decline.

Group 3: (*a*) words made from OT roots with various suffixes: *assığlanmak* for *faydalanmak* 'to utilize'; *kopuzsulluk* for *lyrisme* [F] 'lyricism'; *köğük* for *mısra* 'line of poetry'; *tansıklamak* for *-e hayran olmak* 'to admire'; *yanıtlamak* for *cevaplamak* 'to answer'.

Assığlanmak was Ataç's first attempt at a replacement for *faydalanmak*, in which the *fayda* represents the Arabic *fā'ida* 'use', 'profit', the OT for which was *asığ*. Why he decided to double the *s* is unknown. He then came up with *asılanmak*, no doubt having learned that *ası* was the form *asığ* would have taken had it survived into the modern language. Neither form has endured. He coined *kopuzsulluk* by first adding *-sul* to *kopuz* 'lyre', to make *kopuzsul* 'lyric', and then the abstract-noun suffix *-lik*. *-sul* was not a living suffix, occurring only in *yoksul* 'destitute', described by Clauson (1972: 907) as 'clearly a corruption of *yoksuz*'. *Kopuzsulluk* did not survive its creator.

No more did *köğük*, which he manufactured from *köğ* with the long-obsolete diminutive suffix *-ik*. In so doing he was using the method he later used to create *tilcik*: loading on to a diminutive form of his word for 'metre' the meaning of 'line of poetry'. (The accepted new term for this is *dize*, a deliberate variation of *dizi* 'line'.) *Köğ* for 'metre' is the form he would have found in Atalay's translation of *DLT*. Clauson transcribes it as *kü:g*—i.e. with long *ü*—which is how Dankoff and Kelly (1982–5) also read it. *Küğ* survives, though not in Ataç's sense of 'metre' but rather for 'music'—its first sense was indeed 'tune'. Neither *köğ* nor *küğ* appears in *Tarama Sözlüğü*, but *küğ* is used for 'music' by some musicologists, particularly those at the University of the Aegean (see Chapter 9). *Tansıklamak* was made from *tansık*, which is how the old *tansuk* 'marvellous, marvel' would have appeared had it survived. *Tarama Sözlüğü* does not include the verb but gives *tansık* for *mucize* [A] 'miracle'. Both *yanıtlamak* and the noun *yanıt* 'answer' from which Ataç formed it are commonly used in modern writing.

Group 3: (*b*) words coined by Ataç from Anatolian dialect words: *devinme* for *hareket* 'movement'; *öykünülmek* for *taklit edilmek* 'to be imitated'; *perkitlemek* for *tekit etmek* 'to corroborate'; *yeğinlemek* for *tercih etmek* 'to prefer'; *yöresellik* for *mahallîlik* 'regionalism'. Tekin points out that, as *yeğinlemek* is based on *yeğ* 'good', the *-in-* is superfluous, as is the *-le-* of *perkitlemek*, *perkit-* being a verb-stem anyway. As *perkitmek* is given in *Derleme Sözlüğü* (1963–82) with the required meaning, it is problematic why Ataç did not leave well alone. The *yöre* of *yöresellik* (the only word in this group, apart from *devinmek*, to have won any currency) is shown in *Derleme Sözlüğü* as meaning *çevre* 'surroundings'. The same work shows *devinmek* for 'to move'; on the other hand, it gives *öykünmek* only in the senses of 'to relate, tell' and 'to compete', though the meaning 'to imitate' is given in *Tarama Dergisi*, as is the meaning 'to be sorry'. It was presumably *öykün-mek* that inspired Ataç's invention of *öykü* for 'story', which has largely replaced *hikâye*, though some say that *öykü* is no more than a vulgar mispronunciation of *hikâye*. If so, it is as if we were to discard *nuclear* in favour of the Pentagon's *nucular*.

In view of the rash of *-sel*s and *-sal*s by which the face of written Turkish is blemished, Tekin's comment on *yöresellik* is of historical interest: 'Bunlardan *yöresellik* işlek olmıyan *-sel* ekiyle kurulmuştur. *Kumsal, uysal* gibi pek az birkaç kelimede görülen bu ek bir vakitler *nisbet -î* si yerine teklif edilmiş fakat tutmamıştı' (Of these, *yöresellik* is formed with the unproductive suffix *-sel*. This suffix, which appears in a very few words such as *kumsal* and *uysal*, had at one time been proposed as a replacement for the [Arabic and Persian] adjectival suffix *-î*, but had never caught on). It is fair to add that in 1958, when he wrote this, he was not alone in his judgement.

Group 3: (*c*) coinages produced by dismembering ('ayırma yolu ile') ancient and dialect words—i.e. by taking them apart and putting the pieces together as he fancied: *betke* for *makale* '(newspaper) article'; *dörüt* for *sanat* 'art'; *ep* for *sebep* 'cause'; *söydeşi* for *yani* 'that is to say'; *tükelmek* for *tamamlamak* 'to complete'; *usul* for *aklî* 'intellectual'. None of these won favour. As Tekin says, this method of word-making calls for profound grammatical knowledge. He explains *betke* as derived by Ataç from *biti*, earlier *bitiğ*, in the mistaken belief that *bit-* was the stem of a verb *bitmek* 'to write' (the old word, of Chinese origin, for 'to write' was *bitimek* not *bitmek*); he then added the *-ke* to make a noun of it. It is more likely that he manufactured it from *betik*, his invention for 'book', or from *bete*, his misreading of *biti*, which he went on using for 'letter' until his death. The second syllable, *-ke*, is not an all-purpose noun-suffix but an extremely rare diminutive suffix (Clauson 1972: p. xi); what he thought he was creating was a word meaning 'little writing'. *Dörüt* is the stem of *dörütmek* or *törütmek*, an old word for 'to create', from which he also made *dörütmen* for 'artist'.

With all due respect to Tekin, *ep* 'cause' does not belong in this group but in the first. Ataç would have found it among the equivalents for *sebep* in *Tarama Dergisi*, where it was due to a misreading of *ip* 'rope' in one of the Ottoman sources used by the compilers of that dictionary. There, however, it was given as the Turkish for *sabab* [A] in the sense not of 'cause' but of 'tent rope', the original meaning of the Arabic word.

Söydeşi for 'it means, that is to say', is another oddity that did not take. Tekin supposes that Ataç extracted the first syllable from *söylemek* 'to say' on the correct assumption that the latter was compounded with the denominative verb-suffix *-lemek*, but there was no such noun as *söy*; the *söy* of *söylemek* started life as *söz*. The *-deş* is for the invariable *-daş* '-fellow', which Ataç helped deprive of its invariability.[17] The literal meaning he must have been aiming at was 'its saying-fellow'— i.e. 'which amounts to saying'.

Over *tanmalı* 'wonderful, surprising' one must again take issue with Tekin. His

---

[17] In pre-reform days, the only word in which it appeared as *-deş* seems to have been *kardeş* 'sibling', an Istanbul pronunciation of *kardaş* (earlier *karındaş* 'womb-fellow'), a form used until well into the seventeenth century. *Cep Kılavuzu* (1935) gives *gönüldeş* not *-daş* for *yekdil* 'sympathizer', possibly through a misreading of the phonetic spelling used by Redhouse (1890).

view is that Ataç made it by adding the deverbal suffix -*malı* to *tan*, the noun seen in *tansık* and *tana kalmak* ('to be left to wonderment'), which he took to be a verb-stem meaning 'to wonder'.[18] But there is also a verb *tanmak* 'to be astonished', found in the form *dañmak* in texts of the fifteenth and eighteenth centuries and still used in parts of Anatolia. Ataç presumably made *tanmalı* from the -*me* verbal noun of that word, in which case it belongs in Tekin's list 3(*b*).

As for *usul* for 'intelligent': although *us* originally meant 'intelligence, discrim-ination', *uslu*, once 'intelligent', nowadays means only 'well behaved'. This attempt by Ataç to base a new adjective for 'intelligent' on *us* is rightly criticized by Tekin on the grounds that 'research to date into the Turkish language has failed to come up with a denominal adjective-suffix -*ıl/il*'. Moreover, there was another *usul* [A] 'method, system' in everyday use in Ataç's day and still not extinct. True, it differs from Ataç's *usul* in that, because of its Arabic origin, its final *l* is clear, so that its plural is *usuller*, while 'methodical' is *usullü* and 'unmethodical' *usulsüz* (Lewis 1988: 19),[19] but that would not—indeed did not—make its proposed homograph acceptable.

Group 3: (*d*) words taken from other Turkic dialects or based on such words: *komuğ* for *musiki* 'music'; *ücük* for *harf* 'letter of the alphabet'; *şüyüncü* for *müjdeci* 'bearer of good news'; *tilcik* for *kelime* 'word'; *üycük* for *beyit* 'line of poetry'.

These need not detain us long, since *tilcik*, the only one of them to win any cur-rency at all, has been adequately discussed. The correct form of Ataç's *ücük* is *üjek*, probably of Chinese origin. *Üy* is the form taken by *ev* 'house' in Kirghiz, Uzbek, and those other Eastern dialects in which it does not appear as *öy*. Ataç's reason for making a diminutive of it to replace *beyit* [A] is that 'line of poetry' is a secondary sense of Arabic *bayt*, the primary sense being 'tent' or 'house'.

Group 3: (*e*) compounds made with words from OT and Anatolian or other dialects: *aktöre* or *sağtöre* for *ahlâk* 'ethics'; *bile-duyuş* for *sympathie* [F] 'sympa-thy'; *budunbuyrumcu* for *demokrat* 'democrat'; *düzeyit* for *nesir* 'prose'; *gökçe-yazın* for *edebiyat* 'literature, belles-lettres'; *uza-bilik* for *tarih* 'history'.

To prefix *ak* 'white or *sağ* 'right' to *töre*, the OT for 'customary law', does not seem a particularly felicitous way of expressing the concept of ethics, but some writers do use *aktöre*. *Bile-duyuş*, compounded of *bile*, OT for 'with', and *duyuş*, 'feeling', did not prevail; the new word for 'sympathy' is *duygudaşlık* 'feeling-fellowship', which has not supplanted *sempati*, as may be judged from the fact that the equivalent given in *Türkçe Sözlük* (1988) for *duygudaş* is *sempatizan*.

Tekin passes over the second element of *budunbuyrumcu* in silence, saying only

[18] From this noun *tan* comes the verb *tanlamak* 'to be astonished', in literary use between the thirteenth and eighteenth centuries and still alive in one or two local dialects, including that of the vilayet of Ankara.
[19] Some use the neologism *yöntem*, others still prefer *metot* [F]. In the 1950s Istanbul University had a pair of professors known to their colleagues as Metotlu Cahil ('The Methodical Ignoramus') and Metotsuz Cahil respectively.

that *budun*, an ancient word for 'people', would have become *buyun* had it sur-vived. The ancient word for 'people' was in fact *boḏun*, which by the eleventh century had become *boyun* though, given the existence of *boyun* 'neck', *boyun* 'people' would have stood little chance of acceptance in modern Turkish. As early as 1912, Yakup Kadri [Karaosmanoğlu] made fun of an attempt to replace *millet* 'nation' by *budun* (Levend 1972: 321). But now it has happened, in that *budun* is used to some extent, notably in *budunbilim* for 'ethnography'. The *buyrum* of *buyrumcu* is pure invention, a noun made from the stem of *buyurmak* 'to command'. The *buyruk* of *budunbuyrukçu*, Ataç's offering for 'dictator', was an old Ottoman word for 'command'.

Tekin explains *düzeyit* for 'prose' as illegitimately formed by adding to *düz* 'level' the stem of the old verb *eyitmek* 'to say': 'level-speak'. The somewhat more logical *düzyazı* 'level writing' is used instead. *Gökçe-yazın* was intended to mean 'belles-lettres', *gökçe* being a provincialism for 'beautiful', while *yazın* was Ataç's arbitrary modification of *yazı* 'writing'. The whole expression did not catch on, but *yazın* is current in the sense of 'literature', without having supplanted the time-honoured *edebiyat*.

Categories (*d*) and (*e*) both contain words not in the spirit of the guideline adopted by the Sixth Kurultay, but then no one could have expected it to restrain Ataç's creative urge: 'Türk dili, Türk Milletinin kullandığı dildir. Terimler yapılırken eski tarihlerden beri yaşayıp gelen unsurlar zaman ve mekân itibariyle yakınlık ve uzaklık bakımından dikkate alınmalı ve bugünkü Türkiye Türkçesinin fonetik ve estetiğine uygun olmalıdır' (Turkish is the language used by the Turkish nation. When terms are being made, elements which have survived from ancient times should be considered from the point of view of their proximity and remote-ness in time and place and be in conformity with the phonetics and aesthetics of the present-day Turkish of Turkey) (Kurultay 1949: 146).

No one has yet succeeded in finding an acceptable *Öztürkçe* word for 'history'; *tarih* [A] still holds its ground and will continue to do so. Ataç's *uza-bilik* won no following, any more than his *uza* alone or *uzağı* or *uza-bilim*, or his *uzabilikçi* for 'historian'. *Cep Kılavuzu* (1935) gives *uza* as replacement for *mesafe* [A] 'distance', while *bilik* is OT for 'knowledge', appearing in Ottoman from the fourteenth to the seventeenth century as *bilü* or *bili*. As for *bilim*, which has acquired general currency for 'science' because of its fortuitous resemblance to *ilim* ('*ilm* [A] 'knowledge'), Ataç's first recorded use of it was in 1956, but it had already appeared in 1935, in *Cep Kılavuzu*.

Group 3: (*f*) words made by Ataç from living roots and more-or-less active suffixes: *bağlanç* for *din* 'religion'; *dokunca* for *zarar* 'harm'; *örneğin* for *meselâ* 'for example'; *sorun* for *mesele* 'problem'; *yapıt* for *eser* 'work' (artistic or literary); *yazım* for *metin* 'text'; *yazın* for *edebiyat* 'literature'.

Tekin's conclusion:

Ataç, yaman bir tenkitçi, titiz bir çevirici, kısaca, usta bir edebiyatçı idi; ancak bir dilci değildi. Gerekliliğine inandığı dâvayı yürütebilmek için dilimizdeki yabancı kaynaklı kelimelere türkçe karşılıklar aramış, bulamadığı zaman kendi kurmuştur. Fakat, kelime yaparken bir noktaya dikkat etmemiştir: Yaşıyan köklerden işlek eklerle söz türetmek. Böyle yapsaydı *tilcik*'leri yadırganmaz, kolayca tutunurdu.

Ataç was a remarkable critic and a sensitive translator; in short, a consummate literary man, but he was no language man. To advance the cause in whose necessity he believed, he looked for Turkish equivalents of words of foreign origin in our language and when he could not find them he made them up himself. But in his word-making there was one point he disregarded: the need to derive words from living roots and active suffixes. Had he done so, his *tilcik*s would not have struck people as odd and would have easily gained acceptance.

The criticism sounds reasonable but in its implication that the *tilcik*s did not gain acceptance it is dead wrong. All the words in the last list, with the exception of *bağlanç*, are in everyday use, and all but one with the meanings he assigned to them: *yazım* nowadays means not 'text' but 'spelling'. It is a pity that *bağlanç*, from *bağlan-* 'to be attached', has not had more success, seeing that it was one of Ataç's few correct formations.

Yılmaz Çolpan (1963) does not claim that the thousand-odd neologisms in his glossary of Ataç's words were all originated or resurrected by Ataç, nor were they. He shows *içtenlik* 'sincerity', for example, as having been used by Ataç in 1950, whereas Atay's first recorded use of it is dated 1946. It appears in *Cep Kılavuzu* (1935), for which Atay was largely responsible. Çolpan shows *yır* 'poetry', a respectable old word listed in *Tarama Dergisi*, as first used by Ataç in 1949, but Sadri Maksudî (Arsal 1930: 116) had used it nineteen years before. Nevertheless, even if we halve Çopan's figure, Ataç's contribution to the vocabulary of present-day Turkish unquestionably exceeds that of any other individual.

Aydın Sayılı (1913–93) was born in Istanbul and completed his secondary education at the Atatürk Lycée in Ankara. Atatürk attended the *viva voce* examination for the baccalaureate and was so greatly impressed by Sayılı's performance that he recommended him to the Minister of Education, who sent him to Harvard, where he studied under George Sarton, obtaining his doctorate in 1942. In 1952 he was appointed Professor of the History of Science at Dil ve Tarih-Coğrafya Fakültesi and in 1974 became Chairman of the Philosophy Department of the same faculty. His reputation was worldwide. His best-known work in English (Sayılı 1988) is *The Observatory in Islam and its Place in the General History of the Observatory*.

Unlike many scholars of his age group, he took to *Öztürkçe* enthusiastically, but he did not believe in letting the old words die. He wanted to keep them alive because they might be useful, now or in the future, to express subtle distinctions. Thus he advocates (Sayılı 1978: 400) the retention of *tabiî* alongside the increasingly popular *doğal* for 'natural', because *tabiî* is used 'yadırganmayan bir şey için' (of something not regarded as strange)—i.e. in the sense of 'naturally, of course'. *Tabiî* does in fact survive in this sense, but I fear the credit goes not to Sayılı but to the linguistic conservatism of the people.

His language is eclectic; he uses whatever word best expresses his meaning, whether it belongs to the older or the newer vocabulary. He did not condemn *-sel/sal* but his remarks on it (see Chapter 7) include such Ottoman survivals as *tereddüt, hissedenler, mevcut, çare, vâkıa, taraf, iltifat*, and even the antiquated *selika*. Although he used *Öztürkçe*, he was ready to speak out against its worst features, as we see in the following passage (Sayılı 1978: 399). The word *yanırsız*, which he uses in it for 'unbiased', is the final theme in the present chapter.

Birhayli fena bir başka misal de *kuşku* sözcüğünün *şüphe* yerine kullanılmasıdır. Çünkü *kuşku* sözcüğünde bir itimatsızlık, bir kötü niyet, yahut da hoşlanılmayacak bir sezinleme anlamı vardır. *Şüphe* ise bu bakımdan tarafsız veya yanırsız bir kelimedir. *Kuşku* gibi güzel bir kelimeyi *şüphe* yerine kullanmak onu özel anlamından ayırmak ve aynı zamanda dilimizi *şüphe* ve *kuşku* gibi yakın anlamlı iki kelimeye sahip olmaktan zorla yoksun kılmak demektir.

Another extremely bad example is the use of *kuşku* instead of *şüphe*. For in *şüphe* there is a sense of a lack of confidence, or an evil intent, or a perception of a situation that is going to be unpleasant, whereas *şüphe* in this respect is neutral or unbiased. To use a beautiful word like *kuşku* in place of *şüphe* is to divest it of its proper sense and at the same time to dispossess our language forcibly of a pair of words of related meaning.

His intelligence and erudition marked him off from those responsible for much of the vocabulary of current Turkish. Every page of his book-length article reveals that he thought more deeply about the language than did most of those who shaped its future. The reason he had so little effect on the course of the reform is that, unlike Atay and Ataç, he was not a popular writer but a scholar who wrote for scholars. Discussing *neden*, for example, he mentions that Ottoman had the words *sebep* 'cause' and *illet* 'reason'. *Neden*, which could have replaced *illet*, is now used for both *illet* and *sebep*. But these two words represented two distinct concepts, and two such words exist in all developed languages. 'Cause' is used in relation to nature, and for situations outside one's volition, whereas 'reason' is used for matters coming within one's volition: 'yağmur yağmasının nedeni' (the cause of the rainfall), but 'konuşmak istemesinin sebebi' (the reason for his wishing to speak).

No one seems to have paid any attention to that or his other criticisms and suggestions. He thought it was wrong (Sayılı 1978: 442), for example, that, although *çeviri* was in common use for 'translation', for the verb 'to translate' there was only the old *tercüme etmek* or the non-specific *çevirmek* 'to turn'. He made a verb from *çeviri—çevirilemek*—and used it throughout the article, but it is doubtful if anyone else ever adopted it. Probably not, as it would have been too easily confused with the existing neologism *çevrilemek* 'to explain away, to interpret allegorically'.

He pointed out a flaw in *yüzyıl*, the prevalent replacement for *asır* [A] 'century'—namely, that when you hear 'yedi yüzyıl/yüz yıl' you cannot tell whether what is meant is 'seven centuries' or 'seven hundred years'. And this distinction may sometimes be important. If someone says 'yedi asır kadar önce' (some seven centuries ago), you understand that there may be a margin of error of, say, sixty or seventy years, whereas 'yedi yüzyıl/yüz yıl kadar önce' may imply an error to be measured not in years but in centuries. A valid criticism, but he did not offer an unambiguous alternative to *yüzyıl*; obviously he was hoping that *asır* could be rescued from oblivion.

The trouble was that he was working on too high a plane. One need only open his article at any page to see why his proposals passed over the heads of the wordsmiths. This passage, for example:

Bugün *örtük* ve *açık* sözcüklerini birbirinin karşıtı iki terim olarak kullan larımız vardır. Bunların da terim olarak pek doyundurucu olmadığı söylenebilir. Çünkü *açık* sözcüğü çokanlamlı olduğu gibi, *örtük* de yakın akraba terim türetilmesine pek elverişli değildir. Ayrıca, *örtük* sözcüğü anlamın örtülü olduğunu ifade ediyor. Oysa, burada önemli olan husus anlamın *örtülmesi* değil, örtük biçimde *ifade edilmesi, dile getirilmesidir* ... Bu terimlerin İngilizcedeki karşılıkları *implicit* ve *explicit'*tir ... Fakat *örtük* ve *açık* yerine, yukarıda değinilen yetersizlikleri dolayısıyla, *altgın* ve *üstgün* gibi iki terimin getirilmesi daha isabetli olur. Çünkü bunlardan her ikisi de özel terim vasfını tatmin edici bir şekilde karşıyabileceği gibi, *altgın* sözcüğü anlam bakımından, *örtük* sözcüğüne kıyasla, maksada daha uygun düşer. (Sayılı 1978: 443–4)

There are some amongst us today who use the words *örtük* and *açık* as two antonymous technical terms. One may say that as technical terms they are not very satisfactory. For aside from the fact that *açık* has many meanings, *örtük* is not particularly suited to deriving closely related terms. Moreover, the word *örtük* implies that the meaning is veiled, whereas the important fact here is not that the meaning is veiled but that it is expressed, conveyed, in a veiled way ... The English equivalents of these terms are *implicit* and *explicit* ... But because of the inadequacies of *örtük* and *açık* touched on above, it would be more appropriate to introduce two terms to replace them, such as *altgın* and *üstgün*. Not only would they both meet the definition of a special technical term more satisfactorily; if we consider the word *altgın* from the point of view of meaning, in comparison with *örtük* it is more to the purpose.

Or this, from a discussion of possible equivalents for 'determinism' and 'indeterminism':

Osmanlıcada bu konuda oturmuş ve yerleşmiş terimler pek yoktu. *Muayyeniyet* ve *gayr-i muayyeniyet* sözcüklerinin bu terimlerin fizik alanındaki anlamını karşılamak maksadiyle kullanılabileceği âşıkârdır. Fakat bu anlamlar çok genel ve geniş olduğundan, bu sözcüklerin, gerçek anlamiyle terim sayılmaması gerekir. Ayrıca, bu sözcükler söz konusu felsefî anlamlarını karşılamamaktadırlar. Bu terimlerin felsefî anlamını karşılamak üzere de *icâbiyye* ve *lâicâbiyye* sözcüklerimiz vardı. Fakat bunlar da çok dar bir çevre dışında tanınmamaktaydı. (Sayılı 1978: 502)

Ottoman really had no settled and established terms in this subject. It is manifest that *muayyeniyet* [definiteness] and *gayr-i muayyeniyet* [non-definiteness] could be used for the purpose of representing the meaning of these terms in the field of physics. But since these meanings were very general and broad, these words are not to be regarded as technical terms in the true sense. Moreover, these words cannot meet the philosophical meanings we are talking about. To meet the philosophical meaning of these terms, we also had the words *icâbiyye* [determinism] and *lâicâbiyye* [indeterminism].[20] These, however, were not known outside a very narrow circle.

Sayılı goes on to say that no agreement has been reached on new equivalents for 'determinism' and 'indeterminism', though various terms are in use: *gerektirim*, *gerekircilik*, and *belirlenimcilik* for the first and *belirlenmezcilik* for the second. But obviously these are no more widely used or known than were *icâbiyye* and *lâicâbiyye* in the Ottoman period.

Nevertheless, though his theme is the language of science and teaching, he has time for some less technical terms: 'to translate' and 'century', as we have seen. He considers (Sayılı 1978: 441–2) that insufficient thought was given to the consequences of replacing *kütüphane* by *kitaplık*: what happens to 'librarianship'? In fact the *kitaplıkçılık* he feared has not won the day over *kütüphanecilik*, though *kitaplık bilimi* is used for 'library science'. Another problem he could have added was how to say 'a library of twenty thousand books'; clearly 'yirmibin kitaplık bir kitaplık' won't do, and to say 'volumes' instead of 'books'—'yirmibin ciltlik bir kitaplık'—does not mean the same.

One curious coinage of his which had no success was *yanır*. Speaking of *taraf* [A] 'side' and its derivatives *taraflı* 'partisan' and *tarafsız* 'impartial', he remarks (Sayılı 1978: 402) that some people use the pure Turkish *yan*, *yanlı*, and *yansız* instead. He continues:

Dilimizdeki *kocunmak* ve *yağır* sözcüklerinden bu bakımdan yararlanma yoluna gidilebilir. Bunlardan her ikisi de aslında at için kullanılan sözcükler olmalarına rağmen, *kocunmak* sözcüğü daha genel ve mecazî anlamda da sık sık kullanılmaktadır. Ayrıca bu sözcükler *yanır* ve *gocunmak* biçiminde de telaffuz edilmektedir. *Yağır* veya *yanır* atın omuzları arasındaki yer ve bu yerde eğer vurmasından açılan yara anlamındadır. Yağırı olan at bu yarasından kocunduğu için bu iki sözcük arasında her zaman için hatırlanan bir çağrışım mevcuttur. Bu belirgin anlamıyle, *yağır* veya *yanır* Avrupa dillerindeki *bias* ve *biais* gibi sözcükleri akla getirmektedir.

Kanımca, *yanlı* ve *yansız* yerine *yanırlı* ve *yanırsız* sözcüklerini kullanmak daha yerinde olur. Böylece *yanır* telaffuz şekline aslına yakın özel bir anlam verilmiş olur ve dili bir yerde fakirleştirmek yerine tam tersi yapılmış olur . . . *Tarafsız* veya *yanırsız* karşılığı olarak İngilizcede *neutral* ve bir de gramer terimi olarak *neuter* sözcükleriyle karşılaşır.

From this point of view, one may resort to utilizing the words *kocunmak* and *yağır*, which we have in our language. Although both are originally used of horses, *kocunmak* is frequently used in a more general and metaphorical sense. Moreover, they are also pronounced *yanır* and *gocunmak*.[21] *Yağır* or *yanır* means the horse's withers and the sore made there by saddling. Since the horse with a saddle-sore is scared of this wound he has, there is an

---

[20] The first of these is an Arabic abstract noun of Turkish manufacture, derived from *îğâb* 'making obligatory, making unavoidable'; the *lâ* of the second is the Arabic for 'not'.

[21] *Gocunmak* is an Anatolian pronunciation of *kocunmak*. See Lewis (1988: 4, end of §9).

unforgettable association of ideas between these two words.[22] With this specific meaning, *yağır* or *yanır* calls to mind such words in the European languages as *bias* or *biais* [F].

In my opinion, it will be more appropriate to use *yanırlı* and *yanırsız* instead of *yanlı* and *yansız*. In this way, the pronunciation *yanır* will have been given a special meaning close to its origin and instead of impoverishing the language at one point the exact opposite will have been achieved . . . The sense of *tarafsız* or *yanırsız* is conveyed in English by *neutral* or, as a grammatical term, *neuter.*

It is not surprising that this suggestion did not catch on. The progression from a saddle-sore that makes a horse shy away from a curry-comb, to a bias that makes a person shy away from a course of action, is more than a little far-fetched. But Sayılı did explain the thinking behind his suggestion, which is more than Ataç was in the habit of doing.

---

[22] The reference is to the proverb 'Al kaşağıyı, gir ahıra, yağırı olan gocunur' (Take the curry-comb, go into the stable, and the one with saddle-sores will be scared), much like our 'If the cap fits, wear it.'

7

Ingredients

As we have seen, the reformers' overriding desire was to get rid of Arabic and Persian borrowings, even if the proposed replacements were equally non-Turkish: *hudut* [A] 'frontier' was dislodged by *sınır* [G] (*sýnuron*), *millet* [A] 'nation' by *ulus* [M], *şehir* [P] 'city' by the Sogdian *kent* 'small town, village', *ıstılah* [A] 'technical term' by *terim* [F]. But at least these were natural-born words. This chapter discusses the more noteworthy suffixes used, even invented, in the creation of *Öztürkçe*. The squeamish reader may find some of what follows disturbing.

Before we come on to suffixes, a word about prefixes. At the time when TDK was doing its best to prove that Turkish and the Indo-European languages were akin, efforts were made to create words by using prefixes, against the genius of Turkish. For 'sub-', *ast* was imported from one or other of the Central Asian dialects in which it means 'underside', like Turkish *alt*. It was soon shortened to *as-*, which survives in *asteğmen* 'second lieutenant' and *assubay* 'non-commissioned officer'. In the late 1930s *astüzük* was used for 'supplementary by-laws', *asbaşkan* for 'vice-president', and *askurul* for 'subcommittee'. The first syllable of *yardım* 'help' was prefixed to *direktör* to make *yardirektör* 'assistant director', to *başkan* to make *yarbaşkan* 'vice-president', and to *kurul* to make *yarkurul* 'subcommittee'; this and *asbaşkan* may still be met with occasionally. One other *yar-* survives, in *yarbay* 'lieutenant-colonel', *bay* being the Öztürkçe replacement for *bey* 'commander'. The first syllable of *albay* 'colonel' is also an abbreviation, of *alay* 'regiment', The *gen* of *genel* 'general' was similarly pressed into service as a prefix, a use that survives in *gensoru* 'parliamentary question'. The *tüm* of *tümgeneral* 'major-general' is the first syllable of *tümen* 'division', while the *or* of *orgeneral* 'general' is from *ordu* 'army'. What inspired these truncations was Russian abbreviations like *Sovnarkom* for 'Sovyet Narodnykh Komissarov' 'Council of People's Commissars'. It should be remembered that in those days Turco-Soviet relations were, at least outwardly, cordial.

Another attempt at creating a prefix was *arsı-* 'inter-', an arbitrary corruption of the postposition *arası*, but its use did not go beyond *arsıulusal*, which gave rise to one of the successive designations of the Izmir International Fair: İzmir Beynelmilel Fuarı, İzmir Arsıulusal Fuarı, İzmir Enternasyonel Fuarı, İzmir Uluslararası Fuarı. There is some dispute about the legitimacy of the widely used *öngörmek* 'to foresee', there being no precedent for incorporating an adverb into a verb. There is no such dispute about prefixing *ön* to nouns, as in *önsezi* 'premonition', the *ön* here being an adjective, as in many respectable old words like *önkapı* 'front door' and *önoda* 'antechamber'. So too with *alt*, as in *altgeçit* or *alt geçit* 'underpass'. Now for some suffixes.

-çe/ça. Three old borrowings from Serbo-Croat—*kıraliçe* 'queen', *çariçe* 'tsarina', *imparatoriçe* 'empress'—supplied a feminine suffix, which Turkish lacked. Added to *tanrı* 'god', it made *tanrıça*, the Öztürkçe for *ilâhe* [A] 'goddess'. That was its sole contribution to the language reform.

There is another *-çe/ça* that, unlike the *-ce* of *düşünce* 'thought' and *eğlence* 'amusement', is added to nouns. It is a Persian diminutive suffix, seen in *paça* (*pāča* [P]) 'trotter' from *pā* [P] 'foot', and *lûgatçe* 'glossary' from *lûgat* [A] 'dictionary'. It provided the reform with one or two hybrids like *tarihçe* 'short history', and *dilekçe* 'petition' from *dilek* 'wish'.

-enek. Once occurring in very few words—for example, *görenek* 'usage' and the archaic *değenek* 'stick, wand' (now *değnek*, from *değ-* 'to touch, reach')—it was given new life by İsmet İnönü. On the pattern of *görenek*, he created *gelenek* for 'tradition', which has totally replaced *an'ane* [A], while its adjective *geleneksel* has done the same for *an'anevî* [A] 'traditional'. Other neologisms made with this suffix are *olanak* 'possibility', *seçenek* 'alternative', *yazanak* 'report', and *tutanak* 'minutes of a meeting'.

Apropos minutes, those of the first three Language Congresses (1932, 1934, 1936) were called *Müzakere Zabıtları*; the fourth (1942) *Toplantı Tutulgaları* (*tutulga* is the equivalent given for *zabıtname* in *Cep Kılavuzu* (1935)); the fifth and subsequent ones (1945–); *Tutanaklar*. Those of the Congresses of the Republican People's Party: 1934 *Tutulga*, 1938 *Zabıt*, 1939 *Zabıtlar*, 1947 *Tutanak*.

-ev/-v. The origins of this suffix lie far from Turkey. In Bashkurt and Kazakh the infinitive ends not in *-mek/mak* but in *-v* (preceded by the appropriate vowel after consonant-stems), and in Kirghiz and Tatar *-u* or *-ü*. The respective equivalents in these languages of *almak* 'to take' are *alıv, aluv, alü, alü*, and of *görmek* 'to see' *küriv, körüv, körü, kürü*. Hence several neologisms: *görev* 'duty', *söylev* 'speech', *işlev* 'function', *ödev* 'obligation', *sınav* 'examination', *türev* 'derivative, by-product'. Another was *saylav*, Kazakh and Kazan for 'to choose', used in the early years of the reform instead of *milletvekili* or *meb'us* 'deputy'. *Ödev* is from *ödemek* 'to pay', and for a glimpse of how it struck sensitive Turks we only have to imagine how we would feel if told we should abandon the foreign *obligation* and adopt a new word constructed from an English root and a German suffix, say *paykeit*. Nor can one overlook the possibility that *ödev* owes something to the French *devoir*. As for *görev*, this is how it is explained in Eyuboğlu's (1988) etymological dictionary, a work remarkable for its shiftiness: 'Sözcüğün sonuna getirilen v sesiyle ad türetme, seyrek de olsa, Turk dilinde vardır. *Edilce-v/edilcev* (yapılması, edilmesi gereken), Anadolu halk ağzında ar. **sünnet** karşılığı söylenir … *Gece-v/gecev* (gerçekte gece evi, tarlalarda yapılan, geceleyin ekinleri kollamak için kurulan kulübe)'

(Noun-derivation by adding a *v*, though rare, does exist in the Turkish language. *Edilce-v/edilcev* ('what must be done') is said in popular Anatolian dialect for the Arabic *sünnet*[1]. . . *gece-v/gecev* (in fact *gece evi*, a hut made in the fields and erected for watching the crops by night).) *Edilcev* appears in *Derleme Sözlüğü* (1963–88) (misplaced at v. 1665) as being recorded for *sünnet* at Ünye in the vilayet of Ordu, which makes 'Anadolu halk ağzında' seem a bit of an exaggeration. No explanation is offered for the peculiar-looking *edilce*. Nor does Eyuboğlu strengthen his case by citing another -*v*, in *gecev*, which he himself recognizes as an abraded form of *ev* 'house'. To revert to *görev*: one can see a connection between the notions of obligation and payment, but why should a noun derived from *görmek* 'to see' mean 'duty'? The answer requires a digression.

One of Ataç's neologisms, invented in 1947, is *koşul*, now widely used in writing instead of *şart* [A] for 'condition'. Ataç extracted it from the expression *şart koşmak* 'to impose a condition'. (*Koşmak*, besides meaning 'to run', is also used transitively in the sense of 'to attach', as in 'atı arabaya koştuk' (we hitched the horse to the cart).) The once unproductive noun-suffix -*ul* occurs in a few words such as *çökül* 'sediment' and *kumul* 'sandhill'. Tack it on to *koş*- and you have *koşul*, which should mean, if anything, 'attachment'. But it does not; it means 'condition', though it has not replaced *şart* in the sense of 'prerequisite'. This gives us the clue to *görev*. It will be remembered that *görmek*, besides 'to see', means 'to perform' (compare the English 'to see to'). In the old days when 'duty' was *vazife* [A], 'he has done his duty' was 'vazifesini görmüştür'. Just as *koşul* owes its existence to *koşmak*, which in *şart koşmak* is no more than an auxiliary verb, so *görev* owes its existence to the auxiliary verb *görmek*. I don't think that a Turk of any sensibility could bear to say 'görevini görmüştür'; it has to be 'görevini yapmıştır' or 'görevini yerine getirmiştir'. The lexicographer D. Mehmet Doğan, however, in his volume of essays (1984: 135), perversely combines the Ottoman for 'to perform' with this ill-conceived item of *Öztürkçe*, writing 'görevini ifa etmiştir'.

-*ey/y* is a zombie, like -*it* and -*meç*, raised from its long sleep and put back to work by the reformers. Before they got hold of it, it occurred in a handful of words, notably *kolay* 'easy'; *güney*, common in Anatolian dialects for 'sunny place'; and *kuzay*, *kozay* or *kuzey*, anciently and in dialect 'sunless place'. These forms were explained as follows in an illuminating paper by Jean Deny (1937).[2] *Kol*, besides 'arm', anciently meant 'hand', as it still does in much of Central Asia. *Gün* means 'sun' as well as 'day': 'Gün doğdu/battı' (The sun rose/set). *Kuz* is the side of a mountain out of reach of the sun. The -*ey/y* adds the notion of being in the domain of what is denoted by the noun to which it is suffixed. As Deny puts it, 'Les détails que nous venons de donner permettent donc, à notre avis, de *rattacher en toute sécurité le mot* kol-ay *à la formation de dérivés en* ey *et d'en restituer le sens*

---

[1] The Arabic *sunna* means 'practice of the Prophet'. Its Turkish form *sünnet* has the special sense of 'circumcision'.
[2] I am indebted to Professor Şükrü Elçin for a copy of this article.

primitif dans ces termes: "qui est exposé à l'emprise de la main, qui est sous la main, bien en main, maniable".' Tarama Dergisi (1934) gives *kuzey* as one of ten possible replacements for *şimal* 'north', with a note: 'Gölgede kalan yer man. [= manasına]. "Güney" zıddı' (In the sense of place staying in shadow. Opposite of *güney*). *Kuzey* (the non-harmonic form being due to analogy with *güney*) and *güney* are now usual, even in speech, for 'north' and 'south' respectively.

The reformers, who were unlikely to have seen Deny's paper (and if they had?), added *-ey/ay/y* indiscriminately to verb-stems, nouns, and adjectives. From *ol-* 'to be, happen', *uza-* 'to extend', and *dene-* 'to try', they made nouns: *olay* 'incident', *uzay* 'space', and *deney* 'experiment'; from *yap-* 'to make', the adjective *yapay* 'artificial'; from *yön* 'direction' and *yüz* 'face', the nouns *yöney* 'vector' and *yüzey* 'surface'; from the adjective *düz* 'flat', the noun *düzey* 'level'. In 1938, when the Turkish Navy required names for its new 'Ay' class of submarine, the same hard-working suffix was added to the verbs *atıl-* 'to assail', *batır-* 'to sink', *saldır-* 'to attack', and *yıldır-* 'to daunt': *Atılay, Batıray, Saldıray, Yıldıray*.[3] It is hard to deduce from these examples what the function of *-ay* was supposed to be.

Yüzey, düzey, and *birey* 'individual' all appear in *Cep Kılavuzu* (1935). *Birey*, which had already appeared in *Tarama Dergisi* (1934), is of more respectable ancestry than the rest of what we might, taking a leaf from the Turkish Navy's book, call the Ay class of neologism. *Birey* is the form that *biregü* 'individual', used in Ottoman between the fourteenth and sixteenth centuries, would have taken if it had survived.

-ge. Turkish has an abundance of word-building suffixes but not all of them seem to have a specific meaning.[4] Take *-ge/ga*, for instance. In OT it was used mostly as an ending of names of birds, animals, and insects, many still extant: *karga* 'crow', *çekirge* 'locust', 'grasshopper'. It also appears in a few other nouns, such as *süpürge* 'broom', *dalga* 'wave', *yonga* 'wood chippings'. The reformers used it to make a number of neologisms, including *dizge* 'system' (*diz-* 'to arrange in order'), *genelge* 'circular, notice' (*genel* 'general'), *gösterge* 'indicator' (*göster-* 'to show'), and the question-begging *sömürge* 'colony' (*sömür-* 'to exploit').

-gi/ki is a respectable old suffix, forming numerous nouns from verb-stems: from *duy-* 'to feel', *duygu* 'feeling'; from *as-* 'to hang', *askı* 'hanger'; from *sar-* 'to wrap', *sargı* 'bandage'. A number of successful neologisms have been made with it, such as *bitki* 'plant' from *bit-* 'to grow', and *tepki* 'reaction' from *tep-* 'to kick'. One neologism formed with it, however, has a bad name among conservatives: from *et-* 'to do', *etki* 'influence', 'effect', which has largely supplanted *tesir* [A]. The word exists in the speech of several regions of Western Anatolia, but not in that sense; its meanings are 'ill treatment, distress, excessive difficulty', less commonly

---

[3] *Saldıray* was commissioned in July 1938, the other three in 1939, *Batıray* in March, *Atılay* in May, *Yıldıray* in August.

[4] One is reminded of the Esperanto suffix *-um*: 'suffixe peu employé, et qui reçoit différents sens aisément suggérés par le contexte et la signification de la racine à laquelle il est joint' (Zamenhof 1931: 177).

'witchcraft'. But the conservative scholar Faruk Timurtaş (1979: 47–8) sees more in it to object to than that:

Yardımcı fiillerden prensip itibariyle yeni kelimeler türetilmez . . . 'etmek' kelimesi, bâzan halk ağızlarında, zikredilmesi uygun olmayan veya ayıp sayılan kelimelerin yerini tutmak üzere kullanılır. Meselâ, büyük ve küçük abdestini yapmak 'etmek' kelimesiyle anlatılır. Böyle bir kullanılış İstanbul ağzında ve yazı dilinde de görülür . . . Hiçbir ağızda etki'ye 'tesir' mânâsı verilmemiştir. Bu mânâ sonradan Kurumca uydurulmuştur.

In principle, new words cannot be derived from auxiliary verbs . . . The word *etmek* is sometimes used in popular dialects to replace words that it is unseemly or considered shameful to mention. For example, answering either call of nature is conveyed by the word *etmek*. Such a use is seen both in the spoken language of Istanbul and in the written language . . . In no dialect has *etki* been given the sense of *tesir*. This sense has been concocted *ex post facto* by the Language Society.

-im/m. The flood of new words incorporating this suffix seems to have started with *anlam*, which has now virtually displaced *mânâ* 'meaning'. *Anlam* was one of fourteen alternatives offered in *Tarama Dergisi* (1934), which noted it as used instead of *mânâ* in the vilayet of Konya. *Derleme Sözlüğü* (1963–82), however, shows *añlam* as used in just two villages, not for *mânâ* but for *anlayış* 'sagacity' or *duygu* 'feeling'. Those who recorded it must have either misread their notes or doctored them. *-m* originally indicated a single action, as in *ölüm* 'death', *doğum* 'birth'. Long before the language reform got into its stride, this limitation had begun to weaken, *Yarım* 'a single act of splitting', a verbal noun of *yar-* 'to split', became a concrete noun, 'half'. The meaning of *alım*, from *al-* 'to buy', was extended from a single act of purchase to purchasing in general, and the same happened with *satım* from *sat-* 'to sell', so that 'alım satım' came to mean not a single transaction but buying and selling, business. Similarly *dikim* from *dik-* 'to sew' means not just one stitch but sewing. The suffix has been enormously productive: *basım* 'printing', *dağıtım* 'distribution', *anlatım* 'narration', *oturum* 'session', *seçim* 'election', *üretim* 'production', and countless more. *Kalıtım* 'heredity' was not made from a verb but from Ataç's *kalıt* 'inheritance'. *Ortam* 'environment, ambiance' and *toplum* 'community, society', which one sees and hears all the time, are equally illegitimate, *ortam* being from the noun *orta* 'middle', and *toplum* from the adjective *toplu* 'collective'.

-it/t. An ancient addition to verb-stems: *geçit* 'mountain-pass' or 'parade' from *geç-* 'to pass', *içit* (archaic) 'drink' from *iç-* 'to drink', *binit* (provincial) 'animal for riding' from *bin-* 'to mount'. It has produced many serviceable neologisms: *konut* 'abode' from *kon-* 'to settle', *taşıt* 'vehicle' from *taşı-* 'to carry', *dikit* 'stalagmite' from *dik-* 'to plant', *sarkıt* 'stalactite' from *sark-* 'to hang down', *yakıt* 'fuel' from *yak-* 'to burn'. The ingenious *soyut* 'abstract' from *soy-* 'to strip', which has replaced *mücerret*, was due to Ataç, but to replace its antonym *müşahhas* 'concrete' he added the suffix to the adjective *som* 'solid', not to a verb-stem. Nobody seems to mind; *soyut* and *somut* make a neat pair. *Örgüt* for 'organization', however, has its critics.

It is the result of cross-breeding between *örgü* 'plait' and *organ*, a late nineteenth-century borrowing from the French *organe*. *Örgen*, a face-saving Turkicization of *organ*, will be found in dictionaries but is unlikely to be encountered in real life. A postage stamp issued around 1988 featured *Organ Bağışı* 'Organ Donation', and *Organ Nakli* 'Organ Transplant'. This followed in the tradition of an earlier stamp dedicated to *Sıtma Eradikasyonu* 'the eradication of malaria'. *Örgüt* has acquired a sinister connotation, being used mostly of terrorist organizations, except by some newspapers, notably *Cumhuriyet*, that are committed to *Öztürkçe*. The remainder of the press and most individuals prefer the Ottoman *teşkilât* or the French *organizasyon*.

Other current malformations using *-it/t* are *karşıt* 'contrary', one of Ataç's, from the postposition *karşı* 'opposite', and *eşit* 'equal' from the noun *eş* 'mate'. *Tarama Dergisi* (1934) gave *eşit* as used in Istanbul for 'equal', but the absence of the word from the twelve-volume *Derleme Sözlüğü* (1963–82) makes one wonder.

-meç/maç. A vice to which the reformers were prone was the use of suffixes that had ceased to be productive—that is, that had anciently been used in word formation but were no longer. How would English-speakers receive some Big Brother's decree outlawing the Latin 'corporation' and replacing it with 'bodydom'? Kâmile İmer (1976: 57) has a pertinent observation:

Türetme yoluyla yeni sözcükler yapılırken dilin işlek eklerinin kullanılması dil devrimin bir an önce, uzun süre istemeden başarılı olmasını sağlayabilir. İşleklik yitirmiş eklere bu özelliklerini yeniden kazandırmak güç olmakta, belki uzun süre gerekmektedir. Bu nedenle işlek olmayan eklerle türetilen sözcükler, kökü bilinse bile, dili kullananda kavramla ilgili çağrışıma yol açamamaktadır. Örneğin, *-maç/-meç* ekine (*sarmaç* 'bigudi', *dilmaç* 'tercüman', v.b. [ve başkaları]) Türk Dil Devriminden sonra işlerlik kazandırılmaya çalışılmaktaysa da, şimdilik bu ekle yapılan sözcüklerin dilin işlek ekleriyle yapılan sözcükler oranında tutunmadığı göze çarpmaktadır.

When new words are being made by derivation, the use of the productive suffixes of the language can ensure that the language reform is successful very soon and will not take a long time. It becomes difficult, and may take long, to restore this quality to suffixes that have lost their productivity. That is why words derived with the help of unproductive suffixes, even if their roots be known, are incapable of arousing in the user of the language any relevant association of ideas with the concept. For example, since the start of the language reform there have been attempts to put the suffix *-maç/meç* (as in *sarmaç* 'hair-curler', *dilmaç* 'interpreter', etc.) back to work. At the moment, however, it is obvious that words constructed with this suffix have not caught on to the same extent as words constructed with the productive suffixes of the language.

She does not make it clear that *sarmaç* and *dilmaç* are not on the same level. While *dilmaç* is an old word (though its Turkish origin is far from certain), *sarmaç*, from *sar-* 'to wrap', was a failed attempt to replace *bigudi*, a French word still current among Turkish coiffeurs and their clients. If *dilmaç* really is Turkish, it is the only example of *-maç* attached to a noun and one of the very few examples until modern times of its forming anything other than names of foodstuffs (Clauson 1972: pp. xliii, 500; Doerfer 1963–75: ii, §1010.) Among these names are *tutmaç*, *bulamaç*, and *uğmaç*. Redhouse (1890) defines *tutmaç* as a dish made of stewed mutton in gobbets, with chickpeas. In Redhouse (1968) it is fresh-made pastry cut in strips and cooked with meat and yoghurt. Redhouse (1890) ingeniously but unconvincingly explains it as *tutma aş*, 'holding-food', and either recipe would clearly hold one till the next meal. Doerfer (1963–75: ii, §876) records another popular etymology, no less ingenious but even less plausible: Alexander the Great and his comrades had lost their way and were wandering about with nothing to eat. They said to him, 'Bizni tutma aç' (Don't keep us hungry).[5] Whereupon Alexander, having been supplied with the name, invented the dish. The other two names of dishes are formed from the verbs *bulamak* 'to bedaub' and *uğmak* 'to rub and crumble in the palm of the hand', both being thick soups. Other pre-modern appearances of *-maç* are in *dönemeç* 'bend in a road' (*dön-* 'to turn'), *kanırtmaç* 'lever' (*kanırt-* 'to bend') and *yırtmaç* 'vent in a garment' (*yırt-* 'to tear').

Except in *demeç* 'official statement' (*de-* 'to say'), which may owe something to *démarche*, it has been little used by the reformers. *Günlemeç*, which was *Tarama Dergisi*'s (1934) offering for *tarih* 'date', was spasmodically used during 1934 in draft legislation, notably in the clause 'Bu kanun neşri günlemecinden muteberdir' (This law is in force from its date of publication), but every *günlemecinden* was replaced by *tarihinden* before reaching the statute book.

-men/man. One word that had to go was *mütehassıs* 'expert', not just because its initial *m* and its lack of vowel harmony branded it as Arabic but also because it was too easily confused with another Arabic borrowing, *mütehassis* 'sensitive'. Its replacement was *uzman*, said to have been invented by Köprülü, although he never used it himself. The first syllable was an old word for 'skilled craftsman' and the second might have been the intensive suffix seen in *şişman* 'fat' and *kocaman* 'huge'. But it was not; it was another *-man*, long familiar to Turks in the word *vatman* 'tram-driver' (sometimes used in place of *asansörcü* for the operator of a lift or elevator). For the benefit of readers born since the heyday of the tram or streetcar, it should be explained that *vatman* is the Turkish spelling of the French *wattman*, compounded of the two English words *watt*, the unit of electric power, and *man*.

Fired by the success of *uzman*, the reformers went around adding the suffix to verb-stems, producing such misbegotten words as *öğretmen* 'teacher', *yazman* 'secretary', *okutman* 'lector', and *seçmen* 'voter'. *Koruman* 'trustee' is found in legal language. Less successful was the attempt to replace *cerrah* [A] 'surgeon' by *yarman*, from *yarmak* 'to split'. Its failure was due to the good sense of Turks at large and of Turkish surgeons in particular, who prefer to call themselves *operatör* anyway.

---

[5] For *bizni*, see von Gabain (1950: 92). Alexander the Great's men of course spoke Old Turkic, not modern Turkish.

This suffix also helped to inspire the creation of *teğmen* 'first lieutenant'.[6] After the promulgation of the Surnames Law in 1934, İbrahim Necmi, for many years Secretary-General ('Genel Yazman') of the Language Society, chose 'Dilmen' for his surname, compounded of Turkish *dil* 'language' and non-Turkish *man*.

The suffix appears also in *barmen* 'barman' (which by the mid-1990s had acquired a feminine form, *barmeyd*, replacing the earlier *kadın barmen*), *formen* 'foreman', *sportmen* 'sportsman', and *rekortmen* 'record holder'. It is not clear why the last syllable of all these words except *uzman* (the inspiration for the *man* of which is plausibly reputed to be the second syllable of German *Fachmann* 'expert') is -*men* rather than -*man* as the laws of vowel harmony and the analogy of *vatman* would have led one to expect. It may be significant that Russian uses *rekordmen*, whereas *recordman* is a French invention (1889). In the early 1950s the façade of the İnönü Stadium in Istanbul bore the slogan 'Sportmen, Centilmen İnsandır' (The sportsman is a gentlemanly person), but *sporcu* is more usual nowadays.

Other proposed -*men* words, which fell by the wayside, were *savaşman* 'warrior', *öçmen* 'vengeful', *bakman* 'inspector', *uçman* 'aviator', and *ökmen* 'judge'.

-*sel/sal* is the most controversial of all the products of the language reform. In brief, its origin is the suffix of the French *culturel* and *principal*. The purifiers wanted a native substitute for the Arabic and Persian adjectival suffix -*î* as in *tarihî* 'historical' and *siyasî* 'political'. They failed to find one, because Turkish, thanks to its use of nouns as qualifiers, has no need of an all-purpose adjectival ending. -*li* does not fit the bill; *tarihli* means 'having a history', as in 'şanlı tarihli bir şehir' (a city with a glorious history), or 'bearing a date' as in '4 Haziran tarihli mektubunuz' (your letter dated 4 June), but it does not translate 'historical' as in 'historical research', the Turkish for which is 'tarih araştırmaları'. As Ziya Gökalp (1923: 112–13) pointed out, the use of -*î* ought to be and easily can be avoided;[7] there is no need to say 'Edebî Hafta' for 'Literary Week', the Turkish for which is *Edebiyat Haftası* 'Literature Week'. For 'vital problem' we don't have to say 'hayatî mesele' when we can say 'hayat meselesi'. Gökalp was not calling for the total abandonment of -*î*; he would never have given up *aklî*, for example, the meaning of which—'pertaining to the mind, intellectual'—was quite different from that of *akıllı* 'possessed of mind, intelligent'.

---

[6] *Mülâzim*, the Ottoman term for 'lieutenant', also meant 'adherent', so the *teğ-* must be from *teğmek* (a variation on *değmek* 'to touch'), given in *Tarama Dergisi* (1934) for *temas etmek* 'to make contact' and presumably the source of Atatürk's *teğet* 'tangent'. *Teğmen* may well be an echo of *seğmen* (from the Persian *sagbān* 'dog-keeper'), originally the keepers of the Sultan's hounds, later incorporated in the Janissaries. *Seğmen* or *seymen* survives as the name for the armed and mounted young men in regional costume who feature in processions at weddings and on festal days.

[7] Gökalp made two exceptions: when it was added to Turkish names to make musical terms, such as *varsağı* (now written and pronounced *varsağı*), a ballad-metre of the Varsaks, a Tatar tribe of southern Anatolia, and when it was added to Turkish nouns to make adjectives of colour, such as *kurşunî* 'leaden' and *gümüşî* 'silvery', for it then became a Turkish suffix, words thus formed being exclusive to Turkish.

Unaware or heedless of Gökalp's advice, the reformers took the ending of the French *culturel* and used that.[8] It was not until 1983 that *Türkçe Sözlük* came clean and showed both *kültür* and *kültürel* as borrowed from French; previous editions had shown the noun but not the adjective as a French borrowing, the implication being that the latter was derived from the former by adding a Turkish suffix. In 1934 Ahmet Cevat Emre put a French *-el* on to *ses* 'voice' to make *sesel* for 'vowel', to which for good measure he added *-ik* for the French *-ique*, making *seselik* for 'vocalic'. He also manufactured a word for 'euphonic', *yeğçavlik*, from OT *yeğ* 'good' and *çav* 'voice', plus *-lik* for the French *-lique* as in *vocalique*. Let no kind-hearted reader mistake the *lik* of *yeğçavlik* for the Turkish abstract-noun suffix; the lack of vowel harmony—*lik* not *lık*—shows that it is not.[9] From the obsolete *sü* 'army', İbrahim Necmi Dilmen manufactured *süel* for 'military' in 1935 (*Ulus*, 1 July 1935; Levend 1972: 423).

Until then, Turkish had had no denominal suffix in *l*,[10] but that did not deter the reformers. The Arabic *siyāsa* 'politics, policy' being, as they claimed, obviously derived from the Turkish (actually Mongolian) *yasa* 'law', they saw no need to discard its Turkish form *siyaset*. But *siyasî* 'political' was another matter, because for some inscrutable reason they never claimed that the Arabic suffix *-ī*, whence Turkish *-î*, was originally Turkish. They therefore replaced *siyasî* with *siyasal*.[11] Next for the high jump was *millî* 'national'. The Arabic *millet* having been dislodged by the Mongolian *ulus*, *millî* became *ulusal*—that is to say, the 'pure Turkish' replacement for the Arabic *millî* is half Mongolian and half French, a curiously outlandish way for a Turk to express 'national'.[12] Then there was *kudsî* 'holy', the Arabic *ḳudsī*. *Kuds* plus *-al* should have added up to *kudsal*, but, as the first syllable happened to resemble the Turkish *kut* 'good luck', the *d* of *kudsî* was replaced by the *t* of *kut*, while its *s* was retained, and 'holy' became *kutsal*. As the excuse for this word's existence was that it derived from *kut*, if one subtracted *kut* the remaining *sal* had to be a suffix. Coupled with the fact that the *-al* of *siyasal* and *ulusal* as well chanced to be preceded by an *s*, that seems to have been what

---

[8] The more obdurate *Öztürkçeciler* such as Haydar Ediskun deny this, vigorously but unpersuasively. See the controversy between him and Zeynep Korkmaz in the pages of *Türk Dili*, 15–16 (1965–7). See also Tahsin Banguoğlu, 'Nispet Sıfatları ve -sel, -sal', four articles in *Dünya*, 15–17 Sept. 1965 and 19 Sept. 1965, repr. in Banguoğlu (1987: 264–77).

[9] These two words, *seselik* and *yeğçavlik*, occur in Emre's paper presented to the Second Kurultay: 'Türkçenin Hint-Avrupa Diliyle Mukayesesi', Kurultay 1934 (= *Türk Dili*, 11 (1935), 2–12).

[10] OT had a deverbal adjective-suffix: *-l* after vowels and *-il/ıl* after consonants, as in *kızıl* 'red' from *kız-* 'to be hot'.

[11] Gallagher (1971: 169) says that *siyasal* was 'actually an innovation of the nineteenth century Tanzimat period for the Arabic-Turkish *siyasî*', a dubious assertion for which he gives no evidence.

[12] The National Library has retained its name of Millî Kütüphane. Some years ago the author asked the Librarian how it had escaped becoming Ulusal Kitaplık. With evident glee she replied that its name was enshrined in its charter, which no one had got round to amending and, since the state takeover of TDK in 1983, with luck no one ever would. It is fair to add that a reputable youngish Turkish scholar with whom I discussed the alternative words for 'library' did not find Millî Kütüphane more impressive than Ulusal Kitaplık, but generously told me that *kütüphane* not *kitaplik* is still regularly used of one's personal library.

launched -*sel/sal* on its merry way: *elektriksel* and *fiziksel, kimyasal* 'chemical', *tarihsel* 'historical', and so on *ad infinitum.*

The lusty infant was not slow to extend its sway; having started life as a denominal suffix, it soon became deverbal too: *görsel* 'visual' from *gör-* 'to see', with a matching *işitsel* 'auditory' from *işit-* 'to hear'. For 'educational', *eğitimsel* has an even less legitimate rival: *eğitsel.* And now, to change the metaphor, in the written language -*sel* sweeps all before it.[13] It has even produced a noun, *sorunsal* from *sorun* 'problem', to translate the French *la problématique*, English 'problematic(s)'.

Those who claim -*sel/sal* as an authentic Turkish suffix adduce two words in justification: *uysal* 'compliant' and *kumsal* 'sandy tract'. *Uysal* must be connected with *uy-* 'to conform' (OT *ūd-* 'to follow'), but no one knows quite how. One suggestion is that the ancient deverbal suffix -*l* was added to *uy-sa-* 'to want to conform'; compare *susa-* 'to thirst' and *mühimse-* 'to regard as important' and its *Öztürkçe* replacement *önemse-* (Lewis 1988: 230). The trouble is that -*se-* was never added to verb-stems but only to nouns and adjectives. As for *kumsal*, while Redhouse (1890) and the *Kamus* give it only as a noun, all recent dictionaries, including Redhouse (1968), give it also as an adjective, 'sandy'. One does not have to be a conspiracy theorist to believe that it was not an adjective until the reformers set out to justify their new adjective-suffix -*sel/sal.*

Time was, to express 'psychological illness' you would say 'ruh hastalığı' (illness of the psyche). Now you say 'ruhsal hastalık' (psychish illness), unless you prefer 'psikolojik hastalık'. The use of -*sel/sal* may speed the task of translation from works in West European languages, but it goes against the grain of Turkish and has markedly affected the style of much modern writing, particularly on technical matters. 'Literary criticism', once 'edebiyat tenkidi', became 'edebiyat eleştirisi', then 'yazın eleştirisi'. Some writers talk about 'yazınsal eleştiri', which is a direct translation of 'literary criticism' but to a literate Turk does not convey criticism of literature but criticism which is literary.

Kâmile İmer (1976: 57) strikes a warning note:

Dil devrimi sırasında herhangi bir kavramın anlatımında, onu karşılayacak sözcük dilde bulunamıyor ve türetilemiyorsa yabancı dildeki anlamının etkisi altında yerli dil öğeleriyle çevirme işi yapılabilir. Bu yöntem her ne kadar yerli dil öğelerinin kullanımını sağlamaktaysa da çok başvurulduğunda dilin kendi anlatım özelliklerinden uzaklaşmasına yol açabileceği düşünmeli ve zorda kalmadıkça başvurulmamalıdır. Çünkü her ulusun kavramları adlandırışındaki tutum—kimi benzerlikler olmasına karşın—genel olarak değişiktir.

In the course of language reform, if, in expressing any concept, no word corresponding to it can be found in the language or can be derived, it is possible to do a job of translation with elements of the native language under the influence of its meaning in the foreign language. One must bear in mind that, while this method ensures the use of elements of the native language, if it is resorted to overmuch it can open the way to the language's becom-

---

[13] The author's excuse for changing the metaphor is that, although Turks do not go in much for puns, he imagines that some lovers of the older language must have reflected that *sel* [A] means 'torrent'.

ing distanced from its own characteristic modes of expression, and it should not be resorted to unless one is forced to it. For every nation's attitude in its way of finding names for concepts—despite the existence of some resemblances—is generally different.

Many Turks dislike *-sel* intensely. Nurullah Ataç, the great neologizer, used it and defended it, but he did not like it. Perhaps significantly, it was not mentioned in a TDK brochure on word construction published in 1962 (Dizdaroğlu 1962).[14] Yet its defenders include many writers and scholars whose opinions cannot be brushed aside. This is what Fahir İz,[15] lexicographer and historian of literature, has to say about it:

Bir de -sel eki var ki, o başlı başına bir yazı konusu olabilir. Burada kısaca şunu belirteyim ki, bizim bu eke gereksemeniz sınırlıdır. Avrupa dillerindeki sıfat tamlamaları bizde ad tamlaması olur. Biz, Avrupa dillerinde olduğu gibi mısırsal çarşı, denizsel ticaret, demeyiz Mısırçarşısı, deniz ticareti, deriz.

Fransızca ya da İngilizce değil de Türkçe düşünürsek tarımsal ilaç yerine tarım ilacı, ştiirsel sanat yerine şiir sanatı, parasal sorun yerine para sorunu der de yazarız. Bununla birlikte, kimi durumlarda dilde bu eke gerekseme vardır: sinirsel nefes darlığı, tanrısal komedi v.b. gibi. (İz 1984: 13)

There is also the suffix *-sel*, which could of itself be the subject of an article. Here let me briefly say this: our need for this suffix is limited. The adjective-groups of European languages appear with us as noun-groups. We do not say 'Egyptian Market' and 'maritime commerce', as in the European languages, but 'Egypt Market' and 'sea commerce'.

If we think not in French or English but in Turkish, in place of 'agricultural chemical', 'the poetic art', 'monetary problem', we say and write 'agriculture chemical', 'the poetry art', 'money problem'. Nevertheless, in some situations the language does have a need for this suffix, as in 'nervous shortage of breath', 'The Divine Comedy', and so on.

So erudite a man as Aydın Sayılı (1978: 468) found *-sel* useful and necessary:

Özel terimler kullanma ihtiyacının baskısını kendilerinde hissedenler ve mevcut terimlerin yetersizliğinin yarattığı sıkıntıyı duymak durumunda bulunanlar için sel ve sal eklerinin bir cankurtaran gibi birçok güçlüklere çare getirdiği de bir vâkıa olarak ortadadır. Bu ekleri büyük bir çoğunluk yadırgamamaktadır. İlkin sel ile sal'ı tereddütle karşılamışken sonradan bunlara alışmış, yararlı olduklarını görmüş ve bunlarda Türkçenin selikasına ve estetiğine uymayan bir taraf bulunduğu düşüncesine iltifat etmemeye karar vermiş kimselerin sayısı da az değildir.

It is a manifest fact that for those who feel a pressing need to use special terminology and who find themselves constrained by the inadequacy of existing terms, the suffixes sel and sal are a lifeline remedying a good many difficulties. A large majority do not find these suffixes strange. There are also not a few people who were at first hesitant about sel and sal but have subsequently grown accustomed to them, seen that they were useful, and decided to disregard the notion that there was something about them that did not conform to correct Turkish usage and the aesthetics of the language.

[14] Nor is it mentioned in Korkmaz (1969). In view of Korkmaz's exposure of its illegitimacy during the controversy referred to in note 8 of this chapter, that is hardly surprising.

[15] İz (1984) is a privately printed brochure summarizing the author's previous writings and lectures on *Öztürkçe*.

Peyami Safa, no great admirer of *Öztürkçe*, regarded *-sel* as incorrectly formed and never used it unless he had to, but his taste was offended by having to add the Arabic *-î* to French words. Reproached by a conservative critic for using *fiziksel* instead of *fizikî* for 'physical', he replied that he found words such as *fizikî*, *lojikî*, *matematikî*, and *muzikî* irritating, and preferred the forms in *-sel/sal* (Safa 1970: 189–90). He went on, ' "Dudaksal" demeyelim de "Dudakî" mi diyelim? Yahut yine buyurun Arapçaya: "Şefevî"! Bu gidişle öyle olacak gibi' (Are we not to say *dudaksal* ['labial', from *dudak* 'lip'] but *dudakî*? Or by all means revert to the Arabic: *şefevî*! At this rate, it looks as though that's how it's going to be).

So, like it or not, Turkish is stuck with it, and the language of the intellectuals moves further and further away from that of the people. Social anthropologists and writers in glossy magazines may talk of country life as *kırsal yaşantı*; villagers prefer *kır hayatı*.

-tay. This new suffix was extracted from *kurultay*, originally *kurıltay*, the form taken in Turkish by the Mongolian *ḳurilta* 'assembly of the nobles',[16] borrowed in the thirteenth or fourteenth century. Like the modern reformers who resuscitated it, their forebears must have felt it to be derived from Turkish *kurulmak* 'to be set up' because, in three of the first four citations of the word in *Tarama Sözlüğü* (1963–77), it is used in conjunction with that verb, one example being 'Kurıltay kuralım, meşverete oturalım' (Let us convene an assembly and sit down to take counsel together). *Tarama Sözlüğü* misspells it *kurultay*, although the correct vocalization is shown in the *Kamus*.[17] The last citation in *Tarama Sözlüğü*, from a Turkish translation of an eleventh-century Persian–Persian dictionary, deserves quoting in full, not least because it shows that *kurıltay* was not in use in Turkey in 1789, when the translation was completed:

Gavga [Fa.]: Çığıltı ve ses ve şamata ve arbede ve karkaşa mânasınadır ve encümen ve meclis ve cemaat mânasınadır, Çağatayca kurıltay derler.

Gavga [P]: Confused animal noises, sounds, hubbub, tumult, dispute; also meeting, assembly, gathering; in Chaghatay they say *kurıltay*.

One supposes that the last three words of the Turkish apply only to the second set of meanings.

Once *kurultay* was established, its last syllable was added to the originally Middle Persian *kamu* 'all', the *Öztürkçe* for 'public', making *Kamutay*, intended to replace *Büyük Millet Meclisi* 'Grand National Assembly'. The new suffix was also added to the noun *yargı* 'decision' and to two verb-stems, *danış-* 'to consult' and *sayış-* 'to settle accounts', making *Yargıtay* 'Supreme Court of Appeal', *Danıştay*

---

[16] From *ḳuri-* 'to gather' and the suffix *-lta*. See Poppe (1954: §163) and Doerfer (1963–75): i, §305). The latter discusses the suggested origins of the final *y*, one being that the Turks equated the last syllable of *ḳurilta* with *toy* 'festal occasion, banquet'.

[17] I have corrected the spelling in quoting from *Tarama Sözlüğü*.

'Council of State', and *Sayıştay* 'Exchequer and Audit'.[18] These three survived (though by 1983 *Danıştay* had become *Danışma Meclisi*), but *Kamutay* did not; it never stood much of a chance, because everyone knew *Meclis*, whereas few had ever heard of the other three institutions or cared what those who did know about them might choose to call them. One oddity should be recorded: *kamutay*, with a small *k*, appears in Article 24 of the 1945 Constitution, the Anayasa, where the 1924 Constitution had 'heyet-i umumiye' (plenary body):

1924: Türkiye Büyük Millet Meclisi heyet-i umumiyesi her teşrin-i sani iptidasında bir sene için kendisine bir reis ve üç reis vekili intihab eder.

1945: Türkiye Büyük Millet Meclisi kamutayı her kasım ayı başında kendine bir yıl için bir Başkan, üç Başkanvekili seçer.

The Grand National Assembly of Turkey in plenary session shall, at the beginning of every November, elect for itself a chairman and three deputy chairmen.

Ataç made an *Öztürkçe* word for 'academy' by adding -*tay* to the neologism for 'science': *bilimtay*. This won no currency, doubtless because there is no internationally recognized Turkish Academy: when scholars wistfully talk about one, as they periodically do, the word they use is *Akademi*.

---

[18] The former names were respectively *Temyiz Mahkemesi, Şura-yı Devlet* or *Devlet Şurası*, and *Divan-ı Muhasebat* or *Muhasebat Divanı*.

8

Concoctions

In the Introduction I mentioned three nineteenth-century English neologisms: *birdlore*, *foreword*, and *folklore*. What happened to them? While *birdlore* sank without trace, so completely have *foreword* and *folklore* been accepted into the language that few are aware that they were deliberate inventions. There are parallels in Turkish. Many neologisms have passed away, such as *utku* for 'victory', *tün* for 'night', *yazgaç* for 'pen'. On the other hand, a great many neologisms have become so much a part of the Turkish vocabulary that they are used even by the most vehement opponents of the reform, either because they do not recognize that they are inventions or because they know that the older words will not be understood by a mass audience or mass readership. People nowadays say *genel* because it is the only word they have for 'general', *umumî* being close to obsolescence, though *umumiyetle* is still used for 'generally' alongside *genellikle*. Some neologisms survive but with meanings other than their inventors intended. *Folklor* is current in Turkey for 'folklore', though young people use it for 'folk dancing'. The invention proposed in *Cep Kılavuzu* (1935) for *tayyare* 'aeroplane' was *uçku*, which did not win popular favour, perhaps because it was too reminiscent of *uçkur* 'trouser-belt, pyjama-cord'. *Uçak*, now the only word for 'aeroplane', was originally offered in *Cep Kılavuzu* as a replacement for *tayyare meydanı* 'airfield'.

One would have expected the Language Society to keep records of who invented which neologism and when, but it does not. The result is that, while information about the origin of this or that word may occasionally be gleaned from scholarly works, one is mostly thrown back on anecdotal evidence, either oral or in popular books and articles with no scholarly pretensions. Nor has the Society yet got round to producing the dictionary on historical principles that has been high on its list of priorities since its inception. At the head of the title-page of the first *Tarama Sözlüğü* (1943–57) are the words 'Türkiye Türkçesinin Tarihî Sözlüğü Hazırlıklarından' (Part of the Preparations for the Historical Dictionary of the Turkish of Turkey), but they do not appear in the second (1963–77). Two non-Turkish scholars have gone a long way towards filling the gap, Sir Gerard Clauson with his *Etymological Dictionary of Pre-Thirteenth-Century Turkish* (1972), and Gerhard Doerfer with his *Türkische und Mongolische Elemente im Neupersischen* (1963–75); why has the Society done nothing? Certainly one reason is that the scholars who should have got on with the task in the middle 1930s were reluctant to follow the ethos of the time by ascribing Turkish origins to words that they well knew to be Arabic or Persian. Happily, the Society announced in 1995 that the preparation of a historical dictionary was once more on the agenda. İnşallah, we shall see.

It will be remembered that three methods were prescribed for producing the words required to make Turkish independent of foreign vocabulary: drawing on the resources of the spoken language (why say 'commence' when you can say 'begin'?), and of old texts (why say 'Parliament' when you can resurrect 'Witenagemot'?), and compounding existing words and suffixes (why use 'ornithology' when you can manufacture[1] 'birdlore'?). But in addition—though the Society seems never to have sanctioned, much less prescribed, this fourth method officially—the reformers felt free to use their imagination to invent replacements for the doomed Arabic and Persian words. To enlist the help of Lewis Carrol for this final example, why say 'a white badger with long hind legs and stag-like horns, living chiefly on cheese' when you can fabricate 'tove'?

The Society published a number of works offering guidance on how to create neologisms.[2] Few of the reformers seem to have paid much attention to them, or to Sayılı's (1978) brilliant study. The sad truth is that a great many of the new words were the work of people with no qualifications for the job, a category that included a number of the Society's salaried experts.

Nihad Sâmi Banarlı, who was a consultant to TDK's Technical Terms Commission, tells of an incident at the Sixth Kurultay, in 1949, which did not find its way into the published proceedings (Banarlı 1967). A question was asked from the floor about the principle governing the formation of new technical terms. The ensuing embarrassed silence was eventually broken by Saim Ali Dilemre, the chairman of the Linguistics and Etymology Commission. An amiable doctor of medicine, not of language, he could stand it no longer: 'Arkadaşlar, kemküm etmiyelim. Bizim prensipimiz mirensipimiz yoktu, uyduruyorduk!' (Friends! Let's not beat about the bush. We had no principle or anything of that sort. We've been making them up as we went along!).

Incidentally, one of TDK's two stock responses when accused of *uydurma*, 'faking' (the other being to deny it) was to claim to be continuing a long-established Ottoman practice. Many Ottoman words were in fact manufactured by Turks. *Nezaket* 'politeness' looks Arabic but was made in Turkey from the Persian *nāzuk*, which Turks spell *nazik* and pronounce /nāzik/, as if it were an Arabic present participle like *kâtip* 'writer'. Another such Turkish creation was *felâket* 'catastrophe', on the same Arabic pattern as *nezaket*, from *maflûk*, which, although it appears in dictionaries of modern Arabic as well as of Persian, is not classical Arabic but a Persian invention, quasi-Arabic for 'afflicted', made from the

---

[1] The Language Society did not talk about 'manufacturing' but 'derivation', *türetme*. The Society's opponents prefer *uydurma* 'making up, faking' and some of them call *Öztürkçe* 'Uydurukça' (Fakeish), or 'Kurumca' (Türk Dil Kurumu-ish).

[2] Ağakay (1943), Atalay (1946), Dizdaroğlu (1962), Korkmaz (1969), Özdemir (1973), Hatiboğlu (1974).

Arabic *falak* 'celestial sphere' and so 'destiny'.³ In the main, Ottoman creations were made from Arabic roots in accordance with the rules of Arabic. It was not an Arab but a Turk who was responsible for *tahtelbahir* 'submarine' ('under the sea', whereas the Arabs use *ġawwāṣa* 'diver'). The identity of one such inventor is known: *tayyare* 'aeroplane' was derived from the Arabic *ṭāra* 'to fly' by Fazıl Ahmet Aykaç, an educationalist and minor poet (1884–1967).⁴

Critics of the Society called it 'Alaylılar Derneği' (The Regimentals' Association). *Alaylılar* was an old-fashioned term for army officers risen from the ranks, as distinct from *Mektepliler*, officers who had been through military school. Gültekin (1983: 73–4) defends the former, not very persuasively:

Atatürk, dil çalışmalarını sadece uzmanların işi olarak görmedi. Uzmanların yalnız başlarına bunu başarmaları mümkün değildi. Amaç, konuşma dili ile yazı dili arasındaki farklılığı ortadan kaldırmak, halkın konuştuğu dili geliştirmek olunca, bu çalışmalara bütün bilim ve kültür emekçilerinin, hatta halkın da katılması bir zorunluluktu. Osmanlıcanın tasfiyesi ve Türkçenin geliştirilmesi demokratik bir gelişmeydi. Halkın dil çalışmalarına katılması, bu demokratik gelişmenin sonucudur.

Atatürk did not see working on language just as the business of the experts. It was not possible for the experts to make a success of this on their own. Since the aim was to eliminate the difference between the spoken and the written language and to enhance the language spoken by the people, it was essential that all who laboured in the fields of scholarship and culture, and even the people as well, should participate. The purging of Ottoman and the advancement of Turkish was a democratic advance. The people's participation in the work on language is the consequence of this democratic advance.

There are two flaws in the argument. The first is that most people's participation in the language reform was limited to answering the village schoolmaster's questions, and can rarely have gone beyond 'Round here we don't say spades, we call 'em shovels.'⁵ The second is that there was no excuse for denying the *mektepliler* a voice in vetting the contributions of all the people, including those who laboured in fields of scholarship other than language—in this context, the *alaylılar*. The trouble with the *alaylılar* was that they tended to resort to inventing words unnecessarily, because they gave up too soon on trying to make words from Turkish roots and Turkish suffixes, not having thought deeply enough about either.

³ The adverbial use of the Arabic accusative ending (*tanwīn*), as in *resmen* 'officially' and *şeklen* 'in form', gave rise to some solecisms: from Persian *pişīn* 'in advance' came *peşinen* with the same meaning, as well as an Arabic feminine plural *peşinat* 'down payment'; from Turkish *ayrı* 'separate' came *ayrıyeten* 'separately'. More recently, from the Western *culture* and *normal* came *kültüren* (culturally) and *normalen* (normally), both still heard. Then there is *yakinen*, good Ottoman for 'certainly', often used nowadays to mean 'closely', as if it were not from Arabic *yaqīn* (certain) but Turkish *yakın* (near).
⁴ Some of these Turkish inventions were adopted into Arabic. *Ṭayyāra*, for example, is the usual word for aeroplane in spoken Arabic, though in the written language *ṭā'ira* is preferred.
⁵ One recent contribution made to the language by the people is the growing use of 'Alo'—the 'Hallo' one says when answering the telephone—to mean 'telephone number'; it can be seen preceding the number on shop fronts and even on police cars. An older contribution was *cankurtaran*, literally 'life-saver', for 'ambulance'.

In the early days of the reform, however, someone must have thought to good effect about the suffix -*i* which, added to verb-stems, had made nouns or adjectives such as *yazı* 'writing', *dizi* 'line, row', *dolu* 'full', *ölü* 'dead'. That someone— who, to be fair, may for all we know have been an *alaylı*—had the idea of adding it to more verb-stems. Already in 1934 *Tarama Dergisi* gave *kazı* (from *kaz-* 'to dig') for *hafriyat* [A] 'excavation', and *anı* (from *an-* 'to call to mind') for *hatıra* [A] 'memoire, reminiscence'. The *Kamus* gives 'tercüme etmek' (to translate) as one of the senses of *çevirmek* 'to turn', but *çeviri* 'translation' is not in *Tarama Dergisi*— i.e. it was created after 1934. So were *başarı* 'success', from *başarmak* 'to succeed',[6] and many other benign neologisms. *Cep Kılavuzu* (1935) gave *konu*, from *kon-* 'to be placed', as '= 1. Saded, mevzu; 2. Husus, bab' ('scope', 'subject', 'matter', 'chapter'). *Felsefe ve Gramer Terimleri* (1942) came down in favour of it as the equivalent for *mevzu* 'subject', which by now it has largely replaced.[7]

It must be emphasized that the neologisms singled out here for criticism are in a minority, though a large one; most of those made by compounding existing words and suffixes are blameless. For 'computer', *bilgisayar* 'bit-of-information counter' is neater than the earlier *elektronik beyin* 'electronic brain' or *kompüter;* *altyapı*, literally 'under-structure', is surely preferable to the French borrowing *enfrastrüktür* and, if *netice* [A] 'end, result' had to go, its replacement *sonuç* 'latter end' is not at all bad. Nor is *çağrışım* 'association of ideas', a calque on *tedai* [A], both meaning 'mutual calling'. *Tekel* 'single-hand', one of Aksoy's coinages, has replaced *inhisar* 'monopoly'. And there are many more, ingeniously and regularly formed and not intrinsically unattractive.

English, unlike Turkish, is an unreformed language; if proof of this statement were needed one has only to consider the two words 'osteopath' and 'psychopath' and decide how one would explain to a foreign student the meaning of their final syllable. Or why, given the noun 'destruction' and the verb 'to destroy', the verb belonging to 'construction' is not 'to constroy'. English-speakers take that sort of anomaly for granted, but one cannot help thinking that while the Turks were reforming their language they could have been more logical and systematic. In their words for 'geography', 'geology', and 'geometry'—*coğrafya, jeoloji, geometri*— they still keep three different versions of the Greek *gê* 'earth': *c, je, ge*. They do have a neologism for 'geology'—*yerbilimi*—but not for the other two.

Taken as a whole, the neologisms exhibit very little trace of direction or planning. Nothing in *yazım* 'spelling', *yazın* 'literature', and *yazıt* 'inscription' gives any hint of what they are intended to mean except that they have something to do with writing. *Soru* was an old word for 'question', rarely used since the seventeenth century until it was resurrected to replace *sual* [A], but there is no intrinsic reason

---

[6] 'The secularization of Turkish life finds expression in the replacement of Arabic *muvaffak* "successful" and *mansur* or *muzaffer* "victorious", originally denoting that God has given success or victory, with Turkish *başarılı* and *yener*, which indicate man's own achievement.' (Heyd 1954: 94.)

[7] *Konu* is a calque on a calque: *mawḍūʿ* [A], literally 'placed, put down', whence Turkish *mevzu*, is a calque on the Latin *subiectum*.

why the neologisms *sorun* and *sorum*, both derived from *sor-* 'to ask', should mean respectively 'problem' and 'responsibility' (for which the derivative *sorumluluk* is more usual). *Sorun*, incidentally, can be a bit of a nuisance, since it may mean either 'the problem' or 'your question' (*soru-n*), and as their genitives look and sound identical (*sorun-un, soru-nun*) it is a toss-up whether *sorunun çözümü* means 'the solution of the problem', 'the solution of the question', or 'the solution of your question'; similarly, *yazının* can be the genitive of *yazı* 'writing, article', or *yazın* 'your article', or *yazın* 'literature', though perhaps this is of no great moment.

Another cluster, of words seemingly derived from *kur-* 'to set up', is *kurum* 'society, corporation', *kural* 'rule, norm', *kuram* 'theory', and *kurul* 'committee'. Both *kuram* and *kurum* are old words. *Kuram* occurs in *DLT* with the meaning 'in order of rank' (Dankoff and Kelly 1982–5: iii. 147; Clauson 1972: 660). *Cep Kılavuzu* (1935) gives it as a Turkish equivalent for *bünye* [A] 'physical structure'. There is no apparent justification for that, any more than for its now meaning 'theory', except that somebody or some body said it should. *Kurum* is recorded in *Tarama Sözlüğü* (1963–77) as occurring in two dictionaries, one of the fourteenth century, the other of the eighteenth and nineteenth, in the sense not of 'society, corporation' but of 'form, shape'. Since that was the original meaning of *heyet* [A], used in Ottoman for 'committee', *kurum* may have been resurrected as a calque on *heyet*. As for *kurul*, it looks like an arbitrary truncation of *kurultay*. *Kur*, given in *Cep Kılavuzu* as '= Heyet = Corps', could be another such, but the resemblance between it and *corps* is suspicious. Another and more likely source is suggested by the entry in *Cep Kılavuzu* under 'Genel Başkanlık Kuru': '= Umumî Riyaset Divanı' 'General Presidential Board'. *Kur* for *divan* could be the French *cour*, meaning 'court', just like *divan*.

The assumption behind the change of vocabulary was that the meaning of neologisms constructed from Turkish roots and suffixes would be readily intelligible to everybody, unlike Ottoman words; while a Turk might not know *mefhum* [A] 'concept', he could at once understand *kavram*, manufactured from *kavra-* 'to grasp' plus *-m*. Well, he might, unless he was from one of the many regions of Anatolia where it means 'handful'. And when the suffix was itself a neologism he would be even worse off, especially if it coincided in form with a familiar word. Theoretically, while an unschooled Turk could make nothing of *müselles* [A], he would immediately understand *üçgen* to be a triangle, or could at least guess the meaning from the context. He might if he were a townie, but if he were a villager he would recognize it only as meaning 'three fallow fields'. A villager from the neighbourhood of Isparta would have no difficulty with *özek*, the regular word in those parts for 'centre'. To most other Anatolians, however, it would mean only the pole of an ox-cart. A townie, knowing *öz* 'own' and *ek* 'patch, addition', would never guess that it was the official replacement for *merkez* 'centre'.

The old word for 'conscience' was *vicdan*, Arabic *wijdān*, from the root of *wajada* 'to find'. The new word is a calque on that, *bulunç* from *bulun-* 'to be found' plus the suffix seen in *utanç* 'shame' and *sevinç* 'joy'. The snag is that, if you were not an Arabic scholar, the most you could make of *bulunç* was that it had something to do with being found; 'foundling'?

To replace *kültür* for 'culture', Ziya Gökalp produced *hars*, the Arabic *ḥart* 'tillage, agriculture', which never achieved wide currency. Among possible alternatives for it, *Tarama Dergisi* (1934) offered *ekin* from *ek-* 'to sow'.[8] This second-degree calque is used by some writers but has not superseded *kültür*, while *kültürel* is probably more usual for 'cultural' than *ekinsel*. To country folk *ekin* means what it has always meant, 'crop, sowing'.

Plenty of peculiar creations are to be found in *Felsefe ve Gramer Terimleri*, the little book of philosophical and grammatical terminology published in 1942. They include *almaş* 'alternation', *değşinim* 'mutation', *koram* 'hierarchy', *sonurgu* 'result', *uran* 'industry', *simge* 'symbol', *imge* 'image', and *yöntem* 'system', 'method'. An odd collection; without spending too much time on it, one may say offhand that the first syllable of *almaş* is more likely to derive from the French *alternation* than from *al-* 'to take', that *değşinim* results from a deliberate maiming of *değiş-* 'to change', and that there is no discernible reason why *uran* should mean 'industry'. As for *koram*, it is shown in *Tarama Dergisi* (1934) as meaning *muahharen* 'subsequently' in three Siberian dialects. How it came to be offered as an equivalent of 'hierarchy' is anybody's guess. The suffixes of *almaş* and *sonurgu* confound the imagination. More worth spending a little time on are the last three words in the above selection, *simge, imge, yöntem*, not only because they are all current today but because they have been trawled from the lowest depths to which the language reformers ever sank.

The headwords (in bold italic) of the following notes on the more controversial or otherwise interesting neologisms are in alphabetical order, except for two pairs that are closely connected: *çoğun* comes after *zor*, and *imge* after *simge*.

Araç 'means' and *gereç* 'material' both appear in *Cep Kılavuzu* (1935), *araç* being glossed as '= Vasıta = Moyen', *gereç* as '= Levazım, malzeme = Matériel', and both are current. Like *vasıta* before it, *araç* is used for 'vehicle' as well as for 'means', and is the fashionable new term for 'car'. Timurtaş (1979: 26) does not approve of either *araç* or *gereç*; *araç* was made from *ara* 'space between', but -*ç*, he says, is no longer productive as a denominal suffix. He should have known, however, that the average Öztürkçeci had a mind above that sort of consideration. As for *gereç*, he assumes that it was arbitrarily made by adding -*ç* to *gerek* 'necessary' minus the final *k*, a change for which there is no justification. There is, however, another possibility: that its basis was not *gerek* but the verb *germek* 'to stretch', and that it was intended as a calque on *madde* [A] 'material', which is from the Arabic root M–D–D 'to stretch, extend'. Whatever its origin, it could serve as an example of a word apparently made from a non-existent root and a dubious suffix.

---

[8] TDK published two books on the theme of language and culture. The first, Baydur (1964), was entitled *Dil ve Kültür*; the second, Köksal (1980), *Dil ile Ekin*.

Bağımsızlık is the established replacement for *istiklâl* [A] 'independence'. *Cep Kılavuzu* (1935), in the second part, from Turkish to Ottoman, has *bağınsız* for 'independent', while *Felsefe ve Gramer Terimleri* (1942) has *bağınlaşma* for 'interdependence'. It is not clear who changed the *n* into *m*, and when, but it had happened by 1955. *-ım* is a deverbal suffix, but there is no verb *bağ-*, so the root has to be the noun *bağ* 'tie, bond, impediment'. That is not its only fault, as Timurtaş (1979: 41) notes: 'Bağımsız kelimesi, sadece, bakımsız kelimesinin fonetik değişikliğe uğrayan şekli olabilir. (Türkçede iki sesli arasındaki *k*'lar yumuşayıp *ğ* olmaktadır: toprak-ı toprağı, *ak*'tan ağarmak gibi) (The word *bağımsız* can only be the form taken by the word *bakımsız* ['uncared-for'] when it undergoes phonetic change. (In Turkish, intervocalic *k*s are softened, becoming *ğ*: toprak-ı becomes *toprağı*, and *ağarmak* is from *ak*)). All one can say for *bağımsızlık* is that its meaning is not so unguessable as that of its partner *özgürlük* (see below).

Bay, Bayan. 'Mr', 'Mrs, Miss, Ms'. The purpose of this innovation was to replace the old titles Bey and Hanım, which followed the name, by titles preceding it, as in the Western languages. In OT, *bay* meant 'rich, a rich man', and 'nobleman'. It was so used in Turkish, and the phrase 'bay u geda' [P] (rich man and beggar) occurs in Ottoman poetry into the nineteenth century.

Both *bay* and *bayan* are found in *Tarama Dergisi* (1934), but not as replacements for *Bey* and *Hanım*. Nor do they appear in *Cep Kılavuzu* (1935), which must have been in the press on 26 November 1934, when the Grand National Assembly was debating Law No. 2590: 'Efendi, bey, paşa, gibi lâkab ve unvanların kaldırıldığına dair kanun' (Law on the abolition of such appellations and titles as efendi, bey, and pasha). Several Deputies suggested that *Bay* and *Bayan* could be used in place of *Bey* and *Hanım*, and Dahiliye Encümeni, the Assembly's Committee on Home Affairs, took the same view:

Türkler hususî muhabere ve muhaverelerde bir kimseye ve cemaate hitap ederken adın önünde gelmek şartile erkeğe, ere yani erkişiye bay, kadına da bayan diye hitap edebilirler. Bu tâbirler öz türkçedir ve Türklerin ilk devirlerinde kullanılmıştır. Teveffuk ve imtiyaz ifade etmez.[9]

When addressing somebody or a group of people in correspondence and conversation, Turks may address a male, a man, that is to say, a male person, as 'bay', and a woman as 'bayan', on condition that it precedes the name. These terms are pure Turkish and have been used in the first era of the Turks. They do not express superiority or privilege.

There is no clear reason why *bayan*, a Mongolian word for 'rich', was chosen to be the feminine counterpart of *bay*. Eyuboğlu's etymological dictionary ignores it. *Örnekleriyle Türkçe Sözlük* (1995–6), the Ministry of Education's new four-volume dictionary, does not give etymologies, but the compilers' feelings about

---

[9] *TBMM Zabıt Ceridesi* (1934), Devre iv, Cilt 25: 40–52, at 52 (*Minutes of the Grand National Assembly*, session 4, vol. 25). The odd 'erkeğe, ere yani erkişiye' (a male, a man, that is to say, a male person) must be due to inadequate editing, understandable in view of the speed with which this law was rushed through.

Öztürkçe in general and *bay* in particular are evident from the sole example they give of its use, a couplet by Necip Fazıl Kısakürek, who was, to put it mildly, a rabid reactionary:

> Bir şey koptu benden, her şeyi tutan bir şey;
> Benim adım Bay Necip, babamınki Fâzıl Bey.

> Something has been wrested from me, something embracing everything;
> My name is Bay Necip, my father's was Fâzıl Bey.

Bey has in fact never fallen out of use. Men named, say, Hasan Öztürk have generally been called Hasan Bey in speech and in private correspondence, though the envelope of the letter would be addressed to Bay Hasan Öztürk or, more recently, Sayın Hasan Öztürk. Similarly, letters for his wife Ayşe, though addressed to Bayan or Sayın Ayşe Öztürk, will begin 'Sevgili Ayşe Hanım'. The use of 'Bey' has indeed extended lately: taxi-drivers used to be addressed as Şoför Efendi, but in the late 1990s the usual form is Şoför Bey.

Boyut 'dimension' might have been derived from Turkish *boy* 'length' by suffixing -*it*, but in fact it was one of Atatürk's ingenious essays at providing native etymologies for Ottoman words, in this case *bu'ut*, Arabic *buʿd*. Aksan (1976: 25–6) defends it in a footnote of which the first sentence is mendacious, while the second tries moral suasion to make the first acceptable:

Sözcük Ar. *buut*'un Türkçeleştirilmişi değil, *boy*'dan türetilmiş yeni bir öğedir. Onu Atatürk'ün türettiğini de burada eklemeliyiz.

The word is not the Turkicized form of Arabic *buut*; it is a new item derived from *boy* ['length']. Here we should add that it was Atatürk who derived it.

Budun. Erer (1973: 187–8) has a tale to tell (from Ali Fuad Başgil) about Cemil [Bilsel], who taught Devletler Hukuku, International Law, at the School of Law in Ankara. On his way to class one day in 1932, he ran into Sadri Maksudî and asked him how to translate the name of his subject into *Öztürkçe*, and was immediately told, 'Budunların ara yargısı'. *Budun* is given in *Tarama Dergisi* (1934) as an OT word for 'people'; the true form, as we have seen, was *boḍun*. *Yargı* is shown in the same work as meaning *adalet* 'justice' or *hüküm* 'judgement', but Sadri Maksudî was misusing it in the sense of *hukuk* 'law'. Cemil went into his class and, slightly misremembering what Maksudî had said, began his lecture with 'Budunun ara yargısı . . .'. The students, understanding the first two words in their normal meanings—'of his/her/your thigh' and 'space between'—and recognizing *yargı* as something to do with *yar-* 'to split', began to giggle. The unfortunate lecturer hastily began again, with 'Devletler Hukuku . . .', but it was too late; by that time the class was out of control.

Değin, dek. These old words for 'until' have never quite died, though they have long had difficulty in competing with *kadar* [A], and still do, in spite of the encouragement given to their use by the language reform. 'From Istanbul to Edirne it's level ground all the way' can be expressed as 'İstanbul'dan Edirne'ye değin/dek/kadar hep düz yerlerdir', but saying 'değin' or 'dek' in such a sentence sounds not so much *Öztürkçe* as provincial. In writing they are more frequent, but not as common as *kadar*.

Denli. This word, anciently *teñlig* 'equal', 'as much as', appeared in Ottoman as *denlü*, but by the late seventeenth century it had been driven out of literary use by *kadar*. The reform resurrected it, but while 'Ne denli?' (How much?) and 'bu denli' (this much) are seen in writing, as in 'Bu denli önemli mi?' (Is it so important?), in conversation almost everybody sticks to 'Ne kadar?' and 'bu kadar'.

Doğa has not totally ousted *tabiat* for 'nature', though its adjective *doğal* 'natural' is more common in writing than *tabiî*. In speech, *tabiî* remains in full use for 'of course', 'naturally', though in writing it is often replaced by 'doğal olarak'. *Doğal* appears in *Tarama Dergisi* (1934) as found in Konya for *gubar* [A] 'dust', though with a query. *Cep Kılavuzu* (1935) gives *doğa* for *mizac* 'temperament', and *Felsefe ve Gramer Terimleri* (1942) gives it for 'nature', together with *doğal* for 'natural'. The compilers of the latter work may or may not have known that *doğa* already existed in various regions of Anatolia with such diverse meanings as 'kid', 'turkeycock', 'small-eared lamb born with horns', and 'the flat upper surface of a knuckle-bone'. Timurtaş (Bozgeyik 1995: 76) makes an interesting non-grammatical point:

Batı dillerinde 'nature' var, 'doğ-' mânâsına Lâtince bir kelimeden geliyor. Halbuki bizim inanışımıza göre 'tabiat' doğmuyor, yaratılıyor. Demek ki bu da, mefhum bakımından, mânâ bakımından yanlış. Biz 'doğa' diyemeyiz. Çünkü tabiat kendiliğinden doğmuş değil. Cenab-ı Hak tarafından yaratılmıştır.

The Western languages have 'nature', which comes from a Latin word meaning birth. According to our belief, however, what is called 'nature' is not born but created, which means that this [word *doğa*] is wrong, conceptually and semantically. We cannot say 'doğa', for nature was not spontaneously born; it was divinely created.

Egemenlik. *Cep Kılavuzu* (1935) defines it as '= Hâkimiyet = Souveraineté'. Eyuboğlu (1988: 102) explains *egemen* as *eğe* or *iye* 'owner, master' plus *-men*. *Tarama Sözlüğü* (1963–77) shows *eye* or *iye* as in use from the fourteenth to the sixteenth century, but Eyuboğlu spoils it by citing *egemen* as used 'halk ağzında' (in the popular language) for 'master', an assertion not borne out by *Derleme Sözlüğü* (1963–82). Nor does he explain how the intervocalic g of *egemen* escaped softening to *ğ*. As *egemenlik* is obviously derived from the Greek *hēgemonía* (which Ziya Gökalp had long ago borrowed as *hegemonya*), we need spend no more time on it. It should be noted, however, that it appears on the wall of the Grand National Assembly chamber in the slogan 'Egemenlik Kayıtsız Şartsız Milletindir' (Sovereignty belongs unrestrictedly and unconditionally to the Nation), with an attribution to Atatürk. But Atatürk never said that; the word he used for sovereignty when he enunciated the formula was *hâkimiyet*, in keeping with the Ottoman nature of the rest. In his *Öztürkçe* period he said 'Egemenlik kayıtsız şartsız Ulusundur', leaving the two middle words in Ottoman. *Koşul* for 'condition' was not invented until nine years after Atatürk's death, nor has any one-word substitute for *kayıtsız* yet been devised.

Eşgüdüm 'coordination' is a much criticized word, omitted by at least two dictionaries, Doğan (1988) and *Örnekleriyle Türkçe Sözlük* (1995–6). *Eş* is 'mate' and *güdüm* is 'direction', a noun derived from *güt-*, originally 'to drive (animals) to pasture', more recently 'to manage, to direct' ('güdümlü mermi' means 'guided missile'). *Eşgüdüm* has its following, but most people involved in such matters prefer *koordinasyon*.

Evrensel 'universal'. This looks as if it were deliberately fabricated to resemble its West European equivalent, and so it was, but the closeness of the resemblance was a stroke of luck for whoever first thought of attaching the bogus *-sel* to the ancient and respectable *evren*. *Evren* is a genuine old word for 'universe', explained by Clauson (1972: 13–14) as presumably a derived noun from *evir-* 'to turn': 'if so, the general connotation is of something which revolves; hence "the firmament" which was regarded as a revolving dome . . .' . No doubt via the idea of 'coil', it also meant 'large snake', 'dragon', in which sense it was used in Ottoman from the fourteenth century to the nineteenth. *Türkçe Sözlük* (1988) defines *evren* as the totality of heavenly entities, creation, cosmos, with no mention of snakes or dragons, though it does include the charming old *evren pulu*, literally 'dragon-scale', for 'mica', now *mika*.

Genel is shown in *Cep Kılavuzu* (1935) as '= Umumî = Général'. Doğan Aksan's defence (1976: 32) of *genel*—the conventional one that it was formed by suffixing *-el* to *gen*, OT *keñ* 'wide'—does not explain why an adjective needs reinforcing by an adjectival suffix. Aksan does his best, however, by casually throwing in the words 'gen adından genel'in türetilişi' (the derivation of *genel* from the noun *gen*), doubtless hoping that the reader will have forgotten that he has made it perfectly clear in his previous paragraph that *gen* was an adjective. In the recent innovation *genelde*, *genel* is used as a noun. This looks like a calque on the English expression 'in general', which is what it means.

Gereksinme, Ataç's neologism for *ihtiyaç* 'need', is a puzzle. *Gerek* means 'necessary' or 'necessity', but it is not easy to see what *-sin-* is supposed to mean, especially as this is the only instance of it. There was an OT suffix of the same shape; added to *uluğ* 'great' it made *uluğsunmak* 'to consider oneself great', but, if that was what Ataç had in mind, how did he get from 'consider oneself necessary' to 'need'? The word can only be regarded as an aberration, but it and, even more, *gereksinim* are used (though good writers prefer *gerekseme*, unless they remember the old *hacet*), to an extent that shows Timurtaş's (1979: 51) judgement on it to have been over-optimistic: 'Dilimizin ne gibi bir ihtiyâcı vardı ki, "gereksinme" kelimesi uyduruldu? "İhtiyaç" varken gereksinme'ye muhtaç olacağımızı hiç sanmıyorum' (What sort of need did our language have that led to the fabricating of *gereksinme*? While we have *ihtiyaç* I don't think we shall need *gereksinme*). The question he should have asked himself was how much longer will we have *ihtiyaç*?

İlginç 'interesting'. *Cep Kılavuzu* (1935) gives *ilgi* for the Arabic *alâka* 'interest' and *münasebet* 'relationship'. It was not an invention; it is a legitimate derivative of *il-* 'to tie loosely' and 'to touch'. Its adjective *ilginç*, however, is far from legitimate, manufactured as it was from *ilgi* by adding *-nç*, a suffix previously attached only to verb-stems. Ataç cannot be blamed for this one; his offering for *intéressant* (in 1955) was *ilinç*, properly derived from *il-* on the analogy of numerous existing words such as *sevinç* 'joy' from *sevin-* 'to be pleased', and *gülünç* 'ridiculous' from *gül-* 'to laugh'. It is a pity that, whereas *ilinç*, one of Ataç's relatively few correctly formed inventions, never caught on, the linguistically monstrous *ilginç* did. The probable reason for its success is that people associated it with *ilgi*, which they knew with the meaning 'interest', while *ilinç* conveyed nothing much. The Ottoman for 'interesting' was *alâkabahş* [AP] 'interest-giving', modernized as *alâka uyandırıcı* 'interest-waking', but most preferred *enteresan* [F]. Some still stick to *enteresan*, but *ilginç* is regularly used even in conversation.

Okul 'school'. Under MEKTEP, *Tarama Dergisi* (1934) gives *Okulağ* as having been recorded at Urfa. The entry under MEDRESE is fuller:

Okulağ ('Oku' köküne 'lağ, lak' yer eki getirilerek yapılmış. 'Yayla' ve 'kışla'da olduğu gibi son sessiz düşerek 'okula' şekli de vardır.)

Okulağ (made by the addition of the suffix of place *-lağ/lak* to the root *oku* ['to read']. With the dropping of the final consonant, there is also the form *okula*, as occurs in *yayla* and *kışla*.)[10]

Yes, but never before had *-lağ/lak/la* been suffixed to a verb-stem. The received story of the origin of this most firmly entrenched of all Öztürkçe words is told by Besim Atalay (1940: 40–1):

Bu kelime Yunancaya benzetilerek yapılmamıştır ... Ankarada *Siyasal Bilgiler Okulu* açıldığı zaman Atatürk'e bir tazim telgrafı çekilmiş, bundan pek hoşnut olan O Büyük Adam bir cevap verilmesini istemiş, fakat mektep kelimesi yerine türkçe bir kelime aramışlar, o sıralarda (Urfa)dan Dil Kurumuna bu anlamda *okula* kelimesi gelmiş, kendisine bu söylendiği zaman çok beğenmiş ve mektep için en güzel karşılık olmak üzere kabul buyrulmuş. Aradan bir kaç gün geçtikten sonra kelimenin sonundaki *a* sesi atılarak *okul* şeklinde kullanılmasını emretmişler.

[10] *Yayla*, earlier *yaylak*, means 'summer pasture', from *yaz* 'summer', while *kışla*, from *kış* 'winter', means 'winter quarters' and then 'barracks'.

This word was not made on the analogy of the Greek [*scholē*, whence ultimately French *école*] . . . Atatürk was sent a congratulatory telegram on the opening of the Ankara School of Political Sciences. Very pleased, he wanted a reply to be sent, but they lacked a Turkish replacement for *mektep* 'school'. Around this time the word *okula*, with that meaning, came to the Dil Kurumu from Urfa. When Atatürk was told this, he liked it a lot and it was accepted by him as the best equivalent of *mektep*. A few days later, he directed that the final *a* of the word should be dropped and the word used in the form *okul*.

And indeed *Cep Kılavuzu* (1935) gives 'Okul = Mekteb = Ecole.'

Tahsin Banguoğlu (1987: 303), however, has a more circumstantial story, in no way inconsistent with Atalay's (apart from the latter's first sentence) but adding two pieces of information: the identity of the correspondent from Urfa who had claimed that *okula* was a real word currently used in his native city, and the fact that it was no such thing:

Dikkat ediniz, burda inkılâp hareketinin bilhassa hızı Arapçaya karşıdır. Arapça kelimeleri atmalı da, ne gelirse gelsin. Çünkü Arapçanın hakimiyetinden bıkmış bir nesil. Onun yerine Fransızcası gelse olur. *Schola* Latince. Biri diyor ki 'Efendim bu bizim *okumak* mastarından gelir.' Bir başkası, daha kurnazı, 'efendim diyor, bizim Urfa'da *okula* derler *mektebe*'. Ben doçenttim henüz, Dil Fakültesinde, dedim ki 'bu *okula* kelimesi eğer Urfa'da *mektep* mânâsına varsa ben kendimi asarım, bu Fakültenin kapısına' . . . Ben Türkçe kelime yapımı hakkında bilgime dayanarak konuşuyordum. Ama sonradan yine Kurumdan biri kulağıma eğildi: 'Bizim Urfa mebusu Refet uydurdu' dedi . . . Ondan sonra *okula* demişler, daha sonra *okul* demişler, sonundaki *a*'yı atmışlar.

Mark this well: the thrust of the reform movement is specifically against Arabic. Arabic words have to be discarded come what may, for this is a generation that is fed up with the domination of Arabic. If the French equivalent were to replace it, that's fine. *Schola* is Latin. Somebody says, 'My dear sir, it is is from the stem of our *okumak*.' Someone else, someone craftier, says, 'My dear sir, in my native Urfa they call school *okula*.' I was a lecturer at the time, in the Language Faculty, and I said, 'If this word *okula* exists in Urfa in the sense of school, I shall hang myself from the Faculty gate.' . . . I was speaking on the basis of my knowledge of Turkish word formation. But subsequently someone else from the TDK whispered to me, 'It was Refet, our Deputy for Urfa, who made it up.' . . . After that, they said *okula*. Later on, they said *okul*, chucking away the final *a*.

Some people's refusal to face facts is well exemplified in Eyuboğlu (1988: 237):

OKUL, tr. Okumak'tan ok-ul/okul. Köke gelen ul ekiyle söz üretme: oğ-ul/oğul, koş-ul/koşul (Kır. koşul-taşıl/karışmış, karışık), yumul yumul (halk ağ.).

OKUL, Turkish. From *okumak*, ok-ul/okul. Word production with the suffix ul coming to the root: *oğ-ul/oğul*, *koş-ul/koşul* (Kirghiz *koşul-taşıl* 'mixed, confused'), *yumul yumul* (popular speech).

Was there ever such a farrago? The stem of *okumak* is not *ok*- but *oku*-. If the suffix is -*ul*, the addition sum is wrong; *oku*- plus *ul* makes not *okul* but **okuyul*. If the root of *okul* is the verb-stem *oku*-, its suffix must be *l*. Nor is *oğul* 'son' divisible into *oğ* and *ul*.[11] Enlisting the misbegotten *koşul* in support of *okul* can only be described as impudent. What *yumul yumul* means in popular speech is not immediately ascertainable, as the expression seems to be unknown to the lexicographers or any of the author's Turkish friends. In short, the article can fairly be described as an attempt at blinding the reader with nescience.

Doğan Aksan (1976: 39) sees no fault in *okul*, which he explains as derived from *oku-* and the suffix *-l*; were it not for Banguoğlu's account of the word's origin one might almost have believed him.

Olanak is the *Öztürkçe* for *imkân* [A] 'possibility'. Adile Ayda says of it and of *olasılık*:[12]

icat edilen yeni bir kelime Türk dilinin kurallarına göre yapılmış olsa bile çağrışım yolu ile hoş olmayan, hoşa gitmeyen bir şeyi veya kelimeyi hatırlatıyorsa, üç beş adamdan başkasının bu kelimeyi benimsemesi mümkün değildir. OLANAK ile OLASI kelimeleri bu alanda en iyi örneklerdir.

'Olanak' kelimesi Türkçeyi iyi bilen, zevk sahibi bir Türk için çirkin görünen, kulakları tırmalayan bir kelimedir. Neden? Çünkü insana, şuur plânında değilse bile, şuuraltı plânında 'nak' hecesi ile biten BUNAK, AVANAK kelimelerini hatırlatmaktadır.

even though a newly invented word has been constructed in accordance with the rules of Turkish, if, by an association of ideas, it is reminiscent of some unpleasant or distasteful thing or word, it is impossible that it should be adopted except by a handful of people. The best examples in this category are *olanak* and *olası*.

For a Turk who knows Turkish well and has taste, *olanak* is a word that looks ugly and offends the ear. Why? Because it reminds one, if not on the conscious then on the subconscious level, of words ending with the syllable *nak: bunak* ['imbecile'] and *avanak* ['gullible'].

Olasılık, one of Ataç's inventions, has made great inroads on the domain of *ihtimal* [A]. Some Turkish–English dictionaries will tell you that *olasılık*, like *ihtimal* before it, means 'probability', but Turkish cannot express that concept in a single word; *ihtimal* in fact conveys a lesser likelihood of realization than *imkân* 'possibility'. The proof-text is Hisar (1966: 199): 'ihtimalleri imkânlar halinde duymağa başlayınca' (when he began to feel that the maybes were possibilities). In standard Turkish *-esi/ası* is chiefly used for curses (Lewis 1988: 115); *kör olası* does not mean 'it is possible/probable that he will go blind', but 'may he go blind!' An accurate substitute for *muhtemel* [A], the adjective of *ihtimal*, is *belkili* (characterized by 'perhaps'), though few use it. But all the West European languages have words for 'probable' (*wahrscheinlich, sannsynlig, probabile*), and one would not be surprised if the meaning of *olası* were gradually to shift towards that of 'probable' rather than of 'maybe'.

---

[11] For an effective demolition of the theory that it might be, see Doerfer (1963–75: ii. §82).

[12] Quoted in *Yaşayan Türkçemiz* (1981: ii. 62–3). The second of the three volumes of this spirited, entertaining, and occasionally vituperative compilation on the language reform, published by the conservative newspaper *Tercüman*, is devoted to 'Uydurma, yanlış yapılan, yanlış mânâlandırılan, yanlış kullanılan, Türkçeyi bozan, ne olduğu bilinmeyen kelimeler' (Words that are fake, wrongly constructed, given wrong meanings, wrongly used, ruining Turkish, of unknown pedigree).

Oran, orantı. *Oran* is an old word for 'measure', 'proportion', or 'moderation'. The reform has fixed it in the meaning of 'ratio', in which use it receives unusual praise from the conservative *Temel Türkçe Sözlük* (Tulum 1985–6): 'Kullanılmaması büyük üzüntü sebebi olacak kelimelerdendir' (It is one of those words that it would be a great inconvenience not to use). *Orantı*, the new term for 'proportion', was derived from it by the illegitimate addition of the deverbal suffix *-tı*.

Örnek, örneğin. The first of these has been current for centuries with the meaning 'pattern, example'. Nobody seems to have taken exception to it until Ataç, seeking a replacement for *meselâ* 'for example', thought of adding to *örnek* the old instrumental suffix *-in*. For some reason this evoked much criticism, partly because a good Turkish way of expressing that already existed: *söz gelişi*. It was during the ensuing controversy that *örnek* was charged with being a borrowing from Armenian, which it pretty certainly is not. The word is now part of the language, though there are people who, not feeling quite at home with it, use the old and the new together, saying 'meselâ örneğin', literally 'e.g. for instance'.

Özgürlük, Ataç's successful replacement for *hürriyet* 'freedom', is a mess, both in form and in meaning. *Öz* is 'self' and *gür* is 'abundant'. It could be that the form he first thought of was *özügür*,[13] which he then decided would be more euphonious without the first *ü*, but 'abundant of self' is hardly 'free'. Aksan (1976: 47–8) puts up his usual spirited defence of the indefensible. He finds reason to believe that *özgürlük* was invented before *özgür*, in which case *öz* is an adjective qualifying *gürlük* and the word is therefore 'kurallara uygun bir birleştirme' (a combination in accordance with the rules). Maybe so, but what can it mean other than 'pure abundance'? Certainly not 'freedom'. Emin Özdemir (1969: 23), another zealous partisan of *Öztürkçe*, puts up an ingenious apologia for *özgür(lük)* in which he implicitly acknowledges that no one could guess what it means. He begins by saying that the trouble lies with the writers and language experts who oppose the reform and have not dwelt sufficiently on the structure of *Öztürkçe* words. He goes on: 'Bilindiği gibi bileşik sözcüklerin bir bölüğünde . . . bileştirilen sözcükler sözlük anlamlarından uzaklaşır. *Akbaba, demirbaş* örneklerinde olduğu gibi, *Özgür* sözcüğündeki durum da böyledir' (As is well known, in one category of compound words . . . the words compounded become remote from their dictionary meanings. Just as in the examples *akbaba* and *demirbaş*,[14] so is it with *özgür*). That is to say, a knowledge of the meanings of their components is no help in determining what the compounds mean. This may be expected with natural words that have a history of their own, but not with a word that one man deliberately invented.

---

[13] A *başıbozuk* construction (see Lewis 1988: 259–60).

[14] *Akbaba*, literally 'white father', means 'vulture'. *Demirbaş*, 'iron-head' and so 'stubborn', was the epithet applied by the Ottoman chroniclers to Charles XII of Sweden. After his crushing defeat at Poltava by Peter the Great of Russia in 1709, he took refuge in Turkey, where he remained till 1714. It was presumably because he outstayed his welcome that *demirbaş* came to mean fixtures and fittings, the contents of an inventory.

Saptamak. This verb is *Cep Kılavuzu*'s (1935) replacement for *tespit etmek* 'to establish, confirm'. Whoever devised it was playing the 1930s game of finding what might have been the Turkish etymon of the Arabic word for which a replacement was being sought. There was a suffix *-ta-*, appearing in the archaic *yastamak* 'to lean' and *yaştamak* 'to grow old', superseded since the fifteenth century by *yaslamak* and *yaşlanmak* respectively. So, if *saptamak* had ever existed, its modern equivalent would probably have been *saplamak*. That, however, exists in present-day Turkish with the meaning 'to thrust, pierce'. But your true *Öztürkçeci* has no difficulty in disposing of that kind of objection. Aksan (1976: 48) notes that there is a Kirghiz word *saptamak*, meaning, among other things, 'to wish, claim'. 'Türkiye Türkçesinde *saptamak*'a yeni bir anlam yüklenmiş, bu da yadırganmamış, tutunmuştur' (In the Turkish of Turkey, *saptamak* has been given a new meaning, and this has not been considered odd but has caught on).

Sayın. An old derivative of *saymak* 'to count, to esteem', meaning 'highly regarded', obsolete by the end of the nineteenth century. *Cep Kılavuzu* (1935) dug it up as an alternative to *mübeccel* and *muhterem* 'revered', 'honoured', and it is regularly used before the surname in addressing men or women, having steadily gained ground from *Bay* and *Bayan*. Fewer and fewer bus-conductors have addressed their passengers as 'Baylar' since the late 1970s, the preference being for the old-fashioned 'Beyler'. It is a pity that *Sayın* is not used as a noun, otherwise its plural could have made a neat expression for 'Ladies and Gentlemen'.

There is a modern folk-tale about a Minister of Education's visit to Sivas. Among the welcoming committee were all the local mayors, whom he addressed as 'Sayın Muhtarlar!' The first muhtar, taking *sayın* to be the imperative of *saymak* 'to count' (in military parlance, 'to number off'), said 'Bir!' 'İki!' said the second, 'Üç!' said the third, and so on.

Simge and *imge.* For *timsal* [A] 'symbol', *Cep Kılavuzu* (1935) proposed *sim*. This is recorded as used for 'sign' in the vilayet of Adana, though, in view of the number of Arabs living in that region, the resemblance to the Arabic *sīmā* in the same sense is more than a little suspicious. It never caught on, perhaps because the sort of people who talked about symbols were the intellectuals, to whom *sim* was, if anything, the Persian for 'silver'. So it was given a bit more individuality by the addition of the *-ge* seen in *çekirge* 'grasshopper' and *süpürge* 'broom', and as *simge* it is in active use, being more popular among intellectuals than the French *sembol*. (There is even a Hotel Simge in Istanbul, down the road from the Pera Palas.) It has an adjective *simgesel* 'symbolic' and a derived verb *simgelemek* 'to symbolize'. And *imge*? It was put up as the *Öztürkçe* replacement for *hayâl* [A] 'fancy, image', its alleged origin being the OT *im* 'password', with the addition of the same *-ge*. The connection between 'password' and 'image' seems tenuous, but one only has to spell out *imge* and the French or English *image* to see the true etymology.

Subay 'officer'. This word was a borrowing into Azeri[15] from Mongolian, in which language it first meant 'sterile', then 'childless', then 'light cavalryman' (because he travels the fastest who travels alone), then '(cavalry) officer' (Doerfer 1963–75: iii, §1225). In Azeri it means 'bachelor'. It was brought to Turkey by immigrants from Azerbaijan and is used in several places in Anatolia with the same sense and also that of 'lone, childless'. *Tarama Dergisi* (1934) lists it among possible equivalents for *münferit* 'isolated'.

Terim 'technical term'. Onat, a respectable enough scholar apart from his obsession with the Turkish origin of Arabic, said (1952: 49–50) it was not a corruption of the French *terme* but was the Kirghiz form of the word appearing in the Turkish of Turkey as *derim* 'assembly, gathering'; the form with initial *t* was chosen, he said, because *derim* would have looked like part of *demek* 'to say'. And how do you get from 'gathering' to 'technical term'?

İlim, belli bir konu ile ilgili bilgi topluluğu olduğu gibi, terim de ilim ve sanatların çeşitli bahislerini, meselelerini ayrı ayrı adlar altında derleyip toplayan bilim sözleridir; nitekim *terim* kelimesi de bütün bu sözleri birleşik bir adla anlatmaya yaradığı için bir bilim sözü olarak kabul edilmiştir.

As science is the totality of informating relating to a specific subject, so *terim* is the scientific expressions that collect and assemble the various topics and problems of science and the arts under separate names. So indeed *terim* has been accepted as a scientific word because it serves to express all these words by a common name.

Which is rather like saying 'library' when you mean 'book' or, to use a closer analogy, 'dustbin' when you mean 'rubbish'.

Uygarlık. *Medeniyet* 'civilization' was of Arabic derivation, though it was a nineteenth-century Turk who did the deriving. The *Öztürkçe* replacement found for it was *uygarlık*, an arbitrary coinage based on the name of the Uyghur, a Turkish people who established an advanced civilization in Eastern Turkestan in the tenth to twelfth centuries. So it has far less claim to being pure Turkish than *medeniyet*, which still holds its ground. The adjective *medenî* continues in use in the legal term 'medenî hal', a translation of the French *état civil* 'marital status', sometimes modernized into 'medenî durum'. On the northern approaches to Izmir one sees notices erected by the Karşıyaka municipality, reading 'Yayaya Saygı Uygarlıktır' (Respect for the Pedestrian is Civilization). Assuming an idiot-boy expression, the author asked two affable taxi-drivers the meaning of *uygarlık*, and after briefly conferring they agreed that *uygar* meant the same as *modern* or *çağdaş* (contemporary). It emerged that they did not associate *uygarlık* with *medeniyet*, which they both knew, though the author did not try their patience by asking them to define it.

---

[15] Azeri is the name of the people (and, with the suffix -*ce*, the language) of Azerbaijan. One wishes that BBC newsreaders would stop giving it the vowels of 'canary' instead of 'mastery'.

Yaşam, yaşantı. The first of these neologisms was intended to replace *hayat* [A] 'life', which it has not totally done; in fact one sometimes hears a non-intellectual talking about his or her life as 'yaşam-hayatım'. *Yaşantı* was intended to mean 'way of life', a sense already conveyed unambiguously by *yaşayış*, or 'experience of life, what one lives through'. It is far from being universally popular, because a number of words in *-ntı* express unpleasant ideas: *bulantı* 'nausea', *boğuntu* 'suffocation', *çalkantı* 'agitation', *çarpıntı* 'palpitation', *kaşıntı* 'itching', *kusuntu* 'vomit', *sıkıntı* 'embarrassment', *süprüntü* 'sweepings', *tiksinti* 'disgust', *üzüntü* 'dejection'. Those who do not like *yaşantı* say that to them it conveys not 'experience of life' but 'hayat bozması' (an apology for a life). Not all words in *-ntı* are distasteful—e.g. *gezinti* 'stroll'—though pleasant examples are few and far between.

Yöntem, the neologism for 'method, system', has largely supplanted *usul* [A] and even *metot,* the French *méthode.* Whoever devised it took *yön,* still existing in popular speech in the sense of 'direction', and ostensibly added the suffix seen in *erdem* 'manly virtue'. A word meaning directionness or directiondom may not seem a valid equivalent for 'method', and indeed it is not. In fact I am morally certain that its second syllable is really the second syllable of the French *système.* In case you think my moral certainty no better than an unworthy suspicion, let me tell you what somebody dreamed up to replace the Ottoman *kıyas-ı mukassem* 'dilemma'. It was *ikilem,* compounded of *iki* 'two' and the *lemme* of French *dilemme.* High marks for ingenuity, few for linguistic purity. The same can probably be said of *önder* 'leader'; *Tarama Dergisi* (1934) shows it as used at Polatlı, but *Derleme Sözlüğü* (1964–82) does not show it at all. It looks awfully like *ön* 'front' plus the second syllable of English *leader.*

Zor [P] 'force' and its Öztürkçe derivatives *zorunlu, zorunluk,* and *zorunluluk* have unseated *mecburî* [A] 'obligatory' and *mecburiyet* [A] 'obligation'. All one can say for *zor* and its offspring is that, though their initial *z* brands them as non-Turkish, they are not so conspicuously non-Turkish as *mecburî* and *mecburiyet.* The puzzle here is what the *-un* is supposed to be doing, and how the suffixes *-lu* and *-luk* came to be attached to a non-existent noun, for *zorun* will not be found in the dictionary. The *-un* is the old suffix of the instrumental case, as in Ataç's neologism *örneğin* 'for example', and in *gücün* 'by force', a genuine Turkish synonym of *zorun,* still in use in the late nineteenth century. The *un* of *zorun* is not to be confused with that of *zorunda,* in which the *u(n)* is the third-person suffix and which after an infinitive means 'under an obligation to . . .', like the earlier *mecburiyetinde.*

Çoğun, unlike its sister *zorun*—they share the same suffix—is in the dictionary (though rarely appearing anywhere else), with the meaning 'often'. Its abstract noun *çoğunluk* is in full use, in the sense not of 'frequency' but of 'majority', replacing *ekseriyet* [A].

9

Technical Terms

The Language Society did not forget that Atatürk had wanted the work on technical terms to continue. In 1948 it began publishing glossaries for subjects as varied as statistics and cycling, metallurgy and volleyball; they are listed in Brendemoen (1990: 490–2). Special tribute must be paid to the compilers of *Orta Öğretim Terimleri Kılavuzu* (1963), which provided *Öztürkçe* equivalents of scientific terms for middle schools, with indexes in Ottoman, French, Latin, Greek, English, and German. No less impressive in *Matematik Terimleri Sözlüğü* (1983) ('Dictionary of Mathematical Terms'), a book of over 500 pages. Most of these glossaries, compiled as they were by large editorial bodies, bear no indication of authorship. This one was the work of just two people: Doğan Çoker and Timur Karaçay. But what came of it all? Two examples picked at random from the latter work: it proposed *yöneyler işlencesi* for 'calculus of vectors', and *konaç* for 'coordinate', but these words do not appear in recent dictionaries, neither the Society's own *Türkçe Sözlük* (1988) nor the Ministry of Education's *Örnekleriyle Türkçe Sözlük* (1995–6). It is sad to leaf through these products of manifest ingenuity, industry, and devotion, and to see how little effect they have had; truly love's labour lost.

This chapter discusses the terminology of medicine and law and, more briefly, computing, as being of the most general interest. There are also some remarks on the vocabulary of music, which is a special case.

In Ottoman times, the medical vocabulary was Arabic. Özön, in his dictionary of foreign words (1961*a*) says that after the sixteenth century, when the Jewish refugees from Spain had migrated to Turkey and taken over the medical profession, a number of hybrid Spanish–Italian ('İspanyol–İtalyan kırması') medical terms came into use. Unfortunately he gives no examples.

In 1838 the Tıbhane, the School of Medicine founded in 1827, and the Cerrahhane, the School of Surgery founded in 1832, were amalgamated and moved to Galatasaray. In his speech (which began 'Çocuklar!' (Children!)) at the opening ceremony, Sultan Mahmud II said:

İşbu ebniye-i âliyeyi Mekteb-i Tıbbiye olmak üzere teşkil ve tertip ederek Mekteb-i Tıbbiyei Adliye-i Şahane tesmiye ettim . . . Bunda Fransızca olarak fenn-i tıbbı tahsil edeceksiniz . . . Sizlere Fransızca okutmaktan benim muradım lisanı tahsil ettirmek değildir. Ancak fenn-i tıbbı öğretip refte refte kendi lisanımıza almaktır.   (Ünver 1940: 940)

Having fashioned and arranged these fine buildings to be the medical school, I have named it the Imperial School of Forensic Medicine . . . Here you will study the science of medicine in French . . . My desire in having you taught in French is not to have you study French. It is just to teach you the science of medicine and to bring it gradually into our own language.

For many years the teaching went on in French, most of the teachers being non-Turks, but eventually the students began agitating for Turkish to become the medium of instruction. In 1861 they managed to have some articles on this theme published in the Turkish-language press, which their teachers countered with articles in the French-language press. After a long war of words, Salih Efendi, the Supervisor of the School, took the side of the students, and in 1866 the Ottoman Medical Society, Cemiyet-i Tıbbiye-i Osmaniye, was founded, its first task being to produce a Turkish medical dictionary. From 1870 onwards, medical students had their wish and were taught in Turkish or, to be more accurate, in Ottoman (Uludağ 1940). That did not do them much good; they soon found that a knowledge of French was indispensable, particularly because many of them completed their studies in France.

As the Turkish saying goes, 'o gün bugündür' (it's just the same today). In medical parlance, alopecia is *alopesi*, whereas in common speech it is *saçsızlık* 'hairlessness'. Caesarian, a doctor's word, is *sezaryen*, whereas (umbilical) cord, a mother's and midwife's word, is *göbekbağı* 'navel-tie', with *göbek kordonu* as a more genteel alternative (see Table 9.1).

TDK produced a glossary of medical terms, *Hekimlik Terimleri Kılavuzu*, in 1978, with a revised and enlarged edition in 1980. It was a well-meaning work, inspired by the wish to free medicine 'büyüden, gizemden' 'from spells and mystery'. It does not appear to have made a great difference, one reason being that much of it was *Öztürkçe* that was not intelligible to all. Thus for 'illness' it uses *sayrılık* throughout, a word that had been dropped centuries before in favour of *hastalık* and that, though resurrected in *Cep Kılavuzu* (1935), never caught on.[1] Another reason is that not every practitioner of medicine wants to see it freed from the spells and the mystery; this the author realized some years ago, on reading the following in an Istanbul pathologist's report: 'Mikroskobik [*sic*] bulgular: Stroması ödemli endometrium dokusu görülmektedir. Guddeler sayıca artmış olup, psödistratifiye silendrik epitelle döşelidir. Arada epiteloid histiositler, lenfositler ve Langhans tipi dev hücrelerden oluşmuş yuvarlakça alanlar mevcuttur'. (Microscopic findings: Endometrium tissue with oedematous stroma visible. The glands have increased in number and are covered with pseudo-stratified columnar epithelium. Also present are epitheloid histiocytes, lymphocytes, and roundish areas formed of Langhans-type giant cells).

But worse was to come. Yaman Örs (1989: 18) quotes a specimen of the use of foreign terms in what purports to be medical Turkish:

---

[1] The first meaning of *hasta* [P] was 'tired'. Its use in Turkish for 'ill' is exactly paralleled by the French use of *fatigué(e)* as a euphemism for *malade*.

TABLE 9.1. Names of ailments

Ailment	Doctor's term	Popular term
anaemia	*anemi*	*kansızlık* ('bloodlessness')
appendicitis	*apandisit*	*apandis yangısı* ('appendix inflammation')
cancer	*kanser*	*incitmebeni* ('don't hurt me')
cataract	*katarakt*	*perde* [P] ('curtain')
cholera	*kolera*	
diabetes	*diyabet*	*şeker hastalığı* ('sugar disease')
dysentery	*dizanteri*	*kanlı basur* [A] ('bloody haemorrhoids')
gallstones	*safra* (A) *taşları*	
glaucoma	*glokom*	*karasu* ('black water')
haemorrhoids	*emeroit*	*basur*
leucaemia	*lösemi*	*kan kanseri* ('blood cancer')
lockjaw	*tetanos*	*kazıklı humma/ateş* ('fever with stakes')
malaria	*malarya*	*sıtma* ('heating')
pneumonia	*pnömoni*	*akciğer yangısı* ('lung inflammation'), *batar* ('piercing')
rabies	*kuduz*	
rheumatism	*romatizm*	
scurvy	*iskorbüt*	*tuzlubalgam* ('salty phlegm')
stye		*arpacık* ('little barley-grain'), *itdirseği* ('dog elbow')
tuberculosis	*tüberküloz*	*verem* [A] ('swelling, tumour')
tumour	*tümör*	*ur*
typhoid	*tifo*	*kara humma* ('black fever')
womb	*rahim* [A]	*dölyatağı* ('foetus-bed')

Yapıtında '(Antiepileptik ilaçların) yayılmasının bloke edilmesinde rol oynayan nöronal etkileri arasında eksitasyon eşiğini yükseltmeleri, refrakter periyodu uzatmaları, presinaptik ve postsinaptik inhibisyonu potansiyelize etmeleri sayılabilir. Ayrıca nörofizyolojide spontan repetitif deşarjlara eşlik eden bir durum olarak bilinen posttetanik potansiyalizasyon olayını inhibe ederler; bu olay üzerindeki inhibitör etkileri ile deşarjın yayılmasını önlemeleri arasında ilişki bulunabilir' diyen bir yazar, 'epilepsi türlerinin uluslararası sınıflandırılmasını' verirken, 'psikoduyusal (!) semptomatoloji gösterenlerden', 'ikinci olarak jeneralize olan kısmi tutarıklardan' söz açıyor.[2]

'Among the neuronal effects that play a part in blocking the spread of antiepileptic drugs, there may be counted: raising the excitation-threshold, extending the refractory period, and potentializing pre- and post-synaptic inhibition. Moreover, they inhibit the occurrence of post-tetanic potentialization, which is known in neurophysiology to be a situation accompanying spontantaneous repetitive discharges; there may be a relationship between their inhibiting effects on this occurrence and their preventing the spread of the discharge.'

[2] Örs has no compunction about identifying the writer and his book: O. Kayaalp, *Rasyonel Tedavi Yönünden Tıbbi Farmakoloji* (Ankara: Garanti Basımevi, 1978). The quotation is from pp. 968–9.

The writer of the above, in the course of giving 'the international classification of the varieties of epilepsy', speaks in his work of 'those exhibiting psychosensory (!) symptomatology', and 'secondarily generalized partial seizures'.

Örs then lists a number of individual words, mostly English, used by Turkish doctors, among them *schedule, bowel movement, rounds, background, rule out, fracture, arterial tension, fever, handle etmek, history almak* ('to record a patient's medical history'), and *idantifie etmek*. The list reflects the general advance of English in recent years, and the growing number of Turkish doctors doing postgraduate studies in Britain and America. Örs's source was a three-page communication published in 1968 by the Hacettepe Committee for the Collection of Medical Terms, which commented:

Türkçe karşılığı bulunabilen ve gerçekte uluslararası bilimsel terimlerle de ilgisi olmayan sözcükler ve terimler sık sık kullanılmakta ve yayılmaktadır . . . Yeni yetişen öğrenciler de önce bu terimler karşısında bocalamakla birlikte, sonraları bu duruma katılmakta ve yadırganan yeni bir dil ortaya çıkmaktadır. Öğrenciler böylece, hekimlikte ancak yabancı terimler kullanırlarsa bilgilerinin bilimsel değer kazanacağını sanmaktadırlar . . . Bu yüzden Türkçe bilim dili olarak gelişmemekte ve bir dil kargaşalığı eğitimimizi etkilemektedir.

Words and terms for which Turkish equivalents can be found and which really have nothing to do with international technical terms are frequently employed and are spreading . . . Newly trained students, while at first floundering when they meet these terms, then become part of the situation, and an incongruous new language is emerging. Students think that in this way, if they use only foreign terms in their profession, their knowledge will gain scientific value . . . For this reason, Turkish is not developing as a language of science, and a linguistic chaos is affecting our education.

Örs's comment:

Bu tür örnekleri çoğaltmak, ne yazık ki kolay olacaktır; gerçekten daha nice, nicelerini ekleyebiliriz . . . 'Critère' yerine ölçüt, 'diagnose' yerine tanı kullanmak çok büyük bir çabayı mı gerektirmektedir? Üretilmiş ya da ortaya çıkarılmış birçok Türkçe tıp terimi, yabancı terimlerin anlamını genellikle tümüyle karşılıyorlar. 'Hormon', 'konjenital', 'diffüz', sırasıyle içsalgı, doğuştan, yaygın demektirler, başka da bir şey demek değildirler.

Unfortunately it would be easy to multiply these examples; we really could add very many more . . . Does it call for a great effort to use *ölçüt* instead of *critère, tanı* instead of *diagnose*? Quite a number of Turkish medical terms, derived or brought to light, as a rule completely express the sense of the foreign terms. *Hormone, congenital,* and *diffuse* mean *içsalgı* ['inner secretion'], *doğuştan* ['from birth'], and *yaygın* ['widespread'] respectively, and that is all they mean.

Alluding to the old argument about whether Turks should derive their technical terms from Arabic and Persian, as the Western world does from Greek and Latin, Örs goes on to make a fair point: where, he asks, did the Greeks and Romans get their technical terms from?

Tanı anlamındaki *diagnosis* Yunanca bilgi anlamına gelen bir kökten çıkmıştır. Demek oluyor ki, batı dillerindeki terimler de Türkçe karşılıkları gibi temelde genel dilden, halk dilinden türemiştir. İngilizce tıp dilinde ortaya çıkan *scanning*, Türkçedeki karşılığı olan 'tarama'dan daha mı çok 'bilimseldir'? Fransızca *donneur*'ün 'verici' den daha ileri bir 'bilimsellik' taşıdığı söylenebilir mi?

Diagnosis, meaning recognition, came from a Greek root meaning knowledge. This amounts to saying that terms in the Western languages, like their Turkish equivalents, derived originally from the general language, the popular language. Is *scanning*, which has emerged in English medical language, more 'scientific' than *tarama*, its Turkish equivalent? Can the French *donneur* ['donor'] be said to possess a more advanced scientific quality than *verici*?

Apropos diagnosis, the old term for it was *teşhis* [A]. The new term is *tanı*, the stem of *tanımak* 'to know'. Both terms occur in one and the same document, the pathologist's report referred to above, together with a third, *diagnos*. Such a wealth of synonyms, though appropriate to a literary text, is surely superfluous in a document of this nature; it calls to mind the 'illiyet–nedenlilik–causalité' mentioned at the end of Chapter 1.

There was no mention of the technical terms of medicine in any of the papers presented in 1988 to the first Turkish Medical History Congress (TTK 1992), which suggests that the participants were happy with the status quo. But it was surprising to hear a medical man using in a broadcast talk on curative springs (Ankara Radio, 23 Jan. 1991) the sort of language that might have been immediately intelligible to a professional audience but could have conveyed little to the general public. He mentioned that some springs were beneficial for 'nürolojik ve müsküler komplikasyonlar'. Any lay listener who knew *müsküler* only as the plural of *müskü* 'amulet' and failed to recognize in it the French *musculaire*, could be excused for supposing *komplikasyon* to be the latest Öztürkçe for *büyü* 'magic spell'.

After the change to the Latin alphabet in 1928, the Republic's legal codes, promulgated in 1926, had to be rewritten. The new version of the Civil Code appeared in 1934, when the move to 'purify' Turkish was just getting under way, and the drafters made a conscious effort to keep the language simple. But the passage of more than sixty years has made it virtually incomprehensible except to septuagenarians, since few young lawyers have the time to gain proficiency in Ottoman. For most of them the practice of their profession would be hard indeed were it not for the existence of what may fairly be termed a bilingual edition, in which the 1934 text is given on the left-hand page and a translation into the Turkish of the 1970s on the right. A short sample, Article 414, is enough to demonstrate that we really are talking about two languages, or at least two dialects:

(1934) Küçük üzerindeki vesayet, rüşt veya hâkimin rüşt kararı ile nihayet bulur. Mahkemei asliye, rüşde karar verir iken vesayetin hitamı gününü tesbit ve kararını resmen ilân eder.

(1979) Küçükler üzerindeki korumanlık, erginlikle veya yargıcın erginlik kararıyla sona erer. Asliye mahkemesi erginliğe karar verirken korumanlığın sona erme gününü saptar ve kararını kamusal yoldan duyurur.   (Velidedeoğlu 1979: i. 220–1)

Trusteeship of minors terminates with maturity or the judge's decision of maturity. The court of first instance, when giving its decision of maturity, shall fix the day on which the trusteeship terminates and announce its decision officially.

For the 1934 version's 'resmen' (officially), Velidedeoğlu regularly uses 'kamusal yoldan' (publicly), literally 'through the public way'. He wanted to avoid the Arabic adverb, but 'kamusal yoldan' was not a good substitute. For 'resmen', *Türkçe Sözlük* (1988) offers the half-Turkicized 'resmî olarak', which is current, and 'devletçe', which can serve for 'officially' only when the official body concerned is the state.

Even though the sense of the right-hand pages may not always be crystal clear now, the lawyer can extract the gist from them, while quoting the original text from the left-hand page to impress his client or the court.

There is a similar treatment of the Criminal Code. Here is the text of Article 361 in both versions (Güner 1981: 274–5):

(1926) Her kim iltizam ettiği taahhüdü icra etmeyerek resmî bir daireye veya bir hizmeti âmme ifasına yahut bir musibeti âmmenin önünü almağa elzem olan erzak ve eşyanın fıkdanına sebebiyet verirse bir seneden üç seneye kadar hapse ve yirmi beş liradan aşağı olmamak üzere iki yüz liraya kadar ağır cezayı nakdiye mahkûm olur.

Taahhüdün icra olunmaması failin yalnız ihmal ve teseyyübünden ileri gelmiş ise bir seneye kadar hapse ve yüz liraya kadar ağır cezayı nakdîye mahkûm olur.

(1981) Her kim kabullendiği yüklenmeyi yerine getirmeyerek kamusal bir daireye ya da bir kamu hizmeti yapılmasına yahut bir genel musibetin önünü almaya pek gerekli olan yiyecek ve nesnelerin yokluğuna yol açarsa bir yıldan üç yıla değin hapse ve iki yüz liraya değin ağır para cezasına çarptırılır.

Yüklenmenin yerine getirilmemesin suçu işleyenin yalnız savsama ve özensizliğinden ileri gelmişse bir yıla değin hapse ve yüz liraya değin ağır para cezasına çarptırılır.

Anyone who, by not carrying out the commitment he has undertaken, causes the absence of food and goods essential to an official department or to the performance of a public service or to prevent a general disaster, will be condemned to imprisonment for one to three years and a heavy fine of up to TL200.

If the non-performance of the commitment is due only to carelessness and oversight on the part of the culprit, he will be condemned to imprisonment for up to one year and a heavy fine of up to TL100.

The field in which new words constantly arise is computing, and in this the Turks, like other nations, have been tempted to take the easy course of using the international—i.e. the Anglo-American—terms. Computer people have not succumbed totally to the temptation. For the computer itself, *bilgisayar* is the only name. There are words for the printer (*yazıcı*), the hardware (*donanım* 'rigging'), the software (*yazılım*), and the print-out (*çıkış*),[3] but for the most part the international terms prevail. The purpose of Yalçıner and Şahin's (1993) excellent dictionary is to explain the meaning of computer terms, not to advance the language reform. So its entry

---

[3] For 'print-out', Yalçıner and Şahin (1993) gives not *çıkış* but *yazılı çıktı* 'written output'.

under OCR is '*optik karakter tanıma*. Bkz. [Bakınız 'see'] *optical character recognition*'. Under that heading you find: 'Fotoelektrik dönüştürücüler veya ışıkla kâğıt üzerine yazılmış ya da basılmış olan karakterlerin bulunması, tanınması ve makine diline çevrilmesinde kullanılan bir teknik' (A technique used in the finding, recognizing, and translating into machine language of characters written or printed on paper by photoelectric transformers or by light).

The enter or return key is explained as *enter tuşu* or *return tuşu, tuş* being *touche* [F]. Where a Turkish or *Öztürkçe* term exists, it is shown, as in the entry for graphic mode: *grafik mod, çizgesel mod*. The explanation of 'boot' is *bilgisayarı açmak*, 'to switch the computer on'. The dictionary does not note the new transitive use of *girmek* 'to enter' in the sense of 'to input', but provides an example in 'girilecek' in the following:

garbage in garbage out (GIGO); çöp girerse çöp çıkar
Bir bilgisayar sistemine girilecek veri ile ilgili olarak, verinin hatalı olması halinde üretilecek, çıktının da hatalı olması durumu.

Garbage in, garbage out (GIGO): if garbage goes in, garbage comes out.
In connection with data to be entered in a computer system, the state of affairs where if the datum is wrong the output that will be produced will also be wrong.[4]

The text of an advertisement in the magazine *Nokta* of 31 January 1993 shows why a Turkish computer-user might need such a dictionary: 'MACWORLD TÜRKİYE ses yazı grafik animasyon film multimedya demo disketi hyperdcard [*sic*] üzerinde QuickTime ile hazırlanmış multimedya uygulaması MACWORLD/TÜRKİYE şubat sayısı ile birlikte tüm okurlarımıza bayilerde' (MACWORLD TÜRKİYE sound, writing, graphics, animation, film, multimedia demo disket, multimedia application prepared with QuickTime on hypercard, for all our readers, with the February number of MACWORLD/TÜRKİYE at the newsvendors). The non-harmonic *bayi* (*bā'iᶜ* [A]) '(news)vendor' looks incongruous among all those ultramodern terms, but the word retains its popularity against *gazete satıcısı*.

To give an idea of ordinary people's computer-speak, here are the texts of two letters in *Okur Postası* (Readers' Mail) in the magazine *PC!* of 15 July 1997:

SATILIK 486 PC. 486 DX 2-66, 8 MB RAM, 14" 0.28 SVGA renkli monitör, 3.5" 1.44 FDD, 420 MB HDD, 1 MB ekran kartı, Windows 95 Türkçe klavye + mouse özellikleri olan bilgisayarımı 480 $'a satıyorum.

486 PC FOR SALE. I am selling for $480 my computer with these features: 486 DX 2-66, 8 MB RAM, 14" 0.28 SVGA colour monitor, 3.5" 1.44 FDD, 420 MB HDD, 1 MB screen card, Windows 95, Turkish keyboard + mouse.

PC TAKASI. 14 inç Monokrom ekran çok temiz hard diskli PC bilgisayarımı satmak istiyorum. Yanında yazıcısıyla birlikte 30.000.000 TL. Amiga veya Sega ile takas yapılır.

---

[4] Another example comes from the newspaper *Sabah*, 29 Dec. 1997: 'RP'nin [Refah Partisi'nin] internetine porno sayfa giren muzipler' (the mischievous people who input pornographic pages into the Welfare Party's internet).

PC EXCHANGE. I want to sell my hard-disk PC computer, in very good condition, 14-inch monochrome screen. Along with its printer, TL30,000,000. Will exchange for Amiga or Sega.

TDK has not produced a glossary of musical terms, though in 1954 it published a twenty-seven-page brochure entitled *Terim Anketleri: Müzik*, the work of Turkey's greatest composer, Adnan Saygun (1907–87). With no introductory material, this consisted simply of a list in three columns, headed 'Fransızca' (French), 'Eski Terimler' (Old Terms), and 'Kullanılan veya teklif edilen terimler' (Terms in use or proposed). There was little change from column to column; the terms for 'sharp' and 'flat', for example: '*Dièse*–Diyez–Diyez' and *Bémol*–Bemol–Bemol'. Sometimes a Turkish word was added: '*Allegretto*–Allegretto–Allegretto; çabukça'; '*Allegro*–Allegro–Allegro; çabuk'; '*Appassionato*–Appassionato–Appassionato; heyecanlı'; '*Rallentando*–Rallentando–Rallentando (yavaşlıyarak)'. Rarely does a Turkish word stand alone in the third column: '*Réponse*–Repons; cevap–Cevap'. Rarer yet, an *Öztürkçe* word: '*Transcription*–Transkripsiyon–Çevriyazı'; '*Altération*–Tağyir, tefnin–Değişim'. This is what one would expect of Turkish musicians and musicologists, who adopted Western music complete with its technical terms. In her 252 pages on problems of music, Filiz Ali (1987) mentions no problem of terminology, nor does Sözer (1986) give any hint in his encyclopaedia that an alternative terminology exists.[5] He defines BEMOL: 'Bir notanın doğal sesinden yarım perde (aralık) daha pestleşeceğini (kalınlaşacağını) belirten işaret' (The sign indicating that a note is to be lowered a semitone below its natural pitch). The definition of DİYEZ is on similar lines.

Yet there is an alternative terminology, taught and used in the Department of Music at the University of the Aegean, but consistently disregarded not only by most musicians and musicologists elsewhere but also by Turkish lexicographers, including those of TDK, whom one would have expected to take an interest in an academic haven of *Öztürkçe*. The existence of this terminology is due to Gültekin Oransay, the gifted and influential musicologist who founded the Department, and to Adnan Saygun.[6] Turkish musicians in general use the French terminology, with *do diyez majör* for C sharp major, and *mi bemol majör* for E flat major. The school of Oransay calls these *büyük dikdo* and *büyük yonmi* respectively, using *dik* for sharp and *yon* for flat. For 'composer' it uses not *bestekâr* [P] but *bağdar*, while for 'music' it uses not *müzik* [F] or *musiki* [A] but Ataç's *küğ*, with *küğsel* for 'musical'. Its word for 'singer' is not *şarkıcı* but *ırlagan*, which differs from *dik*, *yon*, and *bağdar* in having an obvious etymology: *ırlamak* is a provincial word for 'to sing'.

[5] Some time before 1986, Bilgi Yayınevi, an Ankara publisher, produced a *Müzik Kılavuzu*, which I have not seen.

[6] Some information about Saygun may be found in Gedikli (1987: 11) and in İlhan (1987). The second of these two articles, however, is not as informative about musical terms as one could have wished.

While we are on the subject of music, here is a perhaps gratuitous note for the benefit of any reader who may have formed the impression that *saz* [P] is the name of the long-necked stringed instrument that holds so important a place in folk-music. The name for this, however, is *bağlama*; *saz* means just 'instrument', be it piano, drum, flute, or anything else. Some musicians use the French *enstrü-man*, some the Turkish *çalgı*, but *saz* is the usual term. Stringed instruments are *telli saz*, percussion instruments are *vurma saz*, wind instruments *nefesli saz*.

10

The New Yoke

The Franglais which so exasperates the Académie Française is as nothing compared with *Türkilizce*,[1] some examples of which we have already met. This development was foreseen in 1954 at the Seventh Kurultay, in a contribution from a schoolmaster named Abdi Tevfik Yegül (Kurultay 1954: 82). He spoke of the questions his pupils were constantly asking him about the new technical terms; why was this one or that one adopted, and would he please explain it?

'Hocam bu Trafik kelimesi ne demektir?' dediler ve çocuklardan birisi devam etti. 'Şemseddin beyin lûgatına babamla birlikte baktık, mânası ticaret, ihtikâr, demiryollarında eşya nakli ve yolcu nakli gibi işlerin yapılması mânasına geliyor' dedi. Çocuk devam etti. 'Babamla Larousse'a da baktık. Burada da trafiğin ticaret ve seyrüsefer anlamına geldiğini' söyledi.

Demek ki bugüne kadar Fransız mandası altına girmiş olan lisanımız bundan sonra kısmen İngiliz mandası altına girecektir. Bunu yapmayalım.

They said, 'Teacher, what does this word "trafik" mean?' One of the children went on: 'My father and I looked at Şemseddin Bey's dictionary [*Kamus*]; it means doing things like commerce, profiteering, and transporting goods and passengers on railways.' The child continued: 'My father and I looked at Larousse as well. There too it meant commerce and traffic.'

That means that our language, which till now has been under French mandate, from now on will come in part under British mandate.[2] Let's not do this.

The same point had been made over seventy years before, by Ahmet Midhat in *Terceman-ı Hakikat* (no. 112 (1881)):

'Vâ esefâ ki, biz şimdiki halde bir lisan dilencisiyiz. Gâh Arabların gâh Acemlerin ve hele şimdi de Frenklerin kapılarını çalarak lâfızca kavaidce sadaka-i ma'rifetini dileniyoruz' (Alas! At present we are mendicants in quest of a language. We knock at doors, sometimes the Arabs' doors, sometimes the Persians', and now particularly the Europeans', begging for a charitable gift of knowledge in the shape of words and rules) (Levend 1972: 129).

The time when TDK's principal business was seeking *Öztürkçe* replacements for Arabic and Persian words has long passed; much of the post-1983 TDK's effort goes into devising and disseminating Turkish equivalents for English words in common use. It sets an example in its journal *Türk Dili* by giving its fax number

---

[1] The earliest use I have spotted of this splendid conflation of *Türkçe* and *İngilizce* is in Başkan (1975).

[2] The speaker's choice of metaphor was due to memories of the years immediately after 1918, when some Turks favoured an American or British mandate over their country.

under the heading 'Belgegeçer (Faks)'. Whether everyone in TDK's offices says 'belgegeçer' (document-passes) rather than 'faks' is another matter; just as one wonders whether all French civil servants really call this useful device by its prescribed name, 'télécopie'. When TDK's campaign was being waged only in the pages of its journal, it did not seem likely to be very effective, preaching as it was to the converted. In 1997, however, the Society began to spread the message wider, by bringing out and circulating to schools a striking poster headed 'Burası Türkiye mi?' (Is this Turkey?). It showed a city street with an abundance of signs such as 'Happy New Year', 'Hotel', 'Real Estate Center', 'Photo Colour', and 'Chicken House'. The French contribution was limited to 'La Famme [*sic*] Boutique'.

It is not hard to see the reason for the present torrent of English. Just as the Turks' acceptance of Islamic civilization led to their adoption of large numbers of Arabic and Persian terms, so, though to a lesser extent, did the increasing exposure of Turkish intellectuals to Western civilization in the nineteenth century bring Italian and, even more, French words surging into their vocabulary.[3] Cevdet Kudret (1966) remarks on the substitution of French words for Arabic, when *hekim* began to be supplanted by *doktor*, *baytar* by *veteriner*, *kâtip* by *sekreter*. He mentions the replacement of the Italian *locanda* 'inn' and *agente* 'agent' (in Turkish used more often for 'agency'), and the Greek *panēgúri* 'festival, fair' by the French *restaurant*, *agence*, and *foire*:

> İş bu kadarla da kalmadı, daha önce girmiş Frenkçe sözcükleri dahi değiştirip yerlerine başka Frenkçe sözcükler aldık: *musiki* yerine *müzik*, *lokanta* yerine *restoran*, *acente* yerine *ajans*, *panayır* yerine *fuar* diyoruz artık . . . Dikkat edilirse, Türkçe *aşevi* en aşaği, en ucuz yemek evleri için kullanılmaktadır. *Lokanta* sözcüğü yavaş yavaş halk arasında da yayılmağa başlayınca, yüksek tabaka kendisi için daha başka bir söz aramış, *restoran*'ı bulmuş. *Aşevi* halkın, *lokanta* orta sınıfın, *restoran* yüksek sınıfın yemek yeridir. Böylece, kendimiz halktan uzaklaştıkça dilimiz de Türkçe'den uzaklaşmaktadır. Frenkçeyi aldıkça, çok inceldiğimizi sanıyoruz. Sözgelimi, halk *ayakyolu*'na ve *aptesane*'ye, orta tabaka *helâ*'ya, biz okumuşlarsa *tuvalet*'e gideriz; son zamanlarda bir de *W.C.* çıktı, arasıra oraya da gidiyoruz.   (Kudret 1966: 74–5)

Nor did it stop there; we have changed European words that had entered earlier also, taking other European words to replace them. Now we say *müzik* instead of *musiki*, *restoran* instead of *lokanta*, *ajans* instead of *acente*, *fuar* instead of *panayır* . . . If you look into it you will see that the Turkish word *aşevi* is used of the commonest and cheapest eating houses. As *lokanta* began to spread gradually among the populace too, the top stratum sought for themselves yet another way of saying it and found *restoran*. *Aşevi* is the eating place of the populace, *lokanta* of the middle class, *restoran* of the upper class. Thus the further we distance ourselves from the populace, the further our language departs from Turkish. The more we adopt European language, the more refined we think we are becoming. In that connection: the populace goes to the *ayakyolu* and the *aptesane*, and the middle

---

[3] Fashions in words do change, without any intervention by a Language Society. Until the Second World War, the colloquial English for 'Are you trying to make fun of me?' was 'Are you taking the mike out of me?' Warriors returning from overseas in or after 1945 were surprised to find that the current expression was—as it still is—'Are you taking the micky?'

class go to the *helâ*, whereas we educated folk go to the *tuvalet*; moreover the *WC* has recently turned up, and now and again we go there as well.[4]

For over a century the usual Turkish for 'furniture' was *mobilya*.[5] The old words *döşeme* and *mefruşat* [A] had ceased to serve; they meant *alaturka*[6] 'Turkish-style' furniture, whereas the new Italian-style furniture brought its own name with it. In those days, 'furnished' was *mobilyalı*. Peyami Safa used *möble*, the French *meublé*, for 'furnished'. More recently, however, *mobilya* has had to compete with another *möble*, not from *meublé* but from *meuble* 'furniture'.[7]

After the irruption of Italian and then French, now, in the American century, it is the turn of English.[8] To some degree the language reform must be held responsible: older people are sometimes aware that the word that comes to their lips may not be understood, but are uncertain about finding the right new word to express what they want to say in what purports to be their mother tongue, so they resort to a foreign and unambiguous word. A far larger class of users of foreign words are professional people—especially doctors, as we have seen in the previous chapter—when they think the obvious word is not sufficiently techni-cal. A friend who at one time edited a Turkish medical magazine told me that when he used *beslenme* for 'nutrition' a doctor corrected it to *nütrisyon*. Nowa-days that doctor would probably have chosen the English *nütrişın*, following the trend illustrated in a cartoon in *Cumhuriyet* of 13 December 1993. It shows two men, both marked as intellectuals by their spectacles, walking along the street. One of them is saying: 'Türkçe yerine İngilizce konuşanlara kıl oluyorum abi . . . operasyon yerine opereyşın, spekülasyon yerine speküleyşın diyenler yüzde sekseni buldu. Hiç olmazsa fifti fifti kullansak yabancı sözcükleri be abi!' Friend, I'm getting fed to the teeth with people who talk English instead of Turkish. The number of those who say 'opereyşın' instead of 'operasyon', 'speküleyşın' instead of 'spekülasyon', has risen to 80 per cent. If at least we were to use [Turkish words and] foreign words fifty fifty, my friend!).

[4] He omits to mention another term used by the *halk*: 'yüz numara' (number one hundred), the door being marked with two zeros. Popular etymology ascribes this to an early Turkish visitor to Paris who mistook the French 'sans numéro' for 'cent numéro', but the French term is 'le numéro cent'.
[5] It still is in popular speech, which also preserves another old Italian borrowing, *familya*, in the sense not so much of 'family' as of 'wife'. *Aile* [A] 'family' is the word used to avoid explicitly saying *karı* 'wife'. To put it bluntly, *familya* is a euphemism for *aile*, once a euphemism for *karı* but now, to the unsophisticated, virtually synonymous with it.
[6] This useful word is borrowed from the Italian *alla turca*. Its antonym is *alafranga*, Italian *alla franca* 'European style'.
[7] Compare the final *es* of *kilometre kare*, one standing for the French mute *e*, the other for *é*. The Turkish form of *neutre* [F] is *nötr* 'neutral', with no final *e*, so *möble* does not need its final *e* to rep-resent *meuble*, except that, if you want to say 'furnished' but scorn both *mobilyalı* and *döşenmiş* as being outmoded, *möbleli* is the word for you, whereas **möbllü* would have been unpronounceable.
[8] English had in fact been the main source of maritime terms since the early 1800s, according to the erudite though sometimes erratic Bedros Effendi Kerestedjian (1912: 143): 'Disons, une fois pour toutes, que les termes de marine et d'instruments de fabrique que [sic] étaient empruntés, autrefois, à l'italien, sont aujourdhui pris généralement de la langue anglaise: les officiers instructeurs de la marine et des fabriques impériales, en Turquie, étant depuis près d'un siècle recrutés en Angleterre.'

The following, from an article by Mümtaz Soysal (1990) is cited not only for its manifest good sense but also for the vigour of its style.[9] The Head of State referred to was President Turgut Özal:

Türkiye Cumhuriyeti'nin devlet başkanı sabah, akşam 'transformasyon' dan söz eder, bakanlar 'sübvansiyone' bile değil, 'sübvanse' edilen girişimleri anlatır . . . Bir okuyucunun isyan ederek duyurduğuna göre, İzmir Belediyesi'nin camdan otobüs durakları 'hem indoor hem outdoor, hem visible, hem invisible' imiş.

Ya halkın kullandığı telefon. Telefonların üzerindeki 'jeton iade holü'ne ne demeli? Haydi 'jeton'la 'iade'yi anladık da, 'hol' nesi? Türkçe 'delik' demek varken İngilizce 'hole' ü imdada çağıran densizi bulup Dil Kurultay'ının bütün üyeleri önünde eşek sudan gelinceye kadar sopaya çekmedikçe, galiba bu çeşit zıpırlıkların sonu gelmeyecek.

The Head of State of the Turkish Republic speaks morning, noon, and night of *transformation*. Ministers talk of enterprises that are not even *subventionné* but *subvensé* . . . According to information supplied by a reader in revolt, the Izmir Municipality's glass bus-shelters are described as being 'both "indoor" and "outdoor", both "visible" and "invisible" '.

And what about the public telephones? What can one say of the words they bear: 'Token Return Hole'? All right, let us concede that we understand *jeton* [F] and *iade* [A]; what is *hole*? Until we find the dim-witted oaf who, it being open to him to say the Turkish *delik*, enlists the aid of the English *hole*, and he is given a sound thrashing in the presence of all the members of the Language Congress, I suppose there will be no end to daftnesses of this kind.[10]

The use of *hol* for 'hole' was particularly ill conceived, because *hol* had long been known to Turks in a different sense; it was another English borrowing, from 'hall' in the sense of a large public room or the entrance hall of a house. But perhaps they may get used to having *hol* with two disparate meanings, as they already have *kot* with five: it means a type of cotton material, the jeans made from it, altitude, and code,[11] and also appears in *kotdışı pazar* 'marché de valeurs non-cotisées', 'unlisted securities market'; this from the French 'cote' 'Stock Exchange quotation'.

Süpermarket now figures in the dictionaries, and so does *süper*, defined in such terms as 'Nitelik, nicelik ve derece bakımından üstün olan' (Superior from the point of view of quality, quantity and degree). *Süperdevlet* is in regular use for 'superpower' but has not yet got into the dictionaries. Sports writers call the player who scores the most goals 'en skorer oyuncu'. The normal word for a bodyguard, or bouncer or chucker-out at a night-club, is *koruma* 'protection', but the with-it word is 'bodyguard', spelled like that. There is, however, no shortage of French.

[9] For the writer's distinction too. Professor Soysal, while Dean of the Faculty of Political Sciences at Ankara, suffered greatly for upholding freedom of thought in the bad days of the early 1970s.

[10] The daftnesses continue, and not only in Turkey. I have in front of me a leaflet entitled 'The Patient's Charter', published by HM Stationery Office in 1991 for the Department of Health. It promises that in due course there will be, *inter alia*, a Turkish version, 'Peyşınt Çartır'.

[11] This makes a verb *kotlamak*. If, when using the telephone, you are asked 'Adınızı kotlar mısınız?' (Will you spell out your name in code?), you should reply, if your name is Mehmet or Meredith, 'Muğla'daki *M*, Edirne'deki *E*' (*M* as in Muğla, *E* as in Edirne) and so on.

The slip of paper your waiter gives you when, dinner over, you ask for 'hesap', will probably have the printed heading 'Adisyon'. The Turkish for 'ambulance' is *cankurtaran* 'life-saver', but the legend you will see on the front of most ambulances in Turkey is *Ambülans*. Mümtaz Soysal (1993)[12] has an ingenious explanation of how this may have come about:

Sözcüklerin doğuşunu, yaşayışını ve ölüşünü izlemek her zaman ilginçtir.

'Ambülans' sözünü alın. Niçin doğdu? Daha doğrusu, çağdaş Türkçenin en güzel sözcüklerinin biri olan 'cankurtaran'ı nasıl öldürdü? Belki de cankurtaranların can kurtarmamaya başlamasıyla birlikte oldu bu değişiklik. Kimbilir, şehir düzenleri bozuldu, yollar tıkandı da, çağrılan cankurtaranlar zamanında gelmeyince hastalar, yaralılar hastaneye kaldırılmadan öldüler. Geç gelen cankurtaran, adıyla çelişen bir araçtır. Adı herhalde bundan değişti.

Oysa, 'ambülans' öyle mi? Adının ne anlama geldiğini bilen yok ki, geç gelince kızılsın. 'Can kurtarmayan ambülans da olabilir' diye düşünmeye başlıyor insanlar ve bu sözde alafrangalıkla birlikte müthiş bir şarklılık, adamsendecilik, olmaması gereken bir hoşgörü yerleşiyor.

It is always interesting to trace how words are born, how they live, and how they die.

Take the word *ambülans*. Why was it born? More to the point, how did it kill off *cankurtaran*, one of the most attractive words in contemporary Turkish? It may well be that this change took place just when the life-savers began not saving lives. Who knows, urban order deteriorated, the roads became clogged, and, when the life-savers that were summoned did not arrive in time, the sick and injured died before being removed to hospital. The life-saver that arrives late is a vehicle that belies its name. It was surely because of this that the name changed.

But is that so with *ambülans*? There is no one who knows what the name means, so why should anyone feel angry when it arrives late? People start to think, 'A non-saver of life may just as well be an ambülans [as anything else],' and in those words, despite the occidental flavour, there nestles a terrible oriental quality, a 'So what?' attitude, a tolerance which ought not to exist.

In an earlier article Soysal (1986) said:

Kendi dilini geliştirmek yerine başkalarının dilini böylesine yalan yanlış benimseyen bir başka toplum da yoktur . . . Radyolarında harfleri bile gâvurca okuyup 'er-aş pozitif' diye kan isteyen ve 'Oşinografi Dairesi'nin bildirilerini okuyan bir toplum bu tarzancayla mı kendi düşüncesini üretecek?

Nor is there any other society that, instead of developing its own language, adopts in so cockeyed a fashion the language of other people . . . A society which even pronounces on its radio the names of the letters of the alphabet in the manner of the heathen, asking for 'er-aş pozitif' [Rh positive] blood, and which reads notices from 'the Department of Oceanography'—is it going to produce its own ideas in this monkey-talk [Tarzanish]?

The pronunciation of 'Rh' as /er-aş/ reflects the French training of many Turkish doctors, while the English-language domination of the field of electronics is

---

[12] The article in entitled 'Atmasyon' (Showing off), from *atma* 'bragging' plus the French suffix of such words as *telekomünikasyon*. See Lewis (1988: 172).

shown by the pronunciation of the abbreviation TV for television; some do say /te-ve/, but /ti-vi/ is at least as common. FM for frequency modulation is universally pronounced /ef-em/, not /fe-me/.

On Fridays, some newspapers' front pages carry a promise that tomorrow's issue will bring next week's television programmes: 'Yarın TV Guide'. Friends I have consulted cannot guess how that last word is pronounced by readers ignorant of English. Even when one knows that *okeylemek* means 'to OK', that *fizibilite raporu* has long been the Turkish for 'feasibility report',[13] and *kalite kontrolü* for 'quality control', one can still be startled by new developments in *Türkilizce*. The programme of the 1998 International Conference on Turkish Linguistics included a paper entitled: 'Türkçe'de Kompleks Predikasyonlar içindeki Gerundium Grubu Ögelerinin Relativizasyonu' ('Relativization of Elements of the Gerund-Group within Complex Predications in Turkish'). If that does not startle you, how about this? The notice outside the places where they measure your vehicle's emission of exhaust-gas reads: 'Egzos Gazı Emisyonu Ölçüm İstasyonu'. Beyond saying that *ölçüm* means 'measurement', just this once I shall break my rule about leaving no Turkish quotation untranslated.

Another new borrowing is -*kolik*, from the suffix of *alcoholic* and its offspring *chocoholic* and *workaholic*, the *Türkilizce* for the last-named being *çalışmakolik* or *işkolik*. Tea addicts are called *çaykolik*. An older such suffix is -*matik* as in *bankamatik*, a cash-dispensing machine. Lately its use has spread in unlikely directions:

Devlet Bakanı Işılay Saygın, ilk kez tapu işlemlerinin bankamatik kartları gibi manyetik kartlarla yürütülmesini sağlayan 'Tapumatik' sisteminin açılışını yaptı. ('Tapular artık tapumatike'. *Hürriyet*, 12 Ağustos 1997, haber) . . .

Bu arada yeri gelmişken üç derginin adından da söz etmeliyim. 'Haftalık Ekonomi, Politik, Finans, Borsa Dergisi PARAMATİK', bilmece-bulmaca dergileri ZEKAMATİK ve ÇÖZMATİK. (Sakaoğlu 1998)

Minister of State Işılay Saygın has performed the opening of the Tapumatik system, which for the first time makes it possible for land-registration operations to be conducted by means of magnetic cards resembling cash-cards ('Title-Deeds at Last Automated', *Hürriyet*, 12 Aug. 1997, news item) [*tapumatike* is a quasi-French past participle from *tapu* 'title-deed' plus -*matik*] . . .

This brings me to[14] the names of three magazines: *Paramatik, the Weekly Journal of Economics, Politics, Finance, and the Stock Market*, and the riddle and puzzle magazines *Zekamatik* and *Çözmatik* [*para* 'money', *zeka* 'intelligence', *çöz*- 'to solve'].

A less obvious example of the influence of English is a new phenomenon: the current greeting *Selâm* in place of *Merhaba*. This is not evidence of increasing religiosity, but is due to the prevalence of English-language films on television, which results in what is called *dublaj Türkçesi* 'dubbing-Turkish'. The aim when dubbing is to use Turkish words requiring lip movements similar to those of the original,

---

[13] There are two correctly derived words for 'feasibility', *olurluk* and *yapılabilirlik*, only nobody much uses them. For 'report' there exists the neologism *yazanak*, but it is nowhere near as common as *rapor*.

[14] Literally, 'At this point, now that its place has come, I must also mention'.

and the lip movements for 'Selâm' are closer to those for 'Hello' than to those for 'Merhaba'. Other such phenomena may be on the way. Another instance of television's effect on speech: according to Hasan Pulur, writing in *Milliyet* of 4 February 1995, *Vay anasını!* is no longer the normal way of expressing surprise, its replacement being *Vavvvv!* 'Wow!'

What Atatürk would have made of all this is an interesting topic for speculation. It is clearly not what he had in mind when he spoke of liberating Turkish from the yoke of foreign languages. Maybe he would have welcomed all the Anglicisms and Gallicisms as evidence of his country's Westernization, preferring them to Arabisms and Persianisms. But what he wanted his countrymen to speak and write was Turkish.

11

The New Turkish

There are two questions we have to address: has the reform eliminated the gap between the language of the intellectuals and the language of the people, and has it impoverished the language? The answer to the first question is that the gap, though not so huge as it once was, is still there. But that is natural, because some people need and use more words than others. No one ever expected the intellectuals to stop talking about bacteriology or astronomy or political science or whatever their particular interests might be. The hope was simply that they would give up the use of Ottoman words for everyday concepts; they would not, so to speak, say 'domicile' when they meant 'house', or 'animadvert on' when they meant 'find fault with', or 'I shall exercise cogitation on this topic' when they meant 'I'll think about it'. And they don't. To that extent the reform has been a success. On the other hand, the spread of *Öztürkçe* and the influx of English have hardly changed the speech habits of non-intellectuals; the language spoken today by the agricultural labourer, the shopkeeper, and the small craftsman is not markedly different from that spoken by their grandparents. These people keep much of the old language alive. To this extent the gap has widened and the reform has failed.

Certainly most of the dispossessed Arabic and Persian words are gone for ever, and many Turks feel that their language has already been damaged beyond repair. Since 1983, however, it has begun to settle down and enjoy a new period of convalescence, although, given the endless deluge of English borrowings, it is too early to say 'of natural development'. In the new TDK's suggested replacements for those borrowings, *Öztürkçe* is far from predominating; some of them are what we may call proper Turkish and what the old TDK would have called Ottoman. The list in *Türk Dili* for November 1997 included *sıhhî* for *hijyenik*, and *fizik tedavi uzmanı* 'physical treatment expert' for *fizyoterapist*. For *kemoterapi* 'chemotherapy' we are even given a choice of adjective: *kimyasal/kimyevî tedavi*. For *enformel* 'informal', *resmî olmıyan*. The best they could do for *klonlamak* 'to clone' was *kopyalamak*, the Italian *kopya* having long since supplanted the Arabic *istinsah* 'copy'.

Aksoy (1982: 115–16) says:

Ben tasfiyeci değilim: Dilden, bütün yabancı sözcüklerin atılabileceğine inanmıyorum. Ama tasfiyecileri suçlamak aklımın köşesinden geçmiyor. Onlar bütün yabancı sözcüklere Türkçe karşılıklar bulma çabası içindeler. Bu, alkışlanacak bir tutumdur. Biliyorum ki 'yüzde yüz başarı' ya ulaşamayacaklardır. Ama çabaları, dile birtakım değerler kazandırabilir. 'Tasfiyeci', dilin zenginleşmesi için hiç çaba göstermeyen 'tutucu'dan daha yararlı bir kişidir. Unutulmamalıdır ki tasfiyeciler var diye dil çığırından çıkmaz. Şimdiye değin birçok tasfiyeci gelmiş geçmiştir. Önerileri ne ölçüde gerçekleşmiştir? Toplum, çalışma verimlerinin hepsini süzgeçten geçirir, işine yarayanı alır.

I am not a purifier: I do not believe that all foreign words can be expelled from the language. Yet it never crosses my mind to find fault with the purifiers. They are endeavouring to find Turkish equivalents for all foreign words, an attitude to be applauded. I know they will not be able to achieve one hundred per cent success, but their endeavours may win a number of valuable items for the language. The 'purifier' is more useful than the 'conservative' who makes no effort to enrich the language. One must not forget that the language won't go off the rails just because of the existence of purifiers. A good many purifiers have come and gone before now. To what extent have their proposals materialized? Society filters all the results of their work and takes what suits its purposes.

It does indeed. That is why *yüklenici*, for example, though correctly formed from a Turkish root and Turkish suffixes (*yükle-n-* 'to take on a burden', and *-ici* denoting regular activity), has not caught on. It was intended to replace *müteahhit* 'contractor', but builders who have spent their working lives with contractors do not know the new word and continue to refer to them as *mutahit*. *Cep Kılavuzu* gave *tecim* for *ticaret* [A] 'commerce', and *tecimer* for *tüccar* [A] 'businessman'. Any businessmen who ever seriously called themselves *tecimer* have left no mark; *tüccar* is still the word. There may be some writers who talk about *tecim*, but if so they are living in the past: *Türkçe Sözlük* (1983) did not include *tecim* though it still gave *tecimsel* for *ticarî* 'commercial'. The 1988 edition includes neither, and marks *tecim evi* for *ticarethane* [AP] 'place of business' as obsolete.

Fahir İz, doyen of scholars of Ottoman and modern literature, does not doubt that the reform has been a success (İz 1984): 'Bügünkü Türkçede dilin yapısına uymayan kırk elli söz vardır. Terimlerde bu sayı yüz dolayındadır. Bunlar yazı diline kazandırılan binlerce söz yanında devede kulaktır' (Present-day Turkish has forty or fifty words incompatible with the structure of the language. In the case of technical terms the figure is around a hundred. Beside the thousands of words won for the written language by the reform, this is insignificant ['the ear on a camel']. He rather skates over the fact that the reform has had little effect on the way ordinary people talk; in his text he mentions just one neologism that has entered the spoken language, the malformed *ilginç* 'interesting'. In his summing-up he says: 'Bügün artık Dil Devrimi'nden geri dönülemeyeceği kesindir. Halkın konuştuğu dili bırakıp tekrar Arapçaya ve Farsçaya dönmek hiçbir zaman söz konusu olamaz' (By now there can definitely be no turning-back from the Language Reform. There can be no question of the people's ever abandoning the language they speak and turning once more to Arabic and Persian). He spoils the effect, however, in the next paragraph:

Artık kimseye seçim yerine intihabat, seçmen yerine müntahip, basın yerine matbuat, yayın yerine neşriyat, başyazar yerine ser-muharrir, yazı kurulu yerine heyet-i tahririye, takma ad yerine nam-i müstear, Akdeniz Adaları yerine Cezayir-i Bahr-i Sefid, Oniki Ada yerine

Cezayir-i İsnaaşer, Kuzey Buz Denizi yerine Bahr-i Muhit-i Müncemid-i Şimalî yazdırmanın ve söyletmenin yolu yoktur.

There is no way of making anyone write and say the Ottoman instead of the *Öztürkçe* for 'election', 'voter', 'the Press', 'publication', 'editor-in-chief', 'editorial committee', 'pseudonym', 'Islands of the Mediterranean', 'Dodecanese', and 'Arctic Ocean'.

The title of his brochure is 'The Turkish of Us All', but who are the 'us'? I cannot believe that any of those words, new or old, with the exception around election time of *seçim* and possibly *seçmen*, are often on the lips of the habitués of the tea houses of Kırklareli or Bayburt. Are these the 'people' who are not going to turn once more to Arabic and Persian? How are they to turn or not to turn 'once more' to two languages they never knew?

The standpoint of Faruk Kadri Timurtaş (1979) is very different, as the title of his book reveals: 'Dictionary of New Words, Fake and Otherwise'. He himself uses *kelime* not *sözcük* for 'word', but *sözlük* for 'dictionary' rather than *lûgat*, which now sounds highly archaic; he thus avoids the cacophonous *sözcükler sözlüğü*. Though not so tolerant of illegitimate creations as Fahir İz, he is no diehard;[1] witness his comment on *içerik*, the new word for *muhtevâ* 'contents' (1979: 54–5).

Son yıllarda uydurmacıların çokça kullandıkları kelimelerden biri de içerik'tir, 'muhtevâ' mânâsına geliyormuş. Dilimizde içeri kelimesi bulunmakla birlikte, içerik diye bir kelime yoktur . . . Muhtevâ kelimesinin artık eskidiği ve herkes tarafından bilinmediği doğrudur ama, bunun karşılığı içerik değildir. Muhtevâ yerine 'iç, öz' kullanılabilir.

Another word much used by the fakers in recent years is *içerik*, purporting to mean *muhtevâ* 'contents'. Although *içeri* exists in our language, there is no such word as *içerik* . . . It is true that *muhtevâ* is antiquated and not known to everyone, but the replacement for it is not *içerik*. *İç* or *öz* may be used instead.

Where he would not agree with Fahir İz is on the number of illegitimate formations in *Öztürkçe*. He lists more than three thousand neologisms, which he places in three categories: words correctly formed, incorrectly formed 'fakes', and words that, though semantically or morphologically incorrect, have become so widely used that they qualify as *galat-ı meşhur*, the Ottoman term for 'error legitimized by usage'. Averaging the results of a spot check of one-fifth of the list shows 40 per cent in the first category, 37 per cent in the second, and 23 per cent in the third, making a total of just under two thousand incorrect forms; a far cry from İz's 'forty to fifty'.

Gültekin devotes a chapter—'Yeni bir Seçkin Dili Tehlikesi var mıdır? (1983: 97–101)—to a discussion of whether there is a danger of the emergence of a new élite language. He decides that there is not:

Türk yazı dili son elli yılda çok büyük değişiklikler geçirdi. Elli yıl önce yazılan birçok yazı bugün anlaşılmıyor, bu normaldır. Ama bundan sonra da aynı ölçüde bir değişiklik süreci

---

[1] He was responsible for a neat linguistic term: *kendileştirmek* literally 'to make one's own' for 'to assimilate', previously *temsil etmek* (Aksoy 1982: 114).

beklememek gerekir. Elli yıl sonra, bugün yazılan yazıların anlaşılmaması gibi bir durum olmamalıdır ve olmayacaktır.

Written Turkish has undergone very great changes in the last fifty years. A good many writings of fifty years ago are unintelligible today; this is normal. But from now on, a process of change of the same order must not be expected. Fifty years ahead there should not and will not be a situation in which what is being written today is unintelligible.

The calm 'bu normaldır' that ends the second sentence gave me a cold grue. Thinking that I might have misunderstood, I searched the dictionaries to see whether *normal* had recently acquired some new significance, but found none. There was no getting round it; when Gültekin says it is normal for something written fifty years ago to be unintelligible, he means exactly that; a shocking tribute to the success of the language reform.

In Chapter 1 I mentioned the 'translations into modern Turkish' and 'simplified versions' of standard authors to be seen in the bookshops. Here is a pertinent comment by Fuat M. Andic, quoted in *Cumhuriyet* of 7 May 1995:

Galiba geçen sene idi, Babıâli'de Yakup Kadri'nin bir kitabını, *Erenlerin Bağından*'ı arıyorum. Hiçbir yerde yok. Onun birçok kitabını basmış bir yayınevi, *Erenlerin Bağından*'ı neden basmadınız sualime 'O kitabı Türkçeleştirecek kimseyi bulamadık' diye cevap verdi. Bin dokuz yüz otuzlu yıllarda basılan ve benim orta mektepte okuduğum bir kitabı bugün Türkçeleştirmek lâzımmış! Çince mi yazmış acaba Yakup Kadri? Üstelik o Türkçeyi anlayıp da uydurmacaya çeviren bulunamıyor!

It must have been last year that I was looking in Babıâli[2] for one of Yakup Kadri's books, *Erenlerin Bağından*. It was nowhere to be found. I asked a publishing firm which had printed a number of his books why they had not printed that one. They replied, 'We haven't been able to find anyone to put it into Turkish.' Apparently a book printed in the Thirties, which I read at middle school, today has to be put into Turkish! Did Yakup Kadri write it in Chinese, I wonder? And, to crown it all, no one can be found to understand that Turkish and turn it into fakeish!

Those who condemn the old TDK and all its works usually round off their argument by saying that parents and children no longer understand one another: 'Baba ile evlât birbirini anlamaz hale gelmiştir.' This is an exaggeration. If the children, busy with their homework, grumble about how much *ev ödevi* their teacher has assigned for this evening, it should not take the parents long to work out that *ev ödevi* is what they used to call *ev vazifesi*. Children will understand what their parents mean by *hakkında* 'about', though they themselves will use *ile ilgili* or *-e ilişkin*. Some of them may even use *hakkında* in school just to show off, and this could be the salvation of some older words. I recall my grandson, at the age of 7, coming home with an involved tale about something that had happened that day at school. It ended with, 'So you see it was the other way round. Or, as you big people would say, *vice versa*.' One's recognition vocabulary is always larger than one's working vocabulary.

---

[2] The street of bookshops, stationers, and newspaper offices, below the Babıâli, the old Sublime Porte.

The reform left the Turks with virtually no choice of levels of discourse. To write as one spoke seemed a laudable aim at a time when 90 per cent of the population could not read much of what was being written, nor fully understand it even if it were read out to them. A minister invited to open a new bridge or conference or exhibition in the old days would never use *açmak* for 'to open'; the only permissible verb was *küşad* [P] *etmek*. But in present-day Turkish it is not easy to rise to a solemn occasion unless one risks baffling most of one's audience by resorting to Ottomanisms.[3] When Turks try to express themselves by employing an Ottoman word, not surprisingly they sometimes get it wrong—for example, 'Müsteşekkiriz' (for 'Müteşekkiriz'), which was an Istanbul waiter's response to being over-tipped. An English approximation might be 'I am gratificated!'[4]

Even well-educated Turks are just as liable to be unclear about the meanings of some neologisms as about the meanings of Ottoman words. There is, for example, a confusing cluster of neologisms beginning with *öz*, in addition to the old words *özen* 'care, attention', *özge* 'other', and *özenti* 'counterfeit': *öze* and *özgü* 'peculiar (to)', *özgür* 'free', *özek* 'centre', *özel* 'private', *özerk* 'autonomous', *özet* 'summary', *özgül* 'specific', and *özgün*, which was intended to replace *aslî* 'original' but is used by many for 'authentic'. But in the latter sense *özgün* does not have the field to itself; in Turkey you can buy audio-cassettes labelled 'Otantik Halk Oyunlarımız' (Our Authentic Folk-Dances). One wonders how much that first word conveys to most people who see it, though it may be no less meaningful to the young than the posters one sees nowadays in Britain advertising 'An Evening of Acoustic Songs'.

It cannot be too often remarked that many of the creators of new words were salaried employees of TDK, the others being enthusiastic amateurs. Very few in either group were experts on the language. Consequently, many of the neologisms were not based on Turkish roots and Turkish suffixes. This fact did not bother the man in the street. He learned the new words first at school, as the steady stream of new coinages from the Language Society was channelled through the Ministry of Education. He then saw them constantly in newspapers and on public notices. Although people with a feeling for language may not have liked the new words, they soon found themselves obliged to use at any rate some of them if they wished to communicate. But in Turkey as elsewhere few knew or cared anything about the origins of the words they used, which is why one hears *bölgevî* for 'regional' and *önemiyyet* for 'importance', both being *Öztürkçe* words with Arabic suffixes.

Despite that sweeping generalization, one must own to being taken aback by a speech made by the Minister of Culture in May 1992. Having publicly expressed

---

[3] For a way in which plain *açmak* can be elevated for a ceremonial occasion, however, see *açılışını yapmak* on page 138.

[4] Of course it is not only Turks who get words wrong. Not every British journalist distinguishes between *mitigate* and *militate*, and one longs to see some public figure sue a newspaper for accusing him of prevarication when all he has been guilty of is procrastination.

his heartfelt thanks to TDK for all the new words it had given the nation, he continued: 'Örneğin, Türk Dil Kurnmunca üretilen Kurul, Kurultay, Yurt, Ülke, Tanrı, Töre, Tüzük, Yargıç, Savcı, Giysi, Ezgi, Isı, Evren ve Amaç gibi sözcükler, Orta Asya'nın değişik bölgelerinde olduğu gibi, bugün Türkiye'de de yaygın bir şekilde kullanılmaktadır' (For example, words produced by TDK, such as *kurul* . . . *amaç*, are widely used today in Turkey as in various regions of Central Asia) (*Sürekli Türk Dili Kurultayı* 1992: 7). Well, not quite. Of those fourteen words, TDK produced just three, none of them used in Central Asia: *kurul* 'committee', *yargıç* 'judge', and *savcı* 'prosecutor'. The rest are centuries older than TDK, except that the old TDK could have claimed any credit there might be for reducing the double *s* of *ıssı* 'warmth' to a single *s*. *Amaç* is a Persian borrowing (*āmāj*).

Here is another part of Mümtaz Soysal's (1986) article 'Türkçenin Düşmanları', already cited in Chapter 10:

Türkçe köklerden kalkarak sağlam bir düşünce ve bilim dili yaratmaktan başka çaremiz yok. Anlaşılır ve bilinir olanı da Türkçeleştirmek hevesine kapılmadan, dili yoksullaştırmayıp tam tersine zenginleştirerek, 'tebliğ' ile 'beyanname' nin farklı kavramların karşılığı olduğunu bilip, 'bildiri' diyerek kesip atmak yerine, 'bildiri, bildirge, bildirim' farklarını yaratarak. Fakat, bir yandan da, geçmişinden kopuk bir toplum olamayacağı için, yeni kuşaklara, birazcık da olsa, Osmanlıcayı da öğreterek. Yabancı dilleri bülbül gibi konuşup ecdadının dilini anlamayan çocuklar yetiştirmiş bizden başka bir toplum yoktur herhalde.

The only expedient open to us is to create a sound language of thought and science by starting from Turkish roots, without yielding to the impulse to Turkicize what is intelligible and familiar, not impoverishing the language but, on the contrary, enriching it; by knowing that *tebliğ* and *beyanname* represent two different concepts ['communication' and 'declaration'] and creating the distinctions *bildiri, bildirge, bildirim* ['communication', 'declaration', 'notification'] instead of cutting the Gordian knot and saying *bildiri*. But also, since no society can exist severed from its past, by teaching the new generations some Ottoman, even if it be only a tiny bit. Surely no society but ours has brought its children up to speak foreign languages fluently but not to understand the language of their forebears.

One of the many significant passages in that article is where Soysal speaks of the need for *bildiri, bildirge*, and *bildirim*, to obviate using *bildiri* in all three senses. Much the same point was made by Ali Püsküllüoğlu in *Cumhuriyet* of 6–7 August 1996, in two articles devoted to the word *söylem*. This neologism was intended to mean *söyleyiş* 'manner of speaking', or *söyleniş* 'pronunciation',[5] though it was perverse to create it when the language already possessed those two regularly formed and unambiguous words. Püsküllüoğlu's thirty-odd citations show that different writers use it in different senses. The days when neologisms were regularly circulated to schools are past; when hearing—or, more often, reading—a new word such as *söylem* for the first time, one knows only that it has something to do with saying. Few will bother to look it up in a dictionary but, like Humpty Dumpty,

---

[5] So *Türkçe Sözlük* (1988). It is not given in *Örnekleriyle Türkçe Sözlük* (1995–6), presumably because the compilers saw no reason for its existence.

will use it to mean just what they choose it to mean. And why shouldn't they? Isn't that what its inventor did? One of Püsküllüoğlu's many examples: 'Tutamayanlar'ı diğer Türk romanlarından ayıran . . . türlü biçemlere ve özyaşamöyküsü, ansiklopedi, günlük, şiir, tiyatro, mektup gibi çeşitli söylemlere yer vermesidir' (What sets *Tutamayanlar* [Atay 1986] apart from other Turkish novels is that it finds room for sundry styles and various *söylem*s such as autobiography, encyclopaedia, diary, poetry, theatre, letters). Here *söylem* must mean 'genre'. In others of Püsküllüoğlu's citations it seems to be used for 'style', 'communication', 'manner', 'contents', 'tone', and 'language'. One also sees it used for 'expression' and for 'rhetoric'.

In Ömer Asım Aksoy's spirited defence of the reform (1982: 115) he gives (with no specific reference) a moving quotation from Falih Rıfkı Atay:

'Vaziyet' sözünün Türkçeye yerleştiği inancında olduğumuzdan lügatte bu kelimeye iki karşılık koymuştuk: 'Position' manasına 'vaziyet' kalacaktı. 'Situation' karşılığı 'durum' kullanacaktık. Siz şu işe bakın: Önceleri alay sözü olarak yazılan ve söylenen 'durum', Türkçeden hiçbir zaman çıkmayacağını sandığımız 'vaziyet' i bütün manaları ile dilden kovdu. Hiç tutmayacağını sandığımız 'genel' aldı yürüdü. Doğrusu benim zevkim 'sel' ve 'sal' nispetlerine isyan etmiştir. Ama ne çıkar bundan, yani benden? . . . Bütün yeni kuşağın dili o. Ben ki yirmi, yirmi beş yıl kadar Türkçenin önünde yürüdüm, yeni kuşak şimdi benim önümdedir. Türkçenin kendi zevkim ölçüleri içinde hapsolmamasına kızmalı mıyım? Hayır.

Because we were confident that the place of *vaziyet* in Turkish was secure, we had put two equivalents for it in the dictionary [*Cep Kılavuzu*]. In the sense of 'position', *vaziyet* would remain. For 'situation' we would use *durum*. Just consider this: *vaziyet*, which we had supposed would never disappear from Turkish, has in all its senses been chased out of the language by *durum*, which in the beginning people used in writing and speech as a joke. *Genel*, which we had supposed would never catch on, is now all the rage. I must say that my taste rebelled against the adjectival suffixes *-sel/sal*, but what effect did that have?—I mean, what effect did I have? That is the language of all the new generation. I, who for some twenty or twenty-five years marched in the vanguard of Turkish, now find the new generation ahead of me. Should I be angry that Turkish is not imprisoned within the dimensions of my taste? No.

Aksoy misses something that can be read between the lines of Atay's generous confession: the disappointment felt by him and his colleagues, who thought they had enriched the language by finding two separate words for the two separate senses of *vaziyet*, only to see it impoverished when *durum* usurped both senses. Nor could they have been best pleased when the new word eventually found for 'position' turned out to be *konum*, which they had offered in *Cep Kılavuzu* as a replacement for *tevdiat* and *mevduat* 'bank deposits' (now *yatırım*).

Agâh Sırrı Levend, Secretary-General of TDK 1951–60 and President 1963–6, said in reply to a question at a meeting of its administrative committee in September 1951: 'Bir anlamda türlü kelimeler bulunması, o dilin zenginliğine delâlet etmez. Meselâ Arapçada "Ayın" kelimesinin 40 anlamı vardır: "deve"nin 50 adı vardır. Bu bir zenginlik değildir' (The existence [in a language] of various words in one meaning is no indication of the richness of that language. In Arabic, for example, the word *ʿayn* has forty meanings, the camel has fifty names. This is not richness) (*Türk Dili*, 1 (1951), 54–5).

One does not like to contradict Levend, but it is indeed richness if you are a desert Arab whose whole way of life depends on camels. One might as well say that English is not a rich language because it has a multitude of names for structures: house, office building, mansion, hut, factory, school, warehouse, block of flats ... The camel has in fact only one generic name in Arabic, *baʿīr*, and a collective noun *ibil* 'camels'. The other names making up Levend's 'fifty' are specific to the age, sex, and use of the individual creature in question: *jamal* is a he-camel, *nāqa* a she-camel, *rāḥila* a she-camel fit to be saddled, *ḥuwār* a baby camel from the time of birth until weaned, and so on and so on.[6]

Never mind about Arabian cameleers; what about Turkish writers who like to have a choice of words? Levend should have remembered that once upon a time Turkish was probably the only language that came anywhere near English in the richness of its vocabulary. It had individual words expressing the senses of to state, to affirm, to declare, to assert, to impart, to communicate, to report, to convey, to comment, to hint, to remark, to narrate, and more. To express all these senses, the Turks for the most part now have to make do with *anlatmak* 'to tell', *söylemek* 'to say', and *bildirmek* 'to inform', with adverbs to supply the nuances. So, for 'to hint', if they wish to avoid or do not know the old *ima etmek*, they have to say 'üstü kapalı söylemek' (to say covertly) or 'dolaylı anlatmak' (to tell indirectly). This is what we might call Basic Turkish. Those who deplore *Öztürkçe* and call it 'Türk Esperantosu' overlook the extreme regularity of Esperanto. Basic English affords a closer analogy, having all the idiosyncrasies of English but none of the subtleties.[7] Various words for seeking knowledge were once available to the Turks. There was *istisfar* 'to ask someone to explain a text', *istiknah*, 'to seek to plumb the depths of a problem', *istilâm*, 'to make an official request for information', *istizah* 'to seek clarification', *istimzaç*, 'to make polite enquiries about someone's well-being or to enquire whether someone is *persona grata* to a foreign government'. Only the last two find a place in *Türkçe Sözlük*, the dictionary most widely used in Turkey, which marks both of them as antiquated.

Orhan Okay (1981: 274) made a shrewd observation about the titles of the Turkish translations of four French philosophical works, the *Pensées* of Pascal, the *Méditations* of Lamartine, the *Réflexions* of La Rochefoucauld, and the *Idées* of Alain. He notes that the 'Thoughts', the 'Meditations', the 'Reflections', and the

---

[6] As to *ʿayn*, 'forty meanings' is an exaggeration, unless *kırk* is being used in its metaphorical sense of 'umpteen', but there may be over twenty, though to get the figure that high you have to count hole, small aperture, eye of a needle, and eyelet as four distinct meanings.

[7] Basic English, with a vocabulary of 850 words, was invented in the late 1920s by Charles Kay Ogden, as a vehicle for international communication. It attracted considerable attention in the 1930s, but nothing has been heard of it since the Second World War and the subsequent emergence of non-basic English as the international language.

'Ideas' all come out in the new Turkish as 'Düşünceler' (Thoughts), whereas the older language offered a choice among *düşünceler, murakabat, tefekkürat, tefelsuf, teemmül,* and *mülahazat.* The same writer also remarks that *takdim etmek* 'to offer humbly', *arzetmek* 'to offer respectfully', *ihsan etmek* 'to bestow', *bahşetmek* 'to confer', *lûtfetmek* 'to offer graciously', and *ita etmek* 'to grant' have all been replaced by *vermek* 'to give' and *sunmak* 'to present'.

Aksoy (1982: 23) positively advocates impoverishment. He comes out strongly against the view that maintaining Ottoman synonyms is a way of enriching the vocabulary and avoiding repetition: 'Yinelemeden kurtulmanın yolu da yabancı sözcüğe başvurmak değil, yazı yazmasını öğrenmektir. Yinelemek zorunlu olan yerlerde ise bundan kaçınmamak gerekir. Arapça ya da Fransızca yazan kişi, bir sözcüğü ikinci, üçüncü kez yinelememek için onun Türkçesini, Almancasını mı kullanır?' (The way to escape repeating oneself is not to have recourse to foreign words; it is learning to write. In places where repetition is unavoidable, one must not abstain from it. Does someone writing in Arabic or French use a Turkish or German equivalent to avoid repeating a word for a second or third time?). He gives short shrift to the objection that *ilişki* 'relation' cannot replace *münasebet* in every-day expressions such as 'ne münasebet?' (what's the relevance of that?),[8] 'münase-betsiz etmeyiniz' (don't behave in an unseemly fashion), and 'münasebet almaz' (it is not seemly). He explains (pp. 57–8) that *münasebet* in these expressions does not mean *ilişki* but is an inseparable part of the whole expression. The question he does not address is whether anyone can be expected to drop these and a host of other expressions which contain non-Öztürkçe words.

An effective voice on the other side is Fatma Özkan (1995: 974–81):

Bir dilde, bir kavram, nesne veya varlığı karşılayan birden fazla kelime varsa, zamanla bu kelimelerin arasında ince anlam farkları doğar. Aralarında böyle nüanslar bulunan kelime-lerden birini dile dolayıp diğerlerini unutturmak, dilimizin ifade imkânlarını daraltır. Meselâ, son zamanlarda, 'beğenme, takdir etme, hoşlanma, hazzetme, zevk alma' kelime-lerinin hepsini birden karşılamak üzere, *keyf alma* sözü dillere pelesenk[9] oldu ... Aynı şekilde, *affedersiniz, kusura bakmayınız, özür dilerim* ibârelerinin yerine, *bağışla* demek, dili-mizin ifâde gücünü azaltmaz mı? Hatta, hepsini bir kenara itip, İngilizce *I am sorry*'nin ter-cümesi olan *üzgünüm* sözüyle meram anlatmak hangi mantıkla açıklanabilir? *Şeref, haysiyet, gurur, kibir, izzetinefis* kelimelerinin yerine sadece *onur*'u koymak; *şüphe, endişe, merak* kelimelerinin yerine yalnızca *kuşku*'yu getirmek, dilimizin kaybı mı, kazancı mıdır?

If a language possesses a plurality of words to express a concept, a thing, or an entity, fine distinctions of meaning eventually arise among them. To let one of them be on everybody's

---

[8] I am reminded that over forty years ago, in the days when Istanbul men about town were still addressing each other as 'Mon cher', I ran into a friend who was in a state of fury at what had just happened to him in a smart shop on İstiklâl Caddesi, where he had gone to buy a tie. It seems that the shop assistant had greeted him with 'Monsieur désire?' Spluttering, he had replied, 'Monsieur mü? Monsieur mü? Quelle münasebet?'

[9] This misuse of *pelesenk* 'balsam' for *persenk* 'buzzword' is not uncommon. 'Buzzword' seems to be our closest equivalent, though one is a little put off by a remark in *Time Magazine* for January 1980: 'The air is thick with devalued buzz words, including "buzz words".'

lips and let the others be forgotten means reducing our language's capacity for expression. For example, *keyf alma* ['relishing'] has recently become the buzzword standing for *beğenme* ['approval'], *takdir etme* ['appreciation'], *hoşlanma* ['liking'], *hazzetme* ['rejoicing'], and *zevk alma* ['taking pleasure']. Similarly, does it not diminish our language's power of expression to say *bağışla* ['spare (me)'] instead of *affedersiniz* ['forgive (me)'], *kusura bakmayın* ['excuse me'], and *özür dilerim* ['I beg pardon']? Even more, what logic can help to explain pushing all of these to one side and expressing your meaning with *üzgünüm*, a translation of the English 'I'm sorry'? Is it a gain or a loss for our language to replace *şeref* ['honour'], *haysiyet* ['self-respect'], *gurur* ['pride'], *kibir* ['self-esteem'], and *izzetinefis* ['dignity'] just by *onur*; to introduce *kuşku* ['suspicion'] alone as a substitute for *şüphe* ['doubt'], *endişe* ['anxiety'], and *merak* ['worry']?

Onur, originally the French *honneur*, is not a creation of the language reform, though its *Öztürkçe* status seems to be due to its being plugged by TRT, the state broadcasting service. It is shown in *Tarama Sözlüğü* (1963–77) as used in several places in the vilayets of Bilecik, Bolu, Ankara, Kayseri, and Hatay, for *kibir* 'self-esteem' and *çalım* 'swagger'.[10] For 'personal honour', ordinary people's speech retains *namus*, originally the Greek *nómos*. (Oddly enough, *onur* appears in the *Oxford English Dictionary* as an obsolete form of *honour*.)

An idea of the dimensions of the impoverishment can be gathered by browsing in a modern Turkish–Turkish dictionary, particularly in the pages containing many words of Arabic origin: those beginning with *m* and, to a lesser extent, *t* and *i*. Look for words that have only a definition, as distinct from those for which a one-word equivalent is given. Every word in the former category represents a failure on the part of the reformers. English has no exact equivalent of the lovely Ottoman word *selika* [A] 'the ability to speak well and write well'. Nor has modern Turkish. *Türkçe Sözlük* (1988) marks it as antiquated. But why did TDK permit it to become antiquated without devising an *Öztürkçe* substitute? Perhaps the cynics' answer is the right one: why bother to create a word for an obsolete concept?

But there are everday concepts that used to be succinctly expressed and no longer are. *Müddet* 'period', *mühlet* and *mehil* 'respite', 'permitted delay', and *vâde* 'term' have all fallen before *süre*, a Frankenstein's monster whose progenitors were the Turkish *sür-* 'to continue' and the French *durée* 'duration'.

For that useful verb *tevil etmek* 'to explain away', 'to interpret allegorically', *Türkçe Sözlük* (1988) gives 'söz veya davranışa başka bir anlam vermek' (to give another meaning to a statement or an action). *Türkçe Sözlük* does not, however, mention here the *Öztürkçe* equivalent, *çevrilemek*, although that word is defined in the same dictionary as 'Çevriye uğratmak ["to subject to translation"], tevil

---

[10] I have had occasion to refer in uncomplimentary terms to Eyuboğlu's etymological dictionary (1988); nevertheless I note his explanation of how this French word entered Anatolian rural dialect, just in case some fact is lurking in it. His story is that it came through the speech of Greek-speaking Anatolian intellectuals who studied French in the foreign schools. That does not begin to explain how the French *honneur* appears in the dialects of a swath of provinces across Central Anatolia but not in the cities where there are or were foreign schools, notably Istanbul, Izmir, and Tarsus. Its use in Hatay is understandable in view of the French influence that for many years was strong in that region.

etmek'. Anyway, it never caught on, probably because it was too easily confused with another neologism, *çevrelemek* 'to surround', and it does not occur in *Örnekleriyle Türkçe Sözluk* (1995–6). So *tevil* may survive.

Consider the nuances of the many words expressing the concept of change. In English, besides *change*, we have *alteration, alternation, mutation, variation, permutation, vicissitudes, deviation, modification, transformation, metamorphosis*. Many of these can be paralleled in Ottoman, i.e. early Republican Turkish: *istihale, tahavvül, tebeddül, tebeddülât, tagayyür, takallüp*, and so forth, whereas the modern Turk's choice is pretty much restricted to *değişmek* 'to change' and *başkalaşmak* 'to become different'. True, biologists if they wish may call on the neologism *değişke* (not in *Örnekleriyle Türkçe Sözlük* (1995–6)), for which *Türkçe Sözlük* (1988) gives: 'Her canlıda dış etkilerle ortaya çıkabilen, kalıtımla ilgili olmayan değişiklik, modifikasyon' (Change unrelated to heredity, which may emerge under external influences in every living thing; modification).

The vast resources of Ottoman Turkish were at the disposal of the reformers. They did not have to perpetuate the whole exuberant vocabulary; they were free to pick and choose, but they deliberately elected to dissipate their heritage. They should have been aware of the danger that their work would lead to a depletion of the vocabulary if they failed to find or devise replacements for the words they were striving to eliminate. Had Sayılı (1978) been written earlier, and had the reformers read it and taken it to heart, they could have done better, but the damage had been done forty years before.

Yet all is not lost. Language is a set of conventions, which ordinarily just grow. What the reformers did was to create conventions; to say that henceforth the tradition will be thus and thus. Once a convention has been established, it makes no difference if it has slowly matured over the centuries or was manufactured last week in an office in Ankara or a study in Istanbul or a café in Urfa. But learning a new word does not automatically banish the old word from one's memory. I had a fascinating conversation in Istanbul with an elderly taxi-driver, who wanted to know what I was doing in Turkey. I told him that I was particularly interested in the language reform. He replied that he had never heard of it; the language was one and unchanging. For 'language', incidentally, he used the old *lisan* [A] and not *dil*. So I asked him, 'What about *önemli* ['important'], which some people now use instead of *mühim*?' 'Oh no,' he answered, 'they're quite different. Suppose the Municipality says that that building over there isn't safe and it's *önemli* to repair it, that means it may be done five or ten years from now. But if they say it's *mühim*, that means work will start tomorrow.' To him the old Arabic word was the more impressive of the two, and he was not aware that *önemli* was totally artificial.

This incident lends support to the view of a Turkish friend, that nuances of meaning are emerging and will continue to emerge between old words and their *Öztürkçe* replacements; he himself did not feel *medeniyet* and *uygarlık* to be synonymous. If he was talking about a particular civilization or the history of civilization, he would use the former, and for 'civilized' he would say 'medenî'. *Uygar*, on the other hand, conveyed to him something more dynamic: civilized and vigorous and progressive. The story in Chapter 8 of the two Izmir taxi-drivers who did not feel that *uygarkık* had anything to do with *medeniyet* is relevant in this context, as is the last sentence of Chapter 7 n. 12.

Fatma Özkan's words quoted above appear to be borne out: 'If a language possesses a plurality of words to express a concept, a thing, or an entity, fine distinctions of meaning eventually arise among them.'

Now that the creation of *Öztürkçe* has been at a virtual standstill since 1983, there are signs that the process of impoverishment has begun to go into reverse. Not that discerning writers waited for 1983 before feeling free to choose whatever words they pleased, though it must be remembered that it took courage to do so when your choice of words could brand you as a communist or a reactionary. One who had such courage was Zeki Kuneralp, and this is what he wrote in the introduction to his memoirs of a long and brilliant career in diplomacy. Unlike him, I shall not apologize for the length of what follows (though I have abbreviated it somewhat), because, like him, I think the matter is important.

Kitapta kullandığım lisandan da bahsetmek isterim, hatta biraz uzunca. Okurlarımdan onun için özür dilerim, ama konu bence mühimdir. Görüleceği gibi eskiye ve yeniye aynı derecede iltifat ettim, ne Osmanlıca, ne de arı Türkçe yazmaktan ürktüm. Her iki şiveyi aynı cümlede kullanmaktan bile çekinmedim. Türkçe kelime bulamadığım vakit, Türkçeleştirilmiş Frenkçeye başvurmakta dahi mazur görmedim. Kökü ne olursa olsun, hangi kelime fikrimi en iyi ifade ediyorsa onu seçtim ... Ya memlekette o anda hakim siyasî havaya uymak, ya ideolojik tercihlerimize iltifat etmek için eski veya yeni dilden yalnız birini kullanır, öbürünü topyekûn reddederiz. Bunun böyle olduğunu anlamak için Ankara'daki malûm otobüs durağının yakın mazimizdeki muhtelif isimlerini hatırlamak kâfidir. Siyasî iktidara göre bu durak isim değiştirmiş, kâh 'Vekâletler', kâh 'Bakanlıklar' olmuştur. Demokrat Parti iktidarının sonuna doğru 'Erkân-ı Harbiye-yi Umumiye Riyaseti' demeğe bile başlamıştık. 27 Mayıs'dan sonra tekrar 'Genelkurmay Başkanlığı' na döndük. Bu biraz gülünçtür, çünkü bir dilin ne partisi, ne de dini vardır. İhtilâlci ve tutucu aynı dili kullanırlar. Aynı dille bir mukaddes kitap yazılabileceği gibi bir aşk romanı da yazılabilir. Dil bir araçtır, gaye değildir, tarafsızdır.

Biz, umumiyetle, bunun farkında değiliz. Meselâ fanatik şekilde arı Türkçe taraftarı isek istediğimiz manayı taşıyan arı Türkçe bir kelime bulmadık mı, diğer bir kelimeye o manayı da yükletiriz, ihtiyacımızı mükemmelen karşılamakta olan Arabî, Farisî veya Frenkçe kelimeyi sosyo-politik inançlarımızdan ötürü kenara iteriz. Böylece lisanımızı fakirleştirir, nüansları yok eder, vuzuhdan yoksun tatsız bir şekle sokarız. Halbuki bir lisan ne kadar çok kaynaktan kelime sağlıyabilirse o nisbette sarahat, renk ve vüs'at kazanır ... Yaşadığımız dünya gittikçe ufalıyor, milletler birbirine yaklaşıyor, dilleri birbirini etkiliyor ve bu suretle hep birden zenginleşiyorlar.   (Kuneralp 1981: 15–17)

I should like to say something, even at some length, about the language I use in this book. For this I ask my readers' pardon, but to my mind the subject is important. It will be seen that I have shown the same regard for the old as for the new; I have not shied away from writing either Ottoman or pure Turkish. I have not even refrained from using both forms of language in the same sentence. Nor, where I have been unable to find the right Turkish word, have I seen any harm in resorting to a Turkicized Western word. I have chosen whichever word best expresses my thought, no matter what its origin ... In order to conform to the political climate prevailing at the time or to gratify our ideological preferences, we use only one of the two languages available to us, the old or the new, rejecting the other entirely. To see that this is so, it is sufficient to recall the various names borne in our recent past by that well-known bus stop in Ankara. This stop has changed its name according to the political party in power, becoming now 'Vekâletler', now 'Bakanlıklar' [both meaning 'Ministries']. Towards the end of the Democrat Party regime, we had even begun to refer to the office of the Chief of the General Staff by its Ottoman name of 'Erkân-ı Harbiye-yi Umumiye Riyaseti'. After 27 May [the day of the 1960 *coup d'état*] we reverted to the modern 'Genelkurmay Başkanlığı'. This is somewhat ludicrous, because a language has no party or religion. Revolutionaries and conservatives may use the same language. A sacred book can be written in any given language, and so can a love story. Language is a means, not an end; it does not take sides.

We generally fail to realize this. For example, if we are fanatical partisans of pure Turkish, when we cannot find a pure Turkish word to express the meaning we want, we load that meaning on to some other word and, for the sake of our socio-political beliefs, cast aside the Arabic, Persian or Western word that perfectly meets our needs. In this way we impoverish our language, we obliterate its nuances, we deprive it of clarity and thrust it into a tasteless form. Whereas, the more numerous the sources a language can draw on for words, the more explicit, the more colourful, the more copious it becomes ... The world we live on is steadily diminishing in size, the nations are growing closer together, their languages are influencing one another and are thereby becoming jointly enriched.   (Lewis 1992: 2–3)

Since Kuneralp wrote that, more and more writers have been doing as he did and using whatever words they prefer. In the pages of any magazine, 'Ottomanisms' may now be seen that twenty years ago one would have thought obsolete: *meçhulümdür* 'it is unknown to me', *-e tâbi* 'subject to', *-e sahip* 'possessing'.

Pleasant though it is for lovers of the old language to see and hear more and more elements of it coming back into use, they should not deceive themselves into assuming that the language reform is over and done with. The effects of fifty years of indoctrination are not so easily eradicated. The neologisms *özgürlük* and *bağımsızlık* have been discussed in Chapter 8. The objection most critics raise to these two words, however, is on grounds not of malformation but of lack of emotional content. Untold thousands of Turks, they say, fought and died for *hürriyet* and *istiklâl*; how many would be ready to fight and die for *özgürlük* and *bağımsızlık*?

There is an answer to this rhetorical question: you do not miss what you have never known. To those who have grown up since the 1950s, *Hürriyet* is the name of a daily newspaper and a square in Beyazıt, while *İstiklâl* is the name of a street in Beyoğlu. To the majority of them, *özgürlük* and *bağımsızlık* mean what *hürriyet* and *istiklâl* meant to older generations and what 'freedom' and 'independence' mean to English-speakers, and yes, they are ready to fight and die for them if need be. If they think about the language reform at all, they see nothing catastrophic in it; the language they have spoken since infancy is their language.

12

What Happened to the Language Society

The years from 1932 to 1950 were TDK's high noon. It had the support of Atatürk's Republican People's Party, which after his death was led by his faithful İsmet İnönü. The Society, however, had no shortage of opponents. Those who disapproved of Atatürk's secularist policies took exception to the change of alphabet and to the language reform, rightly judging that at least part of the purpose behind both was to make the language of the Koran less accessible. There were other opponents, including many who were broadly in favour of the reform but did not approve of eliminating Arabic and Persian words in general use.

The strength of feeling on this matter may be judged from the conciliatory tone of the speech of İbrahim Necmi Dilmen, Secretary-General of TDK, on 26 September 1940 at the eighth Language Festival:

Yabancı dillerden gelme sözlere gelince, bunlar da iki türlüdür: Bir takımı, kullanıla kullanıla halkın diline kadar girmiş olanlardır. Bunları, dilimizin kendi ses ve türetim kanunlarına göre, benimsemekte diyecek bir şey yoktur. Ancak türkçenin kendi dil kanunlarına uymıyan, halkın anlamadığı, benimsemediği sözleri elden geldiği kadar çabuklukla yazı dilimizin de dışına çıkarmak borcumuzdur. (*Türk Dili*, 2nd ser. (1940), 20)

As for words from foreign languages, they are of two kinds. One category is words that with constant use have entered all the way into the language of the people. There is nothing to be said against adopting these in accordance with our language's own laws of phonetics and derivation. But when it comes to words which do not obey the linguistic laws of Turkish and are not understood and not adopted by the people, it is incumbent on us to expel these from our written language too, as quickly as we can.

In those days TDK was set on Turkicizing technical terms. The report on scientific terminology submitted to the Fourth Kurultay (Kurultay 1942: 20) included this:

Gerçekten inanımız odur ki bilim terimleri ne kadar öz dilden kurulursa bilim o kadar öz malımız olur. Terimler yabancı kaldıkça, bilim de bizde başkalarının eğreti bir malı olmaktan kurtulamaz.

Türkçeden yaratılan bir terim, anlamı ne kadar çapraşık ve karanlık olursa olsun, ne demeye geldiğini Türk, çocuğuna, Türk gencine az çok sezdirir.

Indeed it is our belief that scientific terms become our own in so far as they are based on the pure language. So long as they remain foreign, science in Turkey cannot escape being on loan from other people.

A term created from Turkish, however involved and obscure its meaning may be, will give the Turkish child and young person more or less of a perception of what it means.

The 'az çok' was a wise qualification. *Felsefe ve Gramer Terimleri* (1942) had been published in time for that Kurultay; we have seen some examples of its contents in Chapter 8. If children or young persons, in the course of their reading, came across books employing some of the terms prescribed in it, they might well find themselves lacking a perception of the meaning. A word like *insanbiçimicilik* 'human-shape-ism' for 'anthropomorphism' they might work out,[1] but what would they make of *almaş* and *koram*? Or *sanrı* 'hallucination'? Its first syllable could be the noun *san* 'fame' or the stem of *sanmak* 'to suppose'. But might it not be the new *san*, the *Öztürkçe* for *sıfat* 'attribute'? Or could *sanrı* be a misprint for *Tanrı* 'God'? Poor children and young people!

Over the next few years, however, the Society came to see that the steady influx of international terms was unstoppable, and in 1949 it officially changed its attitude: 'Yabancı dillerdeki bilim ve teknik terimlerinin ileri milletlerce müşterek olarak kullanılanları, incelenip kabul edilecek belirli bir usule göre dilimize alınabilir' (Foreign-language scientific and technical terms used in common by the advanced nations may be taken into our language in accordance with a specific method which will be studied and accepted) (Kurultay 1949: 146).

In 1942 a start had been made on modernizing the language of officialdom, hitherto untouched. The building tax, *bina vergisi* to ordinary people, was still *müsakkafat resmi* 'duty on roofed premises' to the tax authorities, while secret sessions of the Assembly, *gizli oturum* to the participants, were recorded in the minutes as *celse-i hafiye*. It was decided that the best way to begin would be to produce an *Öztürkçe* version of the 1924 Constitution, the Teşkilât-ı Esasiye Kanunu (Law of Fundamental Organization). The 1942 initiative did not get very far, but in November 1944 the Parliamentary Group of the governing Republican People's Party set up a commission to prepare a draft, and the result of their labours was Law No. 4695, the Anayasa, 'Mother-Law', accepted by the Assembly on 10 January 1945. Article 104 read: '20 Nisan 1340 tarih ve 491 sayılı Teşkilât-ı Esasiye Kanunu yerine mânâ ve kavramda bir değişiklik yapılmaksızın Türkçeleştirilmiş olan bu kanun konulmuştur' (This law, which has been put into Turkish with no change in meaning and import, replaces the Law of Fundamental Organization no. 491 dated 20 April 1924). That was true, but it is not so much what you say as the way you say it; the new text was certainly intelligible to more people than the old had been, but the Anayasa aroused the ire not only of the habitual opponents of the language reform but also of lawyers and others who felt that the dignity of the Constitution was

---

[1] They might have raised their eyebrows at the form, seeing that in normal Turkish the third-person suffix is always omitted before *-ci* (Lewis 1988: 50).

diminished by the abandonment of the stately Ottoman phraseology.[2] Here is the text of Article 33 in both versions:

(1924) Reisicumhur, hastalık ve memleket haricinde seyahat gibi bir sebeble vezaifini ifa edemez veya vefat, istifa ve sair sebeb dolayısile Cumhuriyet Riyaseti inhilâl ederse Büyük Millet Meclisi Reisi vekâleten Reisicumhur vezaifini ifa eder.

(1945) Cumhurbaşkanı, hastalık ve memleket dışı yolculuk gibi bir sebeple görevini yapamaz veya ölüm, çekilme ve başka sebeplerle Cumhurbaşkanlığı açık kalırsa Büyük Millet Meclisi Başkanı vekil olarak Cumhurbaşkanlığı görevini yapar.

If the President of the Republic is unable to exercise his duties for any reason such as illness or travel abroad, or if the Presidency falls vacant through death, resignation, or other reason, the President of the Grand National Assembly shall provisionally exercise the duties of the President of the Republic.

The drafting of this Constitution was the occasion for modernizing the names of the four months *Teşrin-i evvel*, *Teşrin-i sani*, *Kânun-u evvel*, and *Kânun-u sani* (October–January), into *Ekim*, *Kasım*, *Aralık*, and *Ocak*, because the second and fourth occurred in the text. There had been previous partial modernizations: *Birinci* and *İkinci Teşrin* and *Kânun*, and *İlkteşrin* and *Sonteşrin*, *İlkkânun* and *Sonkânun*. The new name for January preserves the meaning of *kânun* 'hearth'. With the new name for December it became the subject of jokes on the theme that the transition from December to January—*Aralıktan Ocağa*—now meant passing through the gap into the fire.[3]

Tahsin Banguoğlu fought and lost a long fight to save the language from the reformers' worst excesses, a fight that began in 1949, when he was Minister of Education and President of TDK. Early in 1950 he set up an academic committee of the Society with the task of ensuring that work on devising technical terms should continue 'in keeping with the phonetics, aesthetics and grammar of the language'. The Society did not take long to let it slip into oblivion. He was often reviled as an enemy of the reform, which he was not; he contributed at least one successful neologism, *uygulamak* for *tatbik etmek* 'to apply, put into

---

[2] Half a century later, something of the sort began to happen in England. Under the heading 'Legal Reform could Declare Latin Phrases ultra vires', *The Times* reported (28 Oct. 1994): 'Proposals to streamline procedures under which the public can challenge government and local authority decisions in court were unveiled by the Law Commission yesterday. They include replacing Latin terms with English. The report recommends that the names of remedies sought under judicial review should no longer be mandamus, prohibition or certiorari, but mandatory, restraining and quashing orders. It said that although it was recognised that there were limits on the extent to which legal terminology could be made accessible to lay people, it should be as understandable as possible.' In April 1998 an English judge repeated the message. If it happens, we could revive the Dickensian *Özingilizce* for *habeas corpus*: 'have his carcass'.

[3] According to Erer (1973: 136), TDK decided at one time (not specified) to update the remaining months, February–September, into *Kısır*, *Ayaz*, *Yağmur*, *Kiraz*, *Kavun*, *Karpuz*, *Mısır*, *Ayva*, meaning respectively Barren, Frost, Rain, Cherry, Musk-melon, Water-melon, Maize, Quince. These too would have lent themselves to joking; Erer points out that for 'In April the rains begin' one would have to say 'Yağmurda yağmurlar başlar'. True, and what about 'There were no water-melons in July'? And indeed 'There was no rain in April'—'Yağmurda yağmur yağmadı'?

practice'. What made him unpopular with the extremists was his competence as a specialist in the language.

In the May 1950 elections, the Republican People's Party, with 39.9 per cent of the vote, was defeated by the Democrat Party of Adnan Menderes, with 53.3 per cent. TDK's by-laws (*tüzük*) laid down that the Minister of Education was its President *ex officio*. The new Minister ordered the removal of this provision, and in the following February the Society held an Extraordinary Assembly and duly amended its *tüzük*. The Budget Commission recommended a reduction in the Society's annual Ministry of Education grant from TL50,000 (then equal to £2,000) to TL10,000. During the Assembly debate on the Commission's report in February 1951, one Deputy, having affirmed that the Society had 'lost its scientific personality and had become the tool of political aims' and that 'all it did was ruin the language', proposed that its grant be discontinued altogether, a motion which the Assembly voted to accept (Levend 1972: 486). This did not mean the end of the Society's activities, partly because of the receipts from its publications[4] but more because under Atatürk's will it shared the residual income from his estate, after some personal bequests, with the less controversial Historical Society, Türk Tarih Kurumu.[5] The fact that the Minister had severed his connection with it, however, meant that it could no longer channel its output directly into the schools.

One of Menderes's ministers, Ethem Menderes (no relation), believed in *Öztürkçe*, but there was nothing he could do to stem the tide. On 24 December 1952 the Assembly approved a law restoring 'the Law of Fundamental Organization no. 491 . . . together with such of its amendments as were in force up to the date of acceptance of Law no. 4695'. The voting was 341 for and 32 against, with nine abstentions.

The *Öztürkçe* names of ministries and other bodies were also replaced by their previous names, complete with Persian izafets: *Bakanlık* 'Ministry' once more became *Vekâlet*, *Sağlık ve Sosyal Yardım* 'Health and Social Aid' became *Sıhhat ve İçtimaî Muavenet*, *Bayındırlık* 'Public Works' became *Nafia*, *Savunma* 'Defence' became *Müdafaa*, *Genel Kurmay Başkanı* 'Chief of the General Staff' became *Erkân-ı Harbiye-i Umumiye Reisi*, and *Savcı* 'Public Prosecutor' was again *Müddei-i Umumî*. This was the worst blow so far suffered by the Language Society. Most newspapers went with the prevailing wind and moderated their use of neologisms, without abandoning them entirely. Yet the majority of the generation that had grown up since the beginning of the language reform did not share the Democrat Party's attitude.

---

[4] Particularly in demand was TDK's *Türkçe Sözlük*, which had become an essential work of reference not just for devotees of *Öztürkçe* but for anyone wanting to understand the newspapers and the radio.

[5] The two Societies' share rose from TL40,000 in 1938 to TL118,000 in 1941, TL125,000 in 1952, TL269,000 in 1955, TL505,000 in 1960, TL901,000 in 1961, TL1,815,000 in 1964, and TL1,923,000 in 1966 (Kurultay 1966: 117). In 1946, 46% of TDK's income came from the government and 30% from Atatürk's legacy (Heyd 1954: 51).

It was at this time that Falih Rıfkı Atay wrote that the State Radio had been ordered to stop calling members of the Assembly *Milletvekili* and to revert to *Meb'us*, 'giving due weight to the ʿ*ayn* between the *b* and the *u*'.[6]

TDK was now on the defensive. Heyd (1954: 50) wrote:

During the last few years the Society has refrained from suggesting any further neologisms. This moderate attitude is reflected in a small dictionary of foreign (mostly Arabic and Persian) words with their Turkish equivalents, published by the Society in 1953. Its title, *Sade Türkçe Kılavuzu*, seems to indicate that in the present phase 'simple' (*sade*), and not 'pure' (*öz*), Turkish is the Society's slogan.

On 27 May 1960 the Democrats were overthrown by a group of officers, the leading thirty-eight of whom constituted themselves as the National Unity Committee, and the tide turned. The language reform having from the first been attacked by those opposed to Atatürk's other reforms, the officers saw the Democrat Party's attitude to language, exemplified in its restoration of the 1924 Law of Fundamental Organization, as being all of a piece with its policy of undoing Atatürk's work of making Turkey into a secular republic. Shortly after the military takeover, the Society's subsidy was restored. In January 1961 a government circular was sent to all ministries, forbidding the use of any foreign word for which a Turkish equivalent existed. The new Constitution of July 1961 was in 'the new Turkish', though not completely, as is evident from the following sample, the text of Article 34 (the Persian *veya* and words of Arabic origin are shown in italic):

Kamu görev *ve hizmet*inde bulunanlara karşı, bu görev *ve hizmet*in yerine getirilmesiyle ilgili olarak yapılan *isnat*lardan dolayı açılan *hakaret dava*larında, sanık, *isnad*ın doğruluğunu *ispat hakk*ına *sahip*tir. Bunun dışındaki *hal*lerde *ispat* istemenin *kabul*ü, ancak *isnat* olunan *fiil*in doğru olup olmadığının anlaşılmasında kamu yararı bulunmasına *veya* *şikâyet*çinin *ispat*a *razı* olmasına bağlıdır.

In *cases* of *libel* arising from *allegation*s made against those engaged in public duties *and services* in connection with the discharge of these duties *and services*, the defendant *has* the *right to prove* the truth of the *allegation*s. In *situations* falling outside the above, the *acceptance* of the request *to adduce proof* depends on its being in the public interest for it to be determined whether or not the *alleged action* is true, or on the *plaintiff*'s *consent* to the *adducing of proof*.

On 10 September 1962 General Cemal Gürsel, the chairman of the National Unity Committee, who was elected President of the Republic in the following month, sent the Dil Kurumu a personal letter which, apart from one *kadar*, one *resmî*, and a few *ve*s, really was in the new Turkish:

---

[6] This was in an article in *Dünya* (11 Jan. 1953; repr. in *Türk Dili*, 2 (1941), 333–5), entitled 'Şaka Yolu' (By Way of a Joke), so it should not be taken as gospel, but even if his ' "b" ile "u" arasındaki "ayn"ın hakkını vereceksin' was part of the joke, the State Radio no doubt did receive some such order, since *Meb'us* was the term used in the 1924 Constitution, restored in 1952, while the 1945 Constitution used the relatively *Öztürkçe* form *Milletvekili*. *Meb'us* is Arabic (*mabʿūt*), as are *millet* and *vekil*.

İnancım şu ki, Dil Kurumu yıllardan beri sessizce ve inançla çalışmakta ve büyük işler de başarmaktadır. Bu uğraşmada yavaşlık ve elde edilen sonuçlarda yetersizlik varsa, kesin olarak inanıyorum ki, bunun sorumluluğu Dil Kurumu'nda değil, bizlerde ve aydınlardadır. Aydınlar, yazarlar, kurumlar ve kurultaya[7] kadar resmî kurullar, güçlerinin tümüyle değil biraziyle olsun Dil Kurumu'nun çalışmalarına yardımcı olmak zorundadırlar. Bu kişiler ve kurullar, dilimizin özleştirilmesinde sorumluluğun yalnız Dil Kurumu'nda olduğunu sanıyorlarsa yanılıyorlar.   (Levend 1972: 488)

It is my belief that the Language Society has for years now been working quietly and with faith and achieving great things. If there has been any remission in this effort and any inadequacy in the results, I am convinced that the responsibility for this rests not with the Society but with us and the intellectuals. Intellectuals, writers, societies and official bodies all the way up to the Grand National Assembly are under an obligation to assist the Language Society's labours, if not with all their might then at least with a little of it. These individuals and bodies are wrong if they think that the responsibility for purifying our language belongs to the Language Society alone.

Statistical analyses have occasionally been undertaken to see how much of the current vocabulary of the press consisted of 'native' words—i.e. words known, presumed or declared to be of Turkish origin—and how much was 'foreign'—i.e. Arabic or Persian. Unfortunately, no two of them agree. The most reliable is Kâmile İmer's (1973) scholarly study, which goes down only to 1965. Table 12.1 is taken from her summary of word counts of the news sections in five newspapers: *Ulus, Akşam, Cumhuriyet, Milliyet,* and *Hürriyet.* 'Ottoman' at the head of the last column refers to words compounded of Arabic or Persian roots and Turkish suffixes, such as *hatırlamak* 'to remember', and *endişeli* 'anxious'. It will be seen

TABLE 12.1. Origins of vocabulary of five newspapers, 1931–1965 (%)

Year	Turkish	Arabic	Persian	Other	Ottoman
1931	35.0	51.0	2.0	6.0	6.0
1933	44.0	45.0	2.0	4.0	5.0
1936	48.0	39.0	3.0	5.0	5.0
1941	48.0	40.0	3.0	4.0	5.0
1946	57.0	28.0	3.0	7.0	5.0
1951	51.0	35.0	3.0	6.0	5.0
1956	51.0	35.5	2.0	7.5	4.0
1961	56.0	30.5	3.0	6.0	4.5
1965	60.5	26.0	1.0	8.5	4.0

[7] The meaning of *kurultay* here is unclear. It cannot be the Dil Kurultayı (the Language Congress), which is not a committee or official body. The translation is based on the assumption that it is a slip for *Kamutay*, the replacement at one time proposed for 'Büyük Millet Meclisi'. If the assumption is correct, the fault probably lay with a careless proof-reader and a typist too young to remember *Kamutay*.

that the proportion of Turkish words declined soon after the Democrats' coming to power and was not restored until their downfall.

İsmet İnönü had always been an enthusiast for language reform; it will be remembered that he was the author of *gelenek* for 'tradition'. He was personally involved in drafting the 1945 Anayasa. As Prime Minister in a succession of coalition governments in 1962–5, he gave TDK every support; for example, writers of school textbooks were instructed by the Ministry of Education to use 'arı bir Türkçe' (a pure Turkish). But general elections were due in October 1965. In the first few years after the *coup*, the solid block of four million voters who had always turned out for Menderes had kept their heads down, like the Democrat supporters among the newspaper-proprietors and journalists. With the return to civilian rule, however, they began to feel their oats. There was a clear prospect of victory for the Justice Party, whose vice-chairman had declared it to be the continuation of the proscribed Democrat Party. TDK had for some time been alarmed by a stream of press attacks on its 'constant interference with the natural course of the language'. On 29 May 1965, 'her türlü yanlış anlamayı önlemek için' (to prevent any misunderstanding), it produced an uncompromising manifesto, of which these are some extracts:

Atatürk'ün hükümet organları dışında özel bir dernek olarak kurduğu ve özel bir dernek olarak yaşamasını vasiyetiyle sağladığı Türk Dil Kurumu'nun amacı, dilimizin özleştirilmesi ve geliştirilmesidir . . .

Dilin hızla arınması ve gelişmesi için ona kendi yapısına uygun olarak 'müdahale' edilebilir ve edilmelidir. 'Dile müdahale etmemeli; onu zaman içinde kendi kendine gelişmeye bırakmalı.' İlkesi doğru değildir. Dil doğal ve toplumsal bütün olaylar gibi 'müdahale' ile biçim alır . . .

Yabancı sözcükleri atmakla Türkçeyi yoksullaştıracağımız kanısı da yanlıştır. Uygun karşılığı bulunmayan hiç bir yabancı sözcük dilden çıkarılmamıştır; çıkarılamaz da.

Kurum dışında ve yurttaşlar arasında hızla gelişen bir özleştirme akımı vardır. Birçok kimseler ortaya yeni yeni sözcükler atmaktadırlar. Bunların kimisi başarılıdır, tutunmaktadır. Kimisi de başarısızdır. Dil Kurumu'nu yermek isteyenler, başarısız olanları ona mal etmektedir.

Dil Kurumu 'uydurmacı' değildir. Dili zenginleştirmek için şu bilimsel yollardan yararlanır: Halk ağzından derlemeler, eski metinlerden taramalar, türetmeler. Türetmeler dilimizin kök ve eklerinden, dil kurallarına ve dil duygusuna uygun olarak yapılır . . . (*Türk Dili*, 14 (1965), 661–3)

The Turkish Language Society was founded by Atatürk as a private society outside the organs of government, and in his will he ensured its survival as a private society. Its goal is the purification and development of our language . . .

For its speedy purification and development, the language can and should be 'interfered with', in conformity with its own structure. The principle that there must be no interference with the language, but that it must be left to develop by itself with time, is mistaken. Language, like all natural and social events, is shaped by 'interference' . . .

The belief that by discarding foreign words we will impoverish Turkish is also mistaken. No foreign word without an appropriate equivalent has been or can be discarded.

There is a rapidly developing current of purification among citizens outside the Society. A number of people are putting out ever new words. Some of these are successful and catch on; some are unsuccessful. People wishing to disparage the Language Society lay the unsuccessful ones at its door . . .

The Language Society does not make words up. It employs the following scientific ways of enriching the language: gleanings from popular speech, combing through old texts, and derivations.

Derivations are made from the roots and suffixes of our language, in conformity with the rules of language and feeling for language . . .

The manifesto had no perceptible success in mollifying the Society's adversaries. For one thing, they did not have to be particularly well endowed with a feeling for language to know that TDK's 'derivations' were not always from native roots and suffixes.

The Society sometimes found it necessary in the 1960s to disclaim certain ludicrous expressions put into circulation by its opponents to parody some of its coinages. Among the best known are *gök konuksal avrat* 'sky guestish dame' for *uçak hostesi* 'air hostess'; *öz ittirimli götürgeç* 'self-propulsional carry-thing' for *otomobil*; *ayakiter götürgeç* 'foot-pusher carry-thing' for *bisiklet*; *tütünsel dumangaç* 'tobaccoish smoke-thing' for *sigara* 'cigarette'; *içi geçmiş dinsel kişi* 'passed-out religious person' for *İmam bayıldı* 'the Imam swooned' (the name of a highly esteemed aubergine dish); and *ulusal düttürü*, very approximately 'clannish ditty', for *millî marş* 'national anthem'. The reason why unsophisticated people thought these were genuine TDK products is that they found them no different in kind from some of the Society's own creations; how can one tell that a grotesque parody is a parody when the original is itself grotesque?[8]

In the years 1966–9 attacks on the Society intensified and attempts were made, unsuccessfully, to sequester its assets by legal means. In 1967 a sympathetic senator introduced a law compelling all public and private bodies and commercial firms to make their titles, stationery, notices, and trade marks conform to 'the language of the Constitution'. Ingeniously bogged down in a series of committees, it got nowhere. Not that it would have had much effect, because there are an awful lot of words in common use that are not in the text of the Constitution.

On 7 March 1970 a group of conservatives led by Nihad Sâmi Banarlı founded the Kubbealtı Cemiyeti (Under-the-Dome Society). The Kubbealtı is the building in the Topkapı Palace where, in the Ottoman period, the Council of State used to meet, under the presidency of the Grand Vizier. Later the Society promoted itself to Academy: at the beginning of 1972 the first number of its quarterly journal appeared, under the title *Kubbealtı Akademisi Mecmûası*. Its other publications include a respectable series on Turkish calligraphers that

---

[8] The author is reminded of an Ottoman history seminar at an American university, where a participant remarked that the discussion ought to be about Ottoperson herstory. After the seminar, the others present agreed that they had thought she was joking, but none of them could be sure.

continues in the 1990s under the imprint of the Kubbealtı Akademisi Kültür ve San'at[9] Vakfı (Culture and Art Foundation).

There have been other organizations committed to reversing the reform, among them Muallimler Cemiyeti (Society of Teachers), and Türk Dilini Koruma ve Geliştirme Cemiyeti (Society for the Protection and Development of the Turkish Language). In 1967 TDK published *Dil Devrimi üzerine*, a reprint of some newspaper articles on the language reform, at least three of which poured scorn on the latter body for, *inter alia*, calling itself not a *dernek* but a *cemiyet*, its president not *başkan* but *reis*, its secretary-general (Nihad Sâmi Banarlı) not *genel yazman* but *umumî kâtip*, its accountant not *sayman* but *muhâsip*, its members not *üye* but *âzâ*. That particular criticism was a bit unfair; what else could be expected from a society whose *raison d'être* was disapproval of the language reform? Somewhat fairer was the criticism that, if they felt that keenly about the old language, the title they should have chosen was Türk Lisanını Muhafaza ve İnkişaf Cemiyeti.[10]

Neither of these societies seems to have been very vocal since 1983, no doubt because the post-1983 TDK has done nothing much to offend anybody, except, by its very existence, the deposed top people of the pre-1983 TDK.

By the mid-1970s, the proportion of 'Turkish' words, real and invented, in the news columns of the press was regularly as high as 70 per cent, and in some places, notably the leading articles in *Cumhuriyet*, it rose to 90 per cent and more. At that point, many readers would either reach for a dictionary or turn to the sports pages, where the technical terms (e.g. *haf* 'halfback', *bek* 'fullback', *forvet* 'forward'), though scarcely *Öztürkçe*, would be familiar to them. It was common knowledge that Nadir Nadi Abalıoğlu, the editor of *Cumhuriyet*, wrote his editorials in the Turkish he had grown up with, then had them translated into *Öztürkçe*—compare Agop Dilaçar's story of his visit to Necmettin Sadak in Chapter 4.

Bülent Ecevit, Prime Minister in 1973–4, 1978–9, and again in 1998, was an ardent *Öztürkçeci*, some of his utterances being fairly impenetrable, more so perhaps in his speeches than in his writings.[11] He attracted huge crowds wherever he went and, although not every member of those crowds could have understood all he said, his charisma led to a popularization of *Öztürkçe*. When the Justice Party returned to office in 1979, however, the new ministers issued streams of circulars banning neologisms from official correspondence. What was instructive about these circulars was not so much the words they banned as the words they used,

[9] The antiquated spelling *san'at* for *sanat* is worth noting; the use of an apostrophe to mark an original Arabic ʿ*ayn* or *hamza* has long been dropped. Few now are aware that *sanat* is of Arab origin (*ṣanʿa*ʾ), and it passes for Turkish, like *temel* 'basis', 'basic', which lives on unchallenged despite its Greek origin (*themélion*).

[10] As it stands, this can only mean 'Society for Protecting the Turkish Language and for Development'; *Ettirme* should have been inserted after *İnkişaf* to make it transitive.

[11] Mustafa Balbay, however, writing in *Cumhuriyet* (27 Sept. 1990), quotes Professor Şaban Karataş: 'Bülent Bey, yeni kelimeleri kullanmayı sever ... Ama dikkat edin biraz sinirlenince dili değişiyor, Arapça kelimeler kullanmaya başlıyor' (Bulent Bey loves using the new words, but notice that when he becomes a little irritated his language changes and he starts using Arabic words).

ignoring the fact that, for example, the *sözcük* 'word' they employed in the pre-ambles to their blacklists was no less a product of linguistic engineering than the *eşgüdüm* 'coordination' and *olasılık* 'possibility' which they proscribed.

In September 1980 the military again seized power, the politicians having failed to stop rightist and leftist students murdering each other, latterly at an average rate of twenty-two a day. Two years later a new Constitution was promulgated, with some *Öztürkçe*, but not enough to offend any but the most diehard. Much of it was the *Öztürkçe* of 1961: the language of the many passages and whole articles taken over from the 1961 Constitution, among them Article 34 quoted above (Article 39 in the new), was left unaltered. Nor was the language of the additional material as extreme as it might have been—for example, the second clause of Article 12 contains only three inventions, *toplum*, *ödev*, and *sorumluluk*, all of them generally accepted (the words in italic are of non-Turkish origin): '*Temel hak ve hürriye*tler, kişinin topluma, *aile*sine ve diğer kişilere karşı ödev ve sorumluluk-larını da *ihtiva* eder' (The *fundamental rights and freedoms* also *include* the duties and responsibilities of the individual towards society, his *family, and other* persons). One's impression is that the drafters were trying to steer a more or less middle course between the old and the new, with some bias towards the old. For TDK, this was the writing on the wall.

The Society, as Atatürk's heir and a private body, not an organ of the state but what we would call a quango, had assumed that its existence was guaranteed in perpetuity, that it could never be abolished. Nor was it; when the conservatives thought the time was ripe it was simply taken over. A law passed on 11 August 1983 reconstituted it as part of a new Atatürk Kültür, Dil ve Tarih Yüksek Kurumu (Atatürk Cultural, Linguistic, and Historical Institute), linked to the Prime Minister's office, and gave it an almost entirely new Council of Management. The debates on the draft legislation in the Council of State revealed the intensity of the hatred the Society had aroused.[12] A number of legal objections to the proposal were voiced, none of which seemed to be adequately dealt with, but that is not our present concern. Adnan Orel, the spokesman of the National Education Commission, denounced 'Yıllardır dilimize karşı işlendiğine elemle şahit olduğum ihanet' (The treason that, to my sorrow, I have for years seen committed against our language). He continued:

Bu Tasarının kanunlaşmasıyla Türk dili Aziz Atatürk'ümüzün hayata gözlerini yumduğu günden beri içine düşürüldüğü felaketten kurtarılacak, maruz bırakıldığı bir bakıma yangın gibi, sel gibi, zelzele gibi tabiî afetlere benzer; fakat onlar gibi tabiî değil, hayfâ ki, gayrı tabiî bir facianın kurbanı olmaktan halâs edilecektir. Artık millî varlığımızın en hayati, en kıymetil temel unsurlarından, ana direklerden biri olan dilimiz, kurulduğu maksat ve gayeden tamamen ayrılan bir kurumun tasallutundan kurtarılıp devletin sahabetine kavuşturulacak ve işin ehli olan gerçek ilim otoritelerinin şuurlu vicdanlarına, dirayetli ellerine emanet olunacaktır . . .

---

[12] *Danışma Meclisi Tutanak Dergisi*, 19 (June–July 1983), *passim*. Adnan Orel's speech quoted below came on 28 July.

[TDK] . . . canım Türkçeyi fakirleştirmiş, kısırlaştırmış, zayıflatmış, sığlaştırmış, çirkinleştirmiş, hülasa kolunu kanadını kırıp (Tabirimi af buyurun) yolunmuş tavuğa çevirmiştir. O güzelim dilin ahengi, zerafeti, yabancı dillerle kelimeler mefhumlar, mana nüansları bakımından olan muadelet ve paralelliği yok olmuş, hisleri, heyecanları, fikirleri anlatabilmekteki zenginlik ve etkinliği kaybolmuş; akraba dillerle olan münasebeti, diğer Türk lehçeleriyle irtibatı yok edilmiş, Dilimizin asırlar boyunca normal ve tabiî gelişmesinin ona kazandırdığı bize mal olmuş kelimeler, terimler, ifadeyi meram unsurları atılıp, onların yerine Dilimizin ahenk kaidesine, gramerine, yapısına ve hiçbir vasfına uymayan, acayip, çirkin, uydurma kelimeler, terim ve tabirleri üretilip doldurarak, zavallı Dil maskaraya çevrilmiştir.

When this Draft becomes law, the Turkish language will be delivered from the calamity into which it has been plunged since our dear Atatürk closed his eyes to life. What it has suffered resembles in a way such natural disasters as fire, flood, and earthquake, but unlike them is not natural; the language will be saved from being the victim of—alas!—an unnatural disaster. Our language, one of the most vital, most precious constituents and mainstays of our existence as a nation and a state, is about to be freed from the tyranny of an organization that has totally departed from the aim and purpose for which it was established; it will be brought into state ownership and entrusted to the judicious consciences and capable hands of truly scholarly authorities who know their jobs . . .

[TDK] has impoverished our beloved language, has made it sterile, feeble, shallow and ugly; in short, it has broken its legs and wings and turned it into—pardon the expression—a plucked chicken.[13] The harmony and grace of that lovely language has been eliminated, as has its ability to match other languages in words, concepts, and shades of meaning; gone are its richness and effectiveness in expressing feelings, emotions and ideas; annihilated its connection with kindred languages and its relationship with other Turkish dialects. The words, technical terms, and elements for expressing oneself, which were won for it by its normal and natural development over the centuries and have become our own, have been cast away and their places filled by grotesque, ugly, and fake words, terms, and expressions that have been fabricated in no conformity with the rule of harmony of our language, its grammar, its structure, or anything else about it. The unhappy language has become an object of ridicule.

It would be hard to fault him, except in the matter of technical terms. Yet one only has to examine the words employed in his speech, which for the most part were more old-fashioned than those of other speakers in the debate (e.g. *aklıselim* not *sağduyu* 'common sense', *vicdan* not *bulunç* 'conscience', *nesil* not *kuşak* 'generation'), to know that it is not going to be possible to put the clock back. Among his *Öztürkçe* words were *toplum* 'society', *kesim* 'sector', *gözetim* 'supervision', *denetim* 'control', *terim, yönlendirmek* 'to guide', *etkilik* 'effectiveness', *üretmek* 'to produce', and *ödül* 'prize'.[14]

Another speaker described TDK as 'a Society which calls an air hostess "a sky guestish dame"'. This phrase—'gök konuksal avrat'—was a reference to the old

---

[13] It is impolite to mention non-human creatures, cats excepted, without a word of apology. I have heard villagers apologize similarly when speaking of atheists: 'Affedersiniz, dinsizler . . .'.

[14] *Ödül* 'prize', though brought into the standard language by the reform, is not an invention; it is widely used in Anatolia.

spoof mentioned above, and his remark justly brought objections from some of his colleagues: 'That's a lie!' and 'Someone made that up! It's a lie!' The speaker, unruffled, went on to give some authentic examples of TDK's output: 'I have in my hand one of the Society's publications, entitled "Finding equivalents for words of Western origin".[15] It calls *banket* ["verge"] *yol omzu* ["road shoulder"] . . . *Buldozer* it calls *yol düzler* ["road leveller"], and *greyder* ["grader"] *yer düzler* ["earth leveller"].' Other members did not seem to find these specimens of TDK's crimes as heinous as he did, so he gave some more: *genörgütçü* 'gen[eral]-organization-ist' for *bürokrat*, *geçinge* (from *geçinmek* 'to get along, make a living') for *bütçe* 'budget', *düzüngü* for *ideoloji*.[16] His peroration was not at all bad. The Nasrettin Hoca story to which it alludes tells how a passer-by sees the Hoca spooning something into a lake. He asks him what he's up to and the Hoca replies, 'I'm putting ferment in so that the whole lake turns into yoghurt.' 'Silly man!' says the other, 'It won't work.' 'But just suppose it does!'

Millet hayatıyla, devlet hayatıyla dalga geçmektir bu, gayri ciddî hareketlerdir. Efendim, biz üretiriz, salarız, toplum tutarsa onu biz tamam deriz, koyarız. Tamam, tutunmuştur bu kelime, bu 'tilcik' tutunmuştur ve Türk dilinin malı olmuştur. E . . . peki, siz seçip seçip böyle ortaya atacaksınız, bin tane kelime türeteceksiniz, içinden bir tanesi tutacak. O zaman Nasrettin Hoca'nın göle maya çalması gibi bir mesele oluyor. 'Ya tutarsa . . .' Tutmuyor.

This is monkeying with our life as a nation, as a state; this is frivolous behaviour. 'My dear sir, we produce them, we throw them around, and if the public takes to them we say, "Fine," and there we leave it. Very good, this word, this speechlet, has caught on and become part of the Turkish language.' Well, all right, you'll keep picking them out and launching them like this, you'll call a thousand words into being and one of them will catch on. Then comes a problem like Nasrettin Hoca's dropping ferment into the lake. 'But just suppose it works!' It doesn't.

In 1985 a group of disgruntled devotees of the former TDK established Dil Derneği, a new Language Society to carry on the work of the old. One does not hear much of it; although lacking the financial resources of the old TDK, it continues to function but is not churning out *Öztürkçe*. It has produced some useful and scholarly works, notably on applied linguistics (e.g. Dil Derneği 1991).

On 24–8 September 1990 came Birinci Türk Dili Kurultayı (The First Turkish-Language Congress), arranged by the Ministry of Culture. Right in the middle of it, on the 26th, came the annual *Dil Bayramı* (the Language Festival), and the tasteless choice of title, as if the real Birinci Türk Dili Kurultayı (of 1932) had never been, was the target of much criticism. It was doubtless for that reason that its next meeting was called not 'İkinci' (Second) but Sürekli (Continuing) Türk Dili Kurultayı (4–8 May 1992), the proceedings of which were published under that name by the Ministry of Culture. It was not a conspicuous success. Many of the speeches were parochial, being taken up with the numerous defects of TDK's

---

[15]   *Batı Kaynaklı Sözcüklere Karşılık Bulma Denemesi*, ii (Ankara: TDK, 1978).
[16]   *Düzüngü* is a provincial word for *ayna* 'mirror'. Here it might be the result of a clerical error for *düşünü*, once proposed as a replacement for *ideoloji*.

spelling guide, *İmlâ Kılavuzu*, to the evident disappointment of the Central Asian delegates, who had hoped for a serious discussion of the possibility of achieving a common written language.

In 1970 the old TDK had begun suggesting 'yabancı kelimelere karşılıklar'— equivalents for foreign words (no longer Arabic and Persian but English and French) that had entered or were in process of entering the language. It did little to stem the tide; the only examples that linger in the memory are *uzgörüm* for 'television' and *uzgöreç* for 'television receiver', but they had no more success than the *uzaduyum* for 'telepathy' suggested in *Felsefe ve Gramer Terimleri* (1942).

The new TDK began a similar campaign in 1994 in *Türk Dili*, 507: 218–21;[17] (why it felt a need for this has been demonstrated in Chapter 10). The Society had set up a *komisyon* that would meet once a month to discuss possible equivalents for a number of such words in a list previously circulated, and to agree on one or more equivalents for each. The language of the announcement was conservative; some would call it reactionary: *siyasîler* 'politicians', *kelime* 'word', *sirayet eden* 'infecting', *tedbir* 'measure', *taraf* 'side', and even the sentence 'Gün geçmiyor ki batının yeni bir kelimesi . . . arzıendam etmesin' (A day does not pass without a new Western word's . . . putting in an appearance'.[18] There was, however, a sprinkling of *Öztürkçe* (though not a single *-sel*): *araç* 'medium', *kamu kurum ve kuruluşları* 'public associations and institutions', *-e yönelik* 'directed towards'. The first list of foreign words for which substitutes were offered included *şov* 'show' and several of its compounds. For *şov* itself, *gösteri* was proposed. Turkey being as yet little touched by political correctness, for *şovmen* 'showman' the suggestion was *gösteri adamı*, and, for *vanmen şov* 'one-man show', *tek adam gösterisi*. For *talk şov* 'chat-show', *söz gösterisi* or *çene yarıştırma* 'chin-wag', literally 'jaw-racing', and for *talk şovcu*, *çene yarıştırıcı*. It will be seen that *talk şov* has been taken over directly from English with no attempt at Turkicizing it (i.e. not *talk şovu*), just as the French *kilomètre carré* was long ago taken over as *kilometre kare*. For *şovrum* 'show-room', the recommendation was *sergi evi* 'display house'. Regretfully one must add that *şov* still reigns supreme and more often that not is spelled *show*; 'talk-show' is commoner than 'talk şov'.

For *sentır* 'centre', which 'despite the existence in our language of *merkez* [A], is tacked on to the names of various societies and institutions', a return to *merkez* was proposed, so *ticaret merkezi* for trade centre and *iletişim merkezi* (*iletişim* 'communications') for media centre, in preference to *medya sentırı*. Neither appears in *Örnekleriyle Türkçe Sözlük* (1995–6), though it does give *santra*, a football term, as in *santra çizgisi* 'centre line'.

Here we have an indication of how rapidly French is being overtaken as the source of new words: *sentır* is not shown in *Türkçe Sözlük* (1988), though *santr* is.

---

[17] The cover is dated March 1994, the first page February 1994.
[18] The Ottoman *arzıendam* 'putting in an appearance', which is not to be found in the TDK's own *Türkçe Sözlük* (1988), is made up of *ʿarḍ* [A] 'presentation', linked to *endam* (*andām* [P]) 'body') by the Persian izafet.

The replacements proposed for other items in the list displayed the same preference for Turkish words even of Arabic origin; thus for *instant coffee* or *neskafe* the suggestion was *hazır* [A] ('ready') *kahve* and, for *fest fud* 'fast food' *hazır yemek*, while for *konsensüs* 'consensus' a choice was offered between *uzlaşma* and *mutabakat* [A]. The suggested replacement for *fundamentalist* was *köktenci* ('from-the-root-ist') and for *fundamentalizm, köktencilik*. This accords with the view of Western scholars, that in the Islamic context 'radical' is a more appropriate term than 'fundamentalist'. In fact, the word generally used is *köktendinci* 'radical religionist'.

In 1995 the proposals so far made were published in book form,[19] with an interesting introduction in which the aims of the Society are summarized: '1) Türk Dilini araştırmak, 2) Türk Dilini yabancı etkilerden korumak ve geliştirmek' ((1) To research the Turkish language, (2) to protect the Turkish language from foreign influences and to develop it). Words that have entered the language over the centuries, from whatever source, are considered to be Turkish. These include such words as *elektrik, atom, demokrasi*. Even words formed irregularly are acceptable if they are thoroughly entrenched in the language of the people—for example, *kural* 'rule', *önem* 'importance', *bağımsızlık* 'independence', *bilinç* 'consciousness'.

Each month's *Türk Dili* brings its quota of borrowings, with recommendations for Turkish alternatives. In no. 555 (Mar. 1998) came *gurme, sit-com*, and *stand-up*, as in 'stand-up komedyenler'. The Society's proposal for the first was *tatbilir*, although those who see themselves as members of the international community of gourmets may not take kindly to the appellation of taste-knower. Nor is it likely that many people will abandon *sit-com* in favour of its literal translation *durum güldürüsü*, but the suggested abbreviation *durgül* may have more of a chance. The proposal for 'stand-up komedyen' was *sözçatar* 'tacking words together', which does not look very promising, though a pleasant example is given of its use: 'Sözçatarlar Türkiye'de konu sıkıntısı çekmiyorlar' (Stand-up comedians suffer from no dearth of topics in Turkey).

The Society is clearly determined to fight the use of English words for which Turkish equivalents exist or can be devised; *bölüm* should be used rather than *seksiyon, bilgi şöleni* ('knowledge-feast') rather than *sempozyum*.[20] Sadly, there does not seem to be a widespread appreciation of the Society's genuine efforts to undo the worst of the reform while striving to keep new foreign imports at bay; many people seem to be quite unaware that the TDK is not what it used to be.

Even now, though years have passed since the fall of the old TDK, there are still hearts in which the fierce emotions it roused have not died. A book published in

[19] *Yabancı Kelimelere Karşılıklar* (1995: 631). Notice the sign of the times: 'Kelimelere' not 'Sözcüklere'.
[20] *Şölen*, of uncertain origin, was proposed in *Tarama Dergisi* (1934) for *ziyafet* 'feast', and in *Felsefe ve Gramer Terimleri* (1942) for 'potlatch'. The initial ş makes an OT origin unlikely.

1993 affords an example (Mısıroğlu 1993); here is one of its eleven introductory 'Uyarı' (warnings): 'Aziz Genç! Bugün memleketimizin bir numaralı meselesi, enflasyon veya güneydoğu Anadoludaki anarşi değildir! Kıbrıs'ın kaybedilmek üzere olması da değildir! Bütün bunların hepsinden daha ehemmiyetli olan, lisanımızdaki korkunç tahribattır!' (Dear Youth! Today, our nations's number one problem is not inflation or the anarchy in south-eastern Anatolia! Nor is it the fact that Cyprus is on the point of being lost! What is more important than all of these is the terrible devastation of our language!). As usually happens, this sworn enemy of *Öztürkçe* uses some himself: *dinsel,* not *dinî* or even *diynî,*[21] for 'religious' all over the book and, in the above quotations, *uyarı* not *ikaz* for 'warning', and *güneydoğu* not *cenub-u şarkî* for 'south-eastern'. His theme is that the language reform is atheism and that the reformers are enemies of the Koran, Islam, and God. People who say *önsezi* rather than *hiss-i kablelvuku* for 'premonition' are damned. Those who use such bastard words ('piç kelimeler') are either racist Turkists ('ırkçı-Türkçü'), or Kemalists or Communists ('Komonist'). No fair-minded reader who wades through a few pages of this stuff can deny that there had to be a language reform, though not necessarily on the lines of the one that actually happened.

Well, we may put that example down to simple-minded fanaticism, but the same excuse will not do for this one. It is an extract from a letter to the author, written from Istanbul in September 1994 by an old friend, bilingual in Turkish and English. 'Zabanvari Facialar Kurumu' (The Linguistic Tragedies Society) is his quasi-Ottoman term for the Dil Kurumu. For his 'Ulusaldüttürü Turkish', see page 160.

Yesterday we celebrated Dil Bayramı, or some nonsense like that. (I say 'celebrated'—I don't think anyone actually knew.) The radio, however, said something interesting. It quoted somebody on the committee of Zabanvari Facialar Kurumu (or whatever they're called) as saying 'Turks have throughout history always had a written language understood by all. This should happen again.' I hope this means someone has donated a brain to those boys. If they have any sense, they'll abandon the excesses of Ulusaldüttürü Turkish and start talking like me.

The significant thing about that letter is that it was written eleven years after the old TDK had ceased to exist and some twenty years after it had abandoned the excesses. But the man who wrote it has clearly not forgotten, much less forgiven, what it did to the language, and he holds the new TDK (if he is aware of the change) responsible for the sins of the old. In retrospect one can see that it might have helped if the authorities had waited a year or so after the takeover and then quietly given the reborn Society a new name.

---

[21] Pietists wishing to preserve the correct pronunciation of Arabic terms use *iy* to indicate a long *i,* so *iyman* for *iman* /īmān/ 'faith', though they do not usually indicate the length of the *a,* as they could by doubling it. Often they use *iy* to indicate a long *i* where none exists, spelling e.g. *mühim* 'important' as *mühiym.*

Hasan Eren, Secretary-General of the new TDK, told the author some years ago, 'Türk Dil Kurumu'nun esas gayesi, dilde birliğin sağlanmasıdır' (TDK's basic aim is to ensure unity in the language). Given that writers tend to be individualists, one may prophesy that it will be a long time before Turkey's flourishing literary community allows that to happen. But if this prophecy comes true, on present showing the new TDK will not be to blame.

References

ADIVAR, HALİDE EDİP (1962), *Türk'ün Ateşle İmtihanı* (İstanbul: Çan Yayınları).

AĞAKAY, MEHMET ALİ (1943), *Türkçe Felsefe Terimlerinin Dil Bakımından Açıklanması Dolayısiyle Bazı Kelime Yapı Yolları* (İstanbul: TDK).

AKBAL, OKTAY (1984), 'Olan Gençlere Oluyor', *Cumhuriyet*, 5 Apr.

AKSAN, DOĞAN (1976), *Tartışılan Sözcükler* (Ankara: TDK).

AKSOY, ÖMER ASIM (1968), 'Ataç', in TDK, *Ölümünün 10. Yıldönümünde Ataç'ı Anış* (Ankara: TDK), 11–21.

—— (1982), *Dil Gerçeği* (Ankara: TDK).

ALGAR, HAMİD (1988), 'Ahundzâde', in *Türkiye Diyanet Vakfı İslâm Ansiklopedisi* (İstanbul: Türkiye Diyanet Vakfı İslâm Ansiklopedisi Genel Müdürlüğü).

ALİ, FİLİZ (1987), *Müzik ve Müziğimizin Sorunları* (İstanbul: Cem Yayınevi).

ALRIC, ARTHUR (1892), *Un diplomate ottoman en 1836 (Affaire Churchill)* (Bibliothèque orientale elzévirienne, 66; Paris).

ANDAY, MELİH CEVDET (1960), 'Günce gibi', *Yeditepe Dergisi*, 21 (1960).

ARAR, İSMAİL (1981), 'Gazi Alfabesi', in TTK, *Harf Devrimi'nin 50. Yılı Sempozyumu* (Ankara: Türk Tarih Kurumu), 147–67.

—— et al. (1986), *Nutuk-Söylev* (2nd edn., Ankara: Türk Tarih Kurumu; 1st edn., 1981–4).

ARSAL, SADRİ MAKSUDÎ (1930), *Türk Dili için* (n.p. n.d. [Ankara: Türk Ocakları İlim ve Sanat Heyeti]).

ATAÇ, NURULLAH (1952), *Karalama Defteri* (İstanbul: Yenilik Yayınları).

—— (1954), *Diyelim 'Ben'* (İstanbul: TDK).

—— (1964), *Söyleşiler* (Ankara: TDK).

ATALAY, BESİM (1940), *Bir Doçentin Türkçe Okutuşu ve Münakaşalarımız* (İstanbul: Alâeddin Kıral Basımevi).

—— (1939–43), *Divanü Lügat-it-Türk* (5 vols.; Ankara: TDK).

—— (1946), *Türkçe'de Kelime Yapma Yolları* (İstanbul: TDK).

ATATÜRK'ÜN SÖYLEV VE DEMEÇLERİ (1945), i (İstanbul: Türk İnkılâp Tarihi Enstitüsü).

ATAY, FALİH RIFKI (1946), *Yolcu Defteri* (Ankara: Ulus Basımevi).

—— (1951), 'Atatürk ve Dil', *Türk Dili*, 1: 124–6.

—— (1965), '"Hüküm" Nasıl Kurtuldu?', *Dünya*, 16 May.

—— (1969), *Çankaya* (İstanbul: Doğan Kardeş).

ATAY, OĞUZ (1986), *Tutamayanlar* (İstanbul: İletişim).

ATD (1963), *Atatürk ve Türk Dili* (Ankara: TDK).

AYDA, ADİLE (1981), in *Yaşayan Türkçemiz* (1981), ii. 62–3.

BAINBRIDGE, MARGARET (1993) (ed.), *The Turkic Peoples of the World* (London: Kegan Paul International).

BANARLI, NİHAT SÂMİ (1967), 'Diller Çözülürken', *Meydan*, 14 Mar., repr. in Erer (1973), 180–6.

—— (1972), *Türkçenin Sırları* (İstanbul: İstanbul Fetih Cemiyeti).

BANGUOĞLU, TAHSİN (1987), *Dil Bahisleri* (İstanbul: Kubbealtı Neşriyatı).

Başkan, Özcan (1975), 'Terimlerde Özleşme Sorunu', in TDK, *Türk Dili Araştırmaları Yıllığı: Belleten 1974* (Ankara: Türk Dil Kurumu), 173–84.

Baydur, Suat Yakup (1964), *Dil ve Kültür* (Ankara: TDK).

Blochet, E. (1915), 'Le Nom des turcs dans l'Avesta', *JRAS* 305–8.

Bozgeyik, Burhan (1995), *Dil Dâvası: Prof. Dr. Kadri Timurtaş ile Mülâkat* (Istanbul: Bedir Yayınevi).

Brendemoen, Bernt (1990), 'The Turkish Language Reform and Language Policy in Turkey', in G. Hazai (ed.), *Handbuch der türkischen Sprachwissenschaft* (Budapest: Akademía Kiadó, 1990), 454–93.

Buluç, Sadettin (1981), *Osmanlı Devrinde Alfabe Tartışmaları* (Ankara: TTK).

Cep Kılavuzu (1935): *Osmanlıcadan Türkçeye Cep Kılavuzu* and *Türkçeden Osmanlıcaya Cep Kılavuzu* (Istanbul: Türk Dili Araştırma Kurumu).

Clauson, Sir Gerard (1972), *An Etymological Dictionary of Pre-Thirteenth-Century Turkish* (Oxford: Clarendon Press).

Courteille, Pavet de (1870), *Dictionnaire Turk-Orientale* (Paris: Imprimerie Impériale).

Czaplicka, M. A. (1918), *The Turks of Central Asia in History and at the Present Day* (Oxford: Clarendon Press).

Çoker, Doğan, and Karaçay, Timur (1983), *Matematik Terimleri Sözlüğü* (Ankara: TDK).

Çolpan, Yılmaz (1963), *Ataç'ın Sözcükleri* (Ankara: TDK).

Dankoff, Robert, with Kelly, James (1982–5), *Compendium of the Turkic Dialects*, trans. of *DLT*, with introduction and indexes (3 vols., Cambridge, Mass.: Harvard University Press).

Deny, Jean (1937), 'Turc *kol-ay* (cf. grec εὐ-χερής) et la famille des mots en -*ey* (-*ay*)', *Mélanges Émile Boisacq: Annuaire de l'institut de philologie et d'histoire orientales et slaves*, v (Brussels: L'Iinstitut de Philologie et d'Histoire Orientales et Slaves), 295–312.

Derin, Haldun, *Çankaya Özel Kalemini Animsarken (1933–1951)* (Istanbul: Tarih Vakfı).

Derleme Sözlüğü (1963–82): *Türkiye'de Halk Ağzından Derleme Sözlüğü* (12 vols., Ankara: TDK).

Dil Derneği (1991), *Uygulamalı Dilbilim Açısından Türkçenin Görünümü* (Ankara: Dil Derneği).

Dil Devrimi Üzerine (1967) (Ankara: TDK).

Dilâçar, A[gop] (1963), 'Atatürk ve Türkçe', in *ATD* (1963), 41–52.

Dilçin, Cem (1983), *Yeni Tarama Sözlüğü* (Ankara: TDK). [An index in the old letters, and a supplement, to *Tarama Sözlüğü* (1963–77).]

Dilemre, Saim Ali (1933), 'Türk Filolojisi—Türk Dili bir Hint-Avrupa dilidir', in *Kurultay 1932*: 71–81.

—— (1935), 'Eski Dil Mefhumu', *Türk Dili*, 12: 73–83.

Dizdaroğlu, Hikmet (1962), *Türkçede Sözcük Yapma Yolları* (Ankara: TDK).

DLT: Mahmud, Kaşgari, *Dīwān Luġāt al-Turk* (?1079). [For a discussion of the dating, see Dankoff and Kelly (1982–5: i. 6–7).]

Doerfer, Gerhard (1963–75), *Türkische und Mongolische Elemente im Neupersischen* (4 vols., Wiesbaden: Franz Steiner Verlag).

Doğan, D. Mehmet (1984), *Dil Kültür Yabancılaşma* (Ankara: Birlik Yayınevi, 1984).

—— (1988), *Büyük Türkçe Sözlük* (Ankara: Beyan Yayınları).

Ellis, Peter Berresford (1994), *The Druids* (London: Constable).

EMRE, AHMET CEVAT (1960), *İki Neslin Tarihi—Mustafa Kemal Neler Yaptı* (Istanbul: Hilmi Kitabevi).

The Encyclopaedia of Islam (1960–) (2nd edn., London and New York: E. J. Brill).

ERCİLASUN, AHMET BİCAN (1994), 'Atatürk'ün Kaleminden Çıkan Yazılar', *Türk Dili*, 512: 85–91.

EREN, HASAN (1990), '*Uçun* mu, *uçum* mu', in TDK, *Dil Tartışmalarında Gerçekler I* (Ankara: Atatürk Kültür, Dil ve Tarih Yüksek Kurumu), 49–51.

ERER, TEKİN (1973), *Türkiye'de Dil ve Yazı Hareketleri* (Istanbul: İkbal Kitabevi).

ERKİLET, H. E. (1952), 'Dil Devriminde Ordunun Rolü', *Türk Dili* (Dec.), repr. in *Dil Devrimi Üzerine* (Ankara: TDK, 1967), 94–101.

ERTOP, KONUR (1963), 'Atatürk Devriminde Türk Dili', in *ATD* (1963), 53–99.

EYUBOĞLU, İSMET ZEKİ (1988), *Türk Dilinin Etimoloji Sözlüğü* (Istanbul: Sosyal Yayınlar).

FELSEFE VE GRAMER TERIMLERI (1942) (Ankara: TDK).

GALLAGHER, CHARLES F. (1971), 'Language Reform and Social Modernization in Turkey', in Joan Rubin and Björn H. Jernudd, *Can Language be Planned?* (Honolulu: University Press of Hawaii), 159–78.

GEDİKLİ, NECATİ (1987), 'Müzik Araştırmacısı ve Folklorcu olarak Ahmed Adnan Saygun', in İzmir Filarmoni Derneği, *Ahmed Adnan Saygun Semineri Bildirileri* (Izmir), 9–11.

GIBB, E. J. W. (1900–9), *A History of Ottoman Poetry* (6 vols., London: Luzac & Co., for the Trustees of the 'E. J. W. Gibb Memorial').

GÖKALP, ZİYA (1339/1923), *Türkçülüğün Esasları* (Ankara: Matbuat ve İstihbarat Matbaası).

GÜLTEKİN, MEHMET BEDRİ (1983), *Türkçenin Dünü ve Yarını* (Ankara: Kaynak Yayınları).

GÜNER, ŞEFİK (1981), *Türk Ceza Yasasi* (Ankara: TDK).

HATİBOĞLU, VECİHE (1963), 'Atatürk'ün Dilciliği', in *ATD* (1963), 9–22.

—— (1974), *Türkçenin Ekleri* (Ankara: TDK).

—— (1986), ' "Başkan"a Yanlış Denmişti', in Özel *et al.* (1986), 94–8.

HEYD, URIEL (1954), *Language Reform in Modern Turkey* (Jerusalem: Israel Oriental Society).

HISAR, ABDÜLHAK ŞİNASİ (1966), *Fahim Bey ve Biz* (Istanbul: Hilmi Kitabevi; 1st edn., 1941).

İBRAHİM NECMİ (1928), *Yeni Türkçe Dersleri* (Istanbul: Milliyet Matbaası).

İLHAN, SERAP (1987), 'Ahmed Adnan Saygun ve Türkçe Musiki Terimleri', in İzmir Filarmoni Derneği, *Ahmed Adnan Saygun Semineri Bildirileri* (Izmir), 44–5.

İMER, KÂMİLE (1973), 'Türk Yazı Dilinde Dil Devriminin Başlangıcından 1965 Yılı Sonuna kadar Özleşme uzerine Sayıma Dayanan bir Araştırma', *AÜDTC Türkolioji Dergisi*, 5: 175–90.

—— (1976), *Dilde Değişme ve Gelişme Açısından Türk Dil Devrimi* (Ankara: TDK).

İNAN, ABDÜLKADİR (1936), *Türkoloji Ders Hülasaları* (Istanbul: Devlet Basımevi).

İZ, FAHİR (1967), *Eski Türk Edebiyatında Nazım* (Istanbul: İstanbul Üniversitesi).

—— (1984), *Hepimizin Türkçesi*, privately printed brochure (Ankara).

JÄSCHKE, GOTTHARD (1951), *Der Islam in der neuen Türkei* (Leiden: Brill).

KAMUS (1316/1901): Şemsettin Sami [Fraschéry], *Kamus-i Türkî* (Istanbul: İkdam Matbaası). [See also Tulum.]

KARAOSMANOĞLU, YAKUP KADRİ (1963), 'Atatürk ve Türk Dili', in *ATD* (1963), 103–10.

KEMAL, GAZİ MUSTAFA (1927), *Nutuk* (in the old alphabet) (Ankara: Türk Tayyare Cemiyeti).

—— (1934), *Nutuk* (in the Latin alphabet) (3 vols., Istanbul: Devlet Basımevi). [See also Tuğrul *et al.* (1963); Arar *et al.* (1986); Özerdim (1981).]

KERESTEDJIAN, BEDROS EFFENDI (1912), *Dictionnaire de la langue turque* (London: édité par son neveu Haig, M.R.A.S.).

KOLOĞLU, ORHAN (1986), *Miyop Çörçil Olayı: Ceride-i Havadis'in Öyküsü* (Ankara: Yorum Yayınları).

KORKMAZ, ZEYNEP (1969), *Türkçede Eklerin Kullanılış Şekilleri ve Ek Kalıplaşması Olayları* (Ankara: TDK).

——(1985), 'Dil İnkılâbının Sadeleşme ve Türkçeleşme Akımları arasındaki Yeri', *Türk Dili*, 49: 382–413.

——(1992) (ed.), *Atatürk ve Türk Dili: Belgeler* (Ankara: TDK).

[KOŞAY], HAMİT ZÜBEYR, and [IŞITMAN], İSHAK REFET (1932), *Anadilden Derlemeler* (n.p. [Ankara] Cumhuriyet Halk Fırkası).

——[KOŞAY, HÂMİT], and AYDIN, ORHAN (1952), *Anadilden Derlemeler*, ii (Ankara: TDK).

KÖKSAL, AYDIN (1980), *Dil ile Ekin* (Ankara: TDK).

KÖPRÜLÜZADE, MEHMET FUAT (1928), *MilliEdebiyat Cereyanının İlk Mübeşşirleri ve Divan-ı Türkî-i Basit* (Istanbul: Devlet Matbaası).

KRUEGER, JOHN R. (1963) (ed.), *The Turkic Peoples: Selected Russian Entries from the Great Soviety Encyclopedia with an Index in English* (Bloomington, Ind.: Indiana University Press).

KUDRET, CEVDET (1966), *Dilleri Var Bizim Dile Benzemez* (Ankara: Bilgi Yayınevi).

——(1968–70), *Karagöz* (3 vols.; Ankara: Bilgi Yayınevi).

KUNERALP, ZEKİ (1981), *Sadece Diplomat* (Istanbul: İstanbul Matbaası, n.d.).

KURTOĞLU, FEVZİ (1938), *Türk Bayrağı ve Ay Yıldız* (Ankara: Türk Tarih Kurumu).

KURULTAY (1932), *Birinci Türk Dili Kurultayı: Tezler, Muzakere Zabıtları* (Istanbul: TDK, 1933).

——1934: *İkinci Türk Dil Kurultay: Müzakere Zabıtları Tezler* (n.p., n.d.). The proceedings of the 1934 Kurultay seem to have been published only in the form of bound volumes of the issues of TDK's journal *Türk Dili* for September 1934 to December 1935, the numbering of each starting afresh at page 1.

——1936: *Üçüncü Türk Dil Kurultayı: Müzakere Zabıtları, Tezler* (Istanbul: TDK, 1937).

——1942: *Dördüncü Türk Dil Kurultayı: Toplantı Tutulgaları, Tezler* (Ankara: TDK, 1943).

——1949: *Altıncı Türk Dil Kurultayı* (Ankara: TDK, 1950).

——1954: *Yedinci Türk Dil Kurultayı* (Ankara: TDK, 1955).

——1966: *On Birinci Türk Dil Kurultayı* (Ankara: TDK, 1967).

LATÎFÎ (1314/1898), *Teḏkire-i Laṭîfî* (Istanbul: Kitaphane-i İkdam).

LEVEND, AGÂH SIRRI (1965–8), *Ali Şir Nevaî* (4 vols.; Ankara: TDK).

——(1972) *Türk Dilinde Gelişme ve Sadeleşme Evreleri* (Ankara: TDK).

LEWIS, G. L. (1988), *Turkish Grammar* (Oxford: Oxford University Press).

——(1991), 'Etymologist's Quicksand', in Alan Jones (ed.), *Arabicus Felix: Luminosus Britannicus* (Beeston Festschrift) (Reading: Ithaca Press), 236–9.

——(1992), *Just a Diplomat*, trans. of Kuneralp (1981) (Istanbul: Isis Press).

MAUNDEVILLE, SIR JOHN (1886), *The Voyages and Travels of Sir John Maundeville Kt.* (London: Cassell).

MISIROĞLU, KADİR (1993), *Doğru Türkçe Rehberi yahud Bin Uydurma Kelimeyi Boykot* (Istanbul: Sebil Yayınevi).

MÜLLER, GEORGE A. (1910), *Mentone and its Neighbourhood: The Past and the Present* (London: Hodder and Stoughton).

MÜNİF PASHA, ANTEPLİ (1974), 'İmlâ Meselesi', in Mehmet Kaplan and İnci Enginün, *Yeni Türk Edebiyatı Antolojisi*, i (Istanbul: Marmara Üniversitesi Fen-Edebiyat Fakültesi).

NEGROPONTE, NICHOLAS (1995), *Being Digital* (London: Hodder & Stoughton).

NÉMETH, JULIUS [GYULA] (1917), *Türkische Grammatik* (Berlin: Goschen).

NEW REDHOUSE TURKISH–ENGLISH DICTIONARY (1968) (Istanbul: Redhouse Press).

OKAY, ORHAN (1981), 'Kaybolan Nüanslar', in *Yaşayan Türkçemiz* (3 vols., Istanbul: Tercüman Gazetesi Yayınları), i. 273–4.

ONAT, NAIM HÂZIM (1935), 'Türk dilinin Samî dillerle münasebeti', *Türk Dili*, 15: 1–97.

——(1937), 'Güneş Dil Teorisi'ne göre Türkçe–Arapça karşılaştırmalar', in Kurultay 1936: 151–89.

——(1944–9), *Arapçanın Türk Diliyle Kuruluşu* (2 vols., Istanbul: TDK).

——(1952), 'Dilde Uydurma', *Dil Dâvası* (Ankara: TDK), 40–60.

ORTA ÖGRETİM TERİMLERİ KILAVUZU (1963) (Ankara: TDK).

ÖRNEKLERİYLE TÜRKÇE SÖZLÜK (1995–6) (4 vols., Ankara: Millî Eğitim Bakanlığı).

ÖRS, YAMAN (1989), 'Bilim Dili, Hekimlik Dili', in *Bilim Dili Türkçe, Yazın Dili Türkçe* (Ankara: Dil Derneği), 15–22.

ÖZDEM, RAGIP (1939), *Tarihsel Bakımdan Öztürkçe ve Yabancı Sözlerin Fonetik Ayraçları*, 2. (Fasikül, Istanbul: İstanbul Üniversitesi Yayınları).

ÖZDEMİR, EMİN (1969), *Öz Türkçe üzerine* (Ankara: TDK).

——(1973), *Terim Hazırlama Kılavuzu* (Ankara: TDK).

ÖZEL, SEVGİ, *et al.* (1986) (eds.), *Atatürk'ün Türk Dil Kurumu ve Sonrası* (Istanbul: Bilgi Yayınevi).

ÖZERDİM, SAMİ N. (1981), *Açıklamalı Söylev Sözlüğu* (Ankara: TDK).

ÖZGÜ, MELÂHAT (1963), 'Atatürk'ün Dilimiz üzerine Eğilişi', in *ATD* (1963), 23–40.

ÖZKAN, FATMA (1995), 'Türkçe Yanlışları üzerine', *Türk Dili*, 974–81.

ÖZÖN, MUSTAFA NİHAT (1961*a*), *Türkçe–Yabancı Kelimeler Sözlüğü* (Istanbul: İnkılap ve Aka Kitabevi).

——(1961*b*), 'Türkçe Kelime Üretimi ve B. F. Rıfkı Atay', *Gazi Eğitim Enstitüsü Araştırma ve İncelemeleri Bülteni*, 1 (June), 5–42. [The 'B.' in the title stands for 'Bay'.]

POPPE, NICHOLAS (1954), *Grammar of Written Mongolian* (Wiesbaden: Harrassowitz).

PRINGLE, JOHN DOUGLAS (1973), *Have Pen, Will Travel* (London: Chatto & Windus).

REDHOUSE, SIR JAMES W. (1890), *A Turkish and English Lexicon* (Constantinople: Boyajian).

——(1968), *New Redhouse Turkish–English Dictionary* (Istanbul: Redhouse Press).

SAFA, PEYAMİ (1970), *Osmanlıca Türkçe Uydurmaca*, ed. Ergun Göze (Istanbul: Ötüken Yayınevi).

SAKAOĞLU, SAİM (1998), '-kolik ve -matik üzerine', *Türk Dili*, 556: 328–30.

SAYILI, ADNAN (1978), 'Bilim ve Öğretim Dili olarak Türkçe', in Adnan Sayılı (ed.), *Bilim Kültür ve Öğretim Dili olarak Türkçe* (Ankara: Türk Tarih Kurumu), 325–599.

——(1988), *The Observatory in Islam and its Place in the General History of the Observatory* (Ankara: Türk Tarih Kurumu).

ŞEHSUVAROĞLU, BEDİ (1981), *Atatürk'ün Sağlık Hayatı* (Istanbul: Hürriyet Yayınları).

SHORTLAND, EDWARD (1851), *The Southern Districts of New Zealand* (London: Longman, Brown, Green and Longmans).

SILAY, KEMAL (1993), 'The *Türki-i Basit* Movement and its Significance for Turkish Language Reform', *Turkish Studies Association Bulletin*, 17: 123–9. [Abstract of paper read to 1992 MESA conference.]

SOYSAL, MÜMTAZ (1986), 'Türkçenin Düşmanları', *Milliyet*, 2 Nov.

——(1990), 'Dil Savaşı', *Milliyet*, 25 Sept.

——(1993), 'Atmasyon', *Hürriyet*, 17 Jan.

Söz Derleme Dergisi (1939–52): *Türkiyede Halk Ağzından Söz Derleme Dergisi* (6 vols., Istanbul: TDK).

Sözer, Vural (1986), *Müzik ve Müzisyenler Ansiklopedisi* (2 vols., Istanbul: Remzi Kitabevi).

Steiner, Franz (1967), *Taboo* (Harmondsworth: Penguin).

Sürekli Türk Dili Kurultayı (1992) (Ankara: Kültür Bakanlığı).

Tankut, Hasan Reşit (1963), 'Atatürk'ün Dil Çalışmaları', in *ATD* (1963), 111–36.

Tarama Dergisi (1934): *Osmanlıcadan Türkçeye ve Türkçeden Osmanlıcaya Söz Karşılıkları Tarama Dergisi* (2 vols., Ankara: TDTC).

Tarama Sözlüğü (1943–57): *XIII. Asırdan Günümüze kadar Kitaplardan Toplanmış Tanıklariyle Tarama Sözlüğü* (4 vols., Ankara: TDK).

——(1963–77): *XIII. Yüzyıldan beri Türkiye Türkçesiyle Yazılmış Kitaplardan Toplanan Tanıklariyle Tarama Sözlüğü* (8 vols., Ankara: TDK). See also Dilçin (1983).

Taymas, Abdullah (1945–8), *Kırgız Sözlüğü* (2 vols., Ankara: TDK). [Translation of Yudakhin (1940).]

TDK (1988), *İmlâ Kılavuzu* (Ankara: AKDTYK: TDK).

Tekin, Tâlat (1958), 'Ataç'in Dilciliği ve Tilcikleri', *Türk Dili*, 7: 408–13.

Tevfikoğlu, Muhtar (1994), 'Dr. Âkil Muhtar'ın Dolmabahçe'deki Dil Çalışmalarıyla ilgili Notları', *Türk Dili*, 512: 92–113.

Timurtaş, Faruk K[adri] (1979), *Uydurma Olan ve Olmayan Yeni Kelimeler Sözlüğü* (Istanbul: Umur Kitapçılık).

TTK (1981), *Harf Devrimi'nin 50. Yılı Sempozyumu* (Ankara: Türk Tarih Kurumu).

——(1992), *Birinci Türk Tıp Tarihi Kongresi: Kongreye Sunulan Bildiriler 1988* (Ankara: Türk Tarih Kurumu).

Tuğlacı, Pars (1971–4), *Okyanus* (3 vols.; Istanbul: Pars Yayınevi).

Tuğrul, Mehmet, *et al.* (1963), *Söylev (Nutuk)* (Ankara: TDK).

Tulum, Mertol (1985–6), (ed.), *Temel Türkçe Sözlük: Sâdeleştirilmiş vs Genişletilmiş Kâmûs-ı Türkî* (3 vols., Istanbul: Tercüman Gazetesi).

Tunaya, Tarık Zafer (1952), *Türkiye'de Siyasî Partiler* (Istanbul: Doğan Kardeş).

——(1984), *Türkiye'de Siyasal Partiler* (Istanbul: Hürriyet Vakfı Yayınları).

Türkçe Sözlük (1988), (8th edn., 2 vols., Ankara: AKDTYK). [Previous editions were published by TDK.]

Uludağ, Osman Şevki (1940), 'Tanzimat ve Hekimlik', in *Tanzimat* (Istanbul: Maarif Vekâleti), 967–77.

Uşaklıgil, Halit Ziya (1936), *Kırk Yıl* (5 vols.; Istanbul: İnkılap Kitabevi).

Ülkütaşır, M. Şakir (1973), *Atatürk ve Harf Devrimi* (Ankara: TDK).

Ünaydın, Ruşen Eşref (1954), *Atatürk, Tarih ve Dil Kurumları: Hâtiralar* (Ankara: TDK).

Ünver, A. Süheyl (1940), 'Osmanlı Tababeti ve Tanzimat hakkında Yeni Notlar', in *Tanzimat* (Istanbul: Maarif Vekâleti), 933–66.

Velidedeoğlu, Hıfzı Veldet (1979), *Türkçeleştirilmiş Metinleriyle Birlikte Türk Medenî Kanunu ve Borçlar Kanunu* (3 vols.; Ankara: TDK).

von Gabain, Annemarie (1950), *Alttürkische Grammatik* (Leipzig: Otto Harrassowitz).

Yabancı Kelimelere Karşılıklar (1995) (Ankara: AKDTYK: TDK).

Yalçıner, Filiz, and Şahin, Fikret (1993), *Açıklamalı Bilgisayar Terimleri Sözlüğü*, ed. Ali Bayram (Istanbul: Fono Açık Öğretim Kurumu).

Yaşayan Türkçemiz (1981) (3 vols., Istanbul: Tercüman Gazetesi Yayınları).

Yavuz, Kemal (1983), 'XIII–XVI. Asırda Dil Yadigarlarının Anadolu Sahasında Türkçe

Yazılış Sebepleri ve bu Devir Müelliflerinin Türkçe hakkındaki Görüşleri', *Türk Dünyası Araştırmaları* (Dec.).

YORULMAZ, HÜSEYIN (1995), *Tanzimat'tan Cumhuriyet'e Alfabe Tartışmaları* (Istanbul: Kitabevi).

YUDAKHIN, K. K. (1940), *Kirgizsko–Russkiy Slovar'* (Moscow: Akademia Nauk; later edn., Moscow: Sovyetskaya Entsiklopediya, 1965).

YÜCEL, TAHSİN (1982), *Dil Devrimi ve Sonuçları* (Ankara: TDK; 1st edn., *Dil Devrimi*, 1968).

ZAMENHOF, L. L. (1931), *Fundamento de Esperanto* (Paris: Esperantista Centra Librejo).

ZÜRCHER, ERIK JAN (1985), 'La Théorie du "langage-soleil" et sa place dans la réforme de la langue turque', in Sylvain Auroux *et al.* (eds.), *La Linguistique fantastique* (Paris: Denoël), 83–91; Turkish version: 'Güneş-Dil Teorisi ve Türk Dil Reformundaki Yeri', *Birikim*, 2 June 1989.

General Index

Sweden:
  Crown Prince and Princess 56
  King Charles XII 120 n.
Syria 84

Şemsettin Sami Fraschéry 14, 16–17, 30
Şemsüddin Mehmed Karamanoğlu 10
Şeyhülislâm 30
Şinasi 15

Talim ve Terbiye 41
Tankut, Hasan Reşit 40, 60, 73
Tanzimat 12, 14, 51
Tarama Dergisi 21, 44, 50, 52
tasfiyeciler 19, 46
Tatar 19, 50, 95
Tatavlalı Mahremî 12
taxi-drivers 8, 122, 150
technical terms 65–6, 155, 163
Tekin, Talat 82–9
Terceman-ı Ahvâl 12
Thor 45 n.
Tıbbiye-i Adliye-i Şahane 124–5
Tıbhane 124
Times, The 38–9
Timurtaş, Faruk Kadri 98, 115, 116–17, 142
Topkapı Palace 160
Trotsky, Leon 70
Tunalı Hilmi 40
Turcoman 49
Turkicizers 19
Turkish Press 12
Türk Derneği 19
Türk Dil Kurultayı, *see* Kurultay
Türk Dil Kurumu:
  (new) 133, 161, 162–8
  (old) 45, then *passim*
Türk Dili Araştırma Kurumu 45
Türk Dili Tetkik Cemiyeti 45, 67
Türk Dilini Koruma ve Geliştirme Cemiyeti
  161

Türk Tarih Kurumu 45, 156
Türkçe Kanunu 40
Türkçe Sözlük 156
Türkçe Şiirleri 18
Türkî-i basit 12
Türkilizce 134

Union and Progress 21
Ural-Altaic languages 48
Uran, Necdet 43
Uşaklıgil, Halit Ziya 18, 19
Uyghur 60
Uzbek 19, 87
  national motto 71

Ünaydın, Ruşen Eşref 30–1, 33, 45–6

Vaux, Carra de 59
Velidedeoğlu, Hıfzı Veldet 128–9
vocabulary analysis 158–9, 161

Wahby, Taufiq 29 n.
Wall Street Journal 60
word-collection mobilization 49

Yakup Kadri, *see* Karaosmanoğlu
Yalçın, Hüseyin Cahit 30, 31, 32
Yaşayan Türkçemiz 119 n.
Yegül, Abdi Tevfik 133
Yeni Tasvir-i Efkâr 23
Yeni Yazım Kılavuzu 36
'Young Turks' 21
Yunus Emre 39
Yurdakul, Mehmet Emin 18–19, 20
Yusuf Ziya, *see* Özer
Yücel, Tahsin 4, 67, 69

Zamenhof, L. L. 97 n.
Zayączkowski, Ananiasz 62
Ziya Pasha 13, 14
Zürcher, Erik Jan 60

Index of Words, Phrases, and Suffixes

(Ottoman words mentioned in the text and not discussed are excluded from this Index, as are most of the many non-Turkish medical terms on pages 125–7.)